CW01677147

# GARLANDS
## OF FANTASY

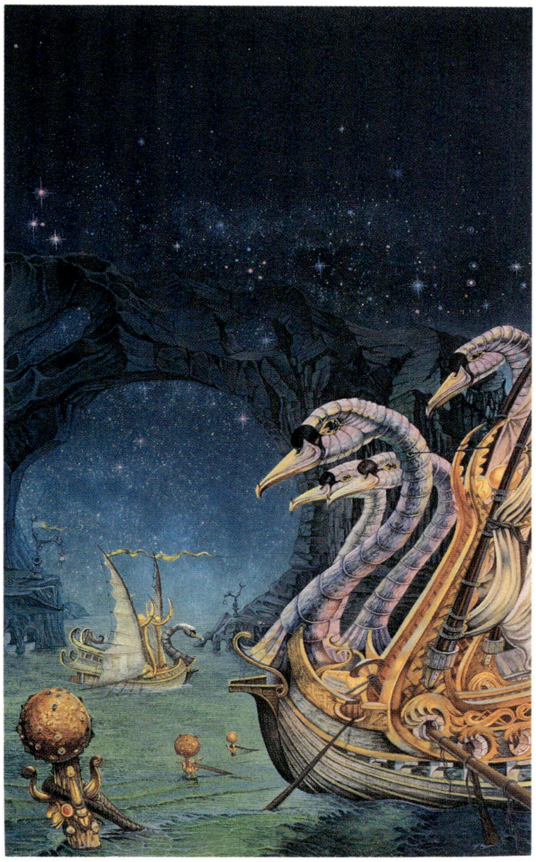

**Haven of the Swans**
Roger 1982
Oils and Acrylic. 8 x 12in (20 x 30cm)
Cover for *The Silmarillion* (paperback), Unwin Hyman.

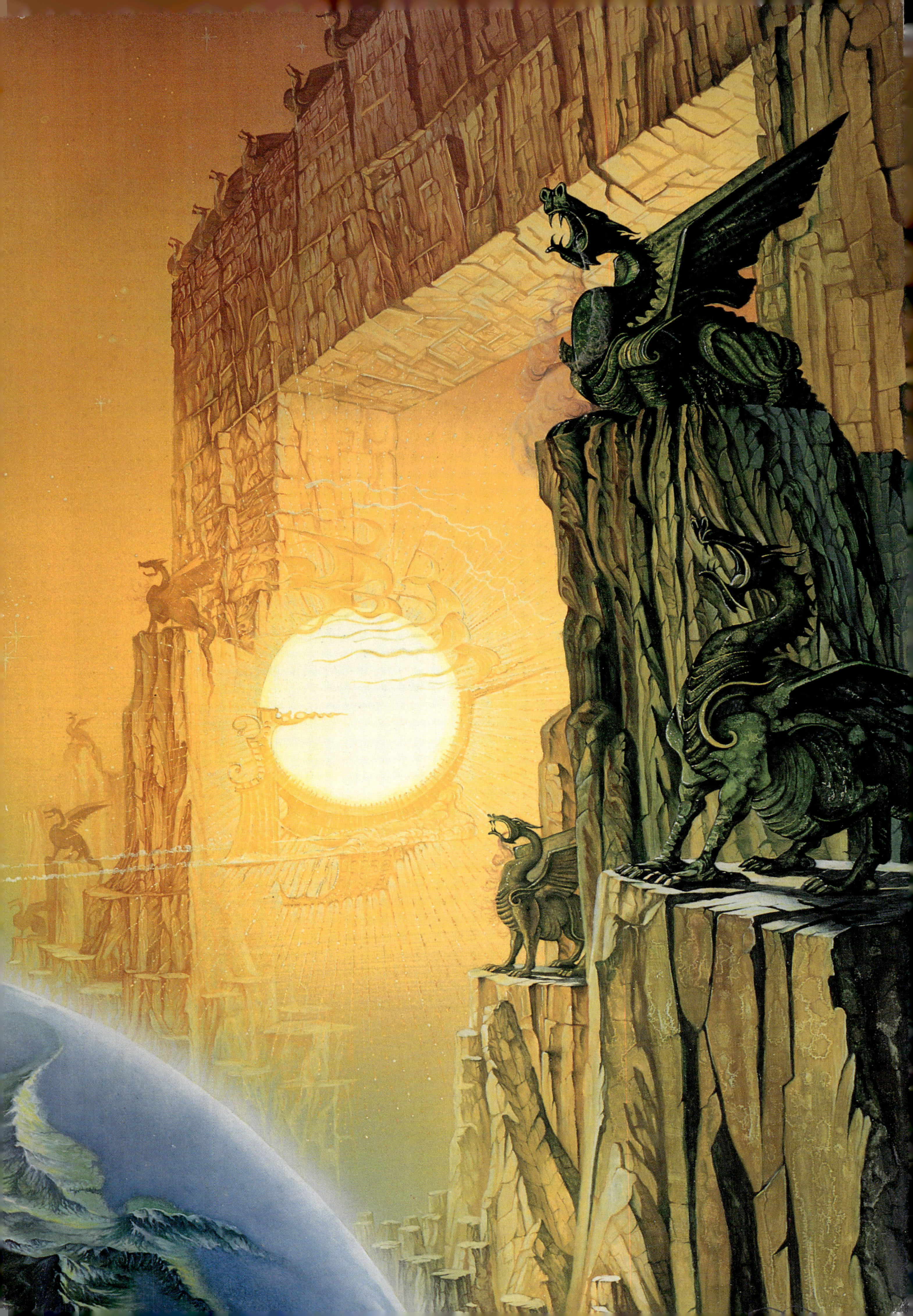

# GARLANDS
# OF FANTASY

## THE ART OF LINDA & ROGER GARLAND

TEXT BY NIGEL SUCKLING

Paper Tiger

TO SETH AND AMY

Paper Tiger
An imprint of Dragon's World
Dragon's World Ltd
Limpsfield
Surrey RH8 0DY
Great Britain

First published by Dragon's World Ltd 1994



**The catalogue record for this book is available from the British Library**
ISBN 1 85028 344 3

Editor: Daniel Giles
Designer: Karen Ferguson
Art Director: John Strange
Editorial Director: Pippa Rubinstein

Printed in Singapore

**(Page 2) Tale of the Sun and Moon**
Roger 1983
Oils and Acrylic. 10 x 13in (25 x 33cm)
Cover for *The Book of Lost Tales: Part 1*, Unwin Hyman.

**(Opposite) Smaug**
Roger 1987
Oils and Acrylic. 12 x 19in (30 x 48cm)
Cover for *The Hobbit* (50th anniversary edition), Unwin Hyman.

# CONTENTS



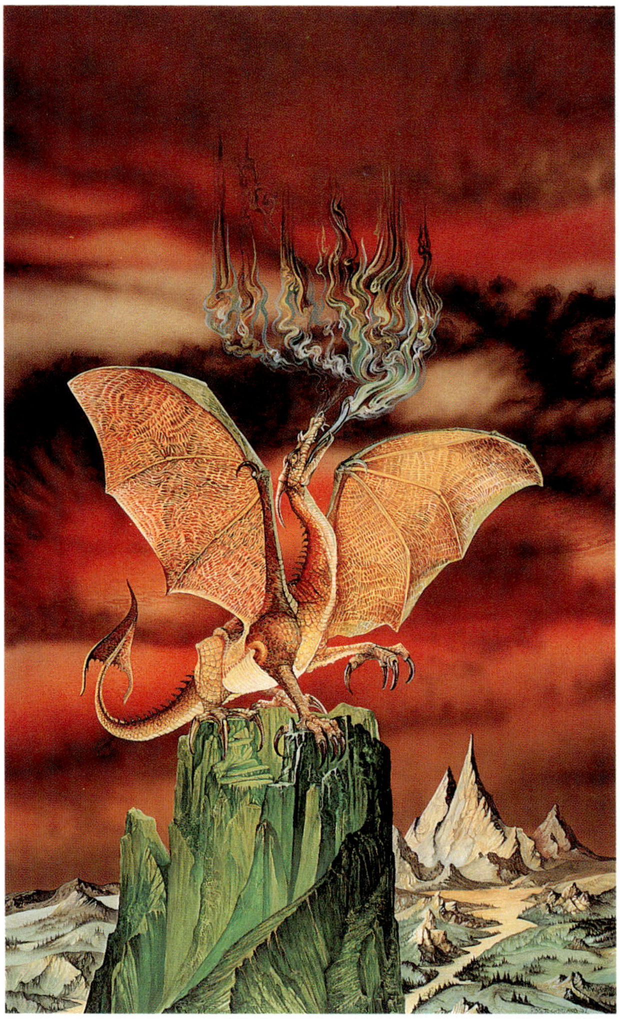

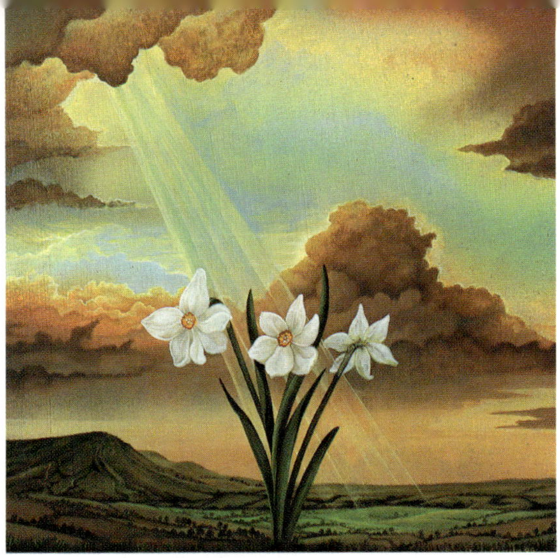

# INTRODUCTION

*"The Garlands have an unusual partnership; both are artists in the same line of work, but neither eclipses the other."*

Four miles or so south of Launceston, on the winding road to Plymouth, a small sign tucked into the hedge and saying 'Gallery' is the first hint of the Garlands' Cornish retreat. On a couple of bends and one meets a larger sign in a spacious turning which declares, beneath a wrought iron dragon, 'TOLKIEN AND SYMBOLIST PAINTINGS'. Across the lake-filled valley sits a granite farm complex with a touch of ecclesiastic elegance, having once belonged to the church.

In one wing, a converted barn, Linda and Roger Garland have their home and the gallery, which for several years has been their mainstay. The other buildings are occupied by Roger's retired parents and his twin brother's family who run the farm.

The house feels more like a converted church than a barn, the upstairs living room having three tall, Gothic arched windows facing east towards the green hills bordering Dartmoor. The gallery is tucked away at the back of the building directly under the Garlands' studio and houses a changing display of their own work, plus some by other artists.

Do they mind selling original paintings as opposed to the reproductions available? Linda: 'Not really, though we're happier selling each other's pictures so it must be a slight wrench.'

The Garlands have an unusual partnership: both are artists in the same line of work, but neither eclipses the other. They do have particular areas of interest, but there is also a large overlap in which it is impossible for an outsider to tell who has done what. This has occasionally led to calls from clients saying they don't care which is available, as long as one of the Garlands takes on the commission.

So does both of them being artists cause complications? Roger: 'Mostly it seems an advantage because we understand each other's problems, particularly the importance of deadlines.'

The only real drawback, it appears, comes from both of them being in an insecure profession, so at times their flat and hectic periods have coincided, with all that entails.

△ Narcissus
Linda 1989
Oils. 7 x 7in (18 x 18cm)
Book cover, Prism Press.

This work was produced for a book about 'channelling' – working out illness by concentrating on the parts of the body which are diseased. To illustrate this Linda came up with the idea of a ray of sunlight, and from where it falls on the ground springs the flower, which is a symbol of spring and rejuvenation. It is commonly believed that channelling can even cure such dreadful diseases as cancer.

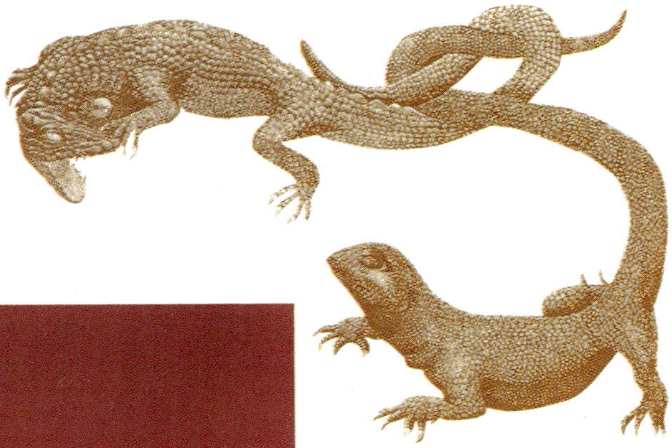

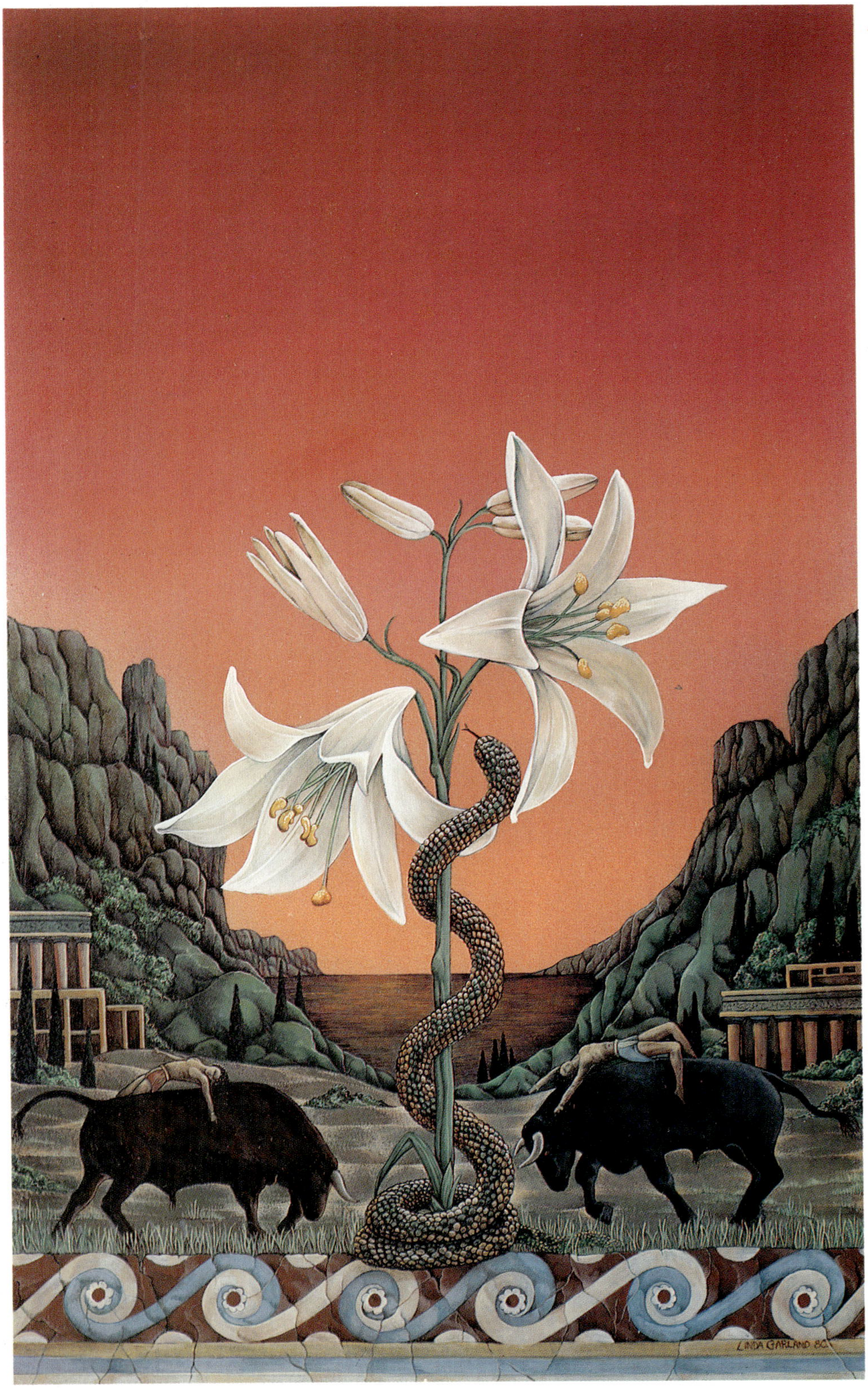


◁ **The Lily and the Bull**
Linda 1980
Oils and Acrylic. 11 x 17in
(28 x 43cm)
Book cover, Corgi.

This was a story for teenagers featuring the bull races that used to take place at the palace of Minos in ancient Crete. The challenge was to produce a design that would work equally as a cover and a painting in its own right.

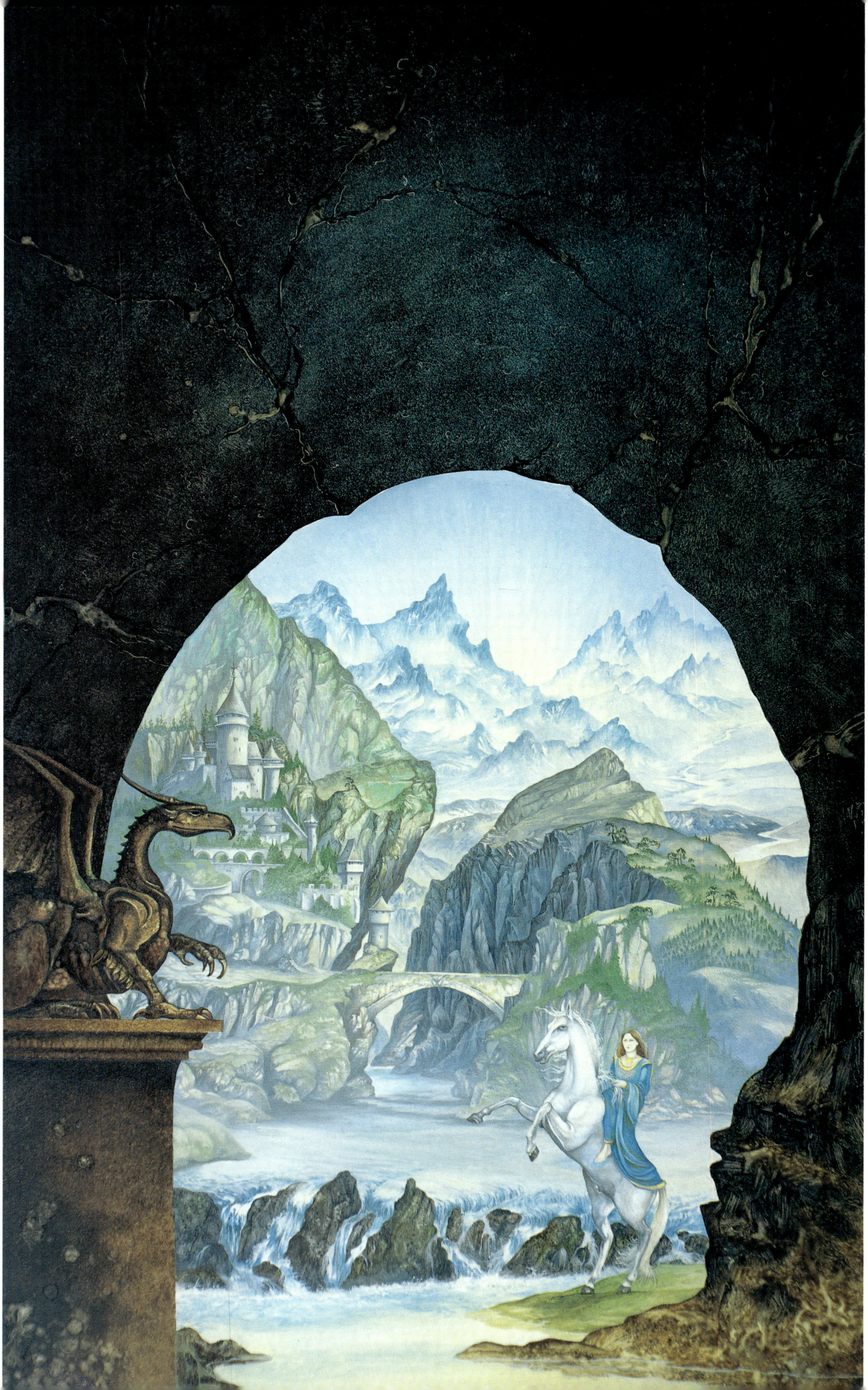

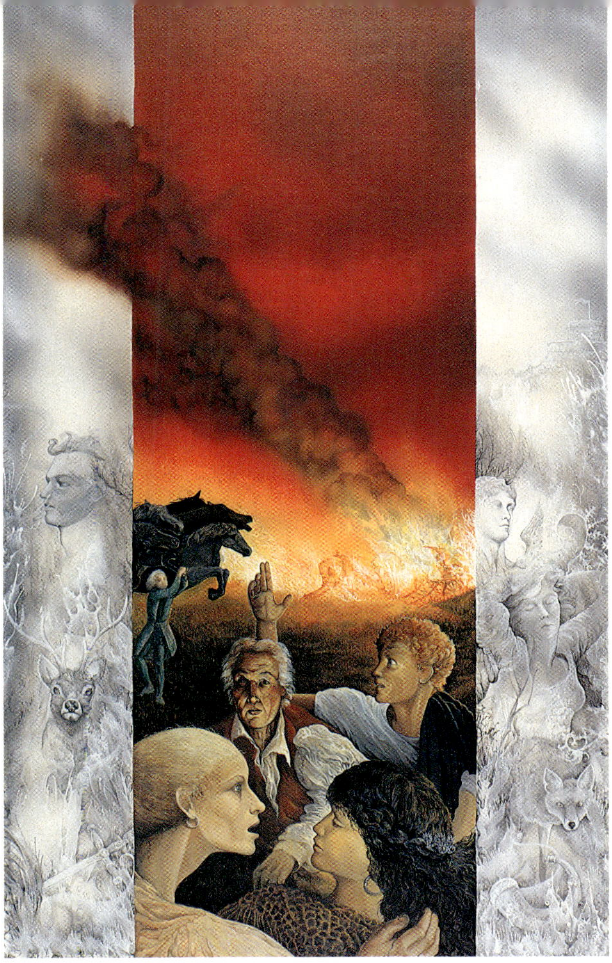

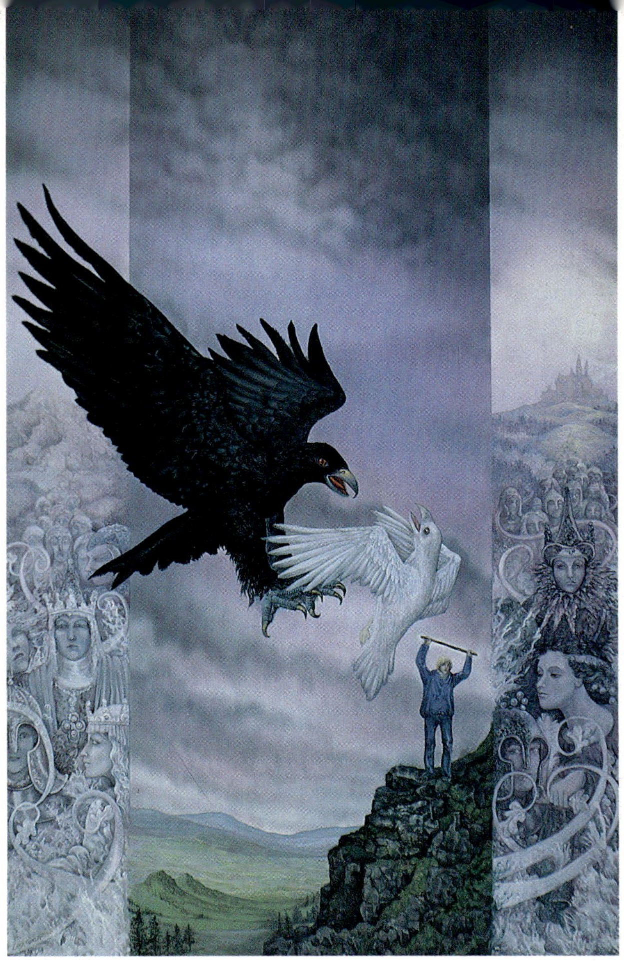

△ **Fireshaper's Doom**
Linda 1988
Oils and Acrylic. 11 x 17in (28 x 43cm)
Book cover. Orbit.

Produced as a sequel to *Windmaster's Bane*, all the characters shown feature in the story. Those with finer features belong to the fairy race, or Sidhe.

◁ **Horsegirl**
Roger 1987
Oils. 11 x 18in (28 x 46cm)
Book cover, Headline Press.

Roger's brief for this picture was simple: 'Just do one of your fantasy landscapes with a horse in it.' He did not even see a synopsis of the text. The picture was well received, and the only change required was to paint the horse black. The arch is a favourite device on book covers and allows space for lettering at the top, while also drawing the eye in to the picture.

▷ **Windmaster's Bane**
Linda 1987
Oils and Acrylic. 11 x 17in (28 x 43cm)
Cover for a book by Tom Deitz, Orbit.

This painting was commissioned for a story about two separate parallel worlds which start to interface and unbalance each other. The parallelity suggested the picture's format, the margins being executed with a 'controlled accident' technique in which blobbed paint is sprayed about with an empty airbrush and then manipulated into whatever images arise.

They met at college in Wolverhampton, where Linda was studying Fine Art and Roger Graphics and Design. After graduating, they moved to London in search of work and there married, choosing Friern Barnet church purely on account of its wonderful stained glass windows. They only learned it was a favourite venue for High Society nuptials when they found their own modest ceremony sandwiched between two sumptuous affairs bristling with cut-glass accents.

What work they did find was mostly of the very casual kind, for which their degrees were totally irrelevant – serving petrol and slaving in the Bond Street Wimpy, for instance. Linda: 'A sad indictment of art school is they give you no idea of what's going to happen afterwards. It feels like being taken up a ladder and pushed off. The only thing you're qualified for is teaching.'

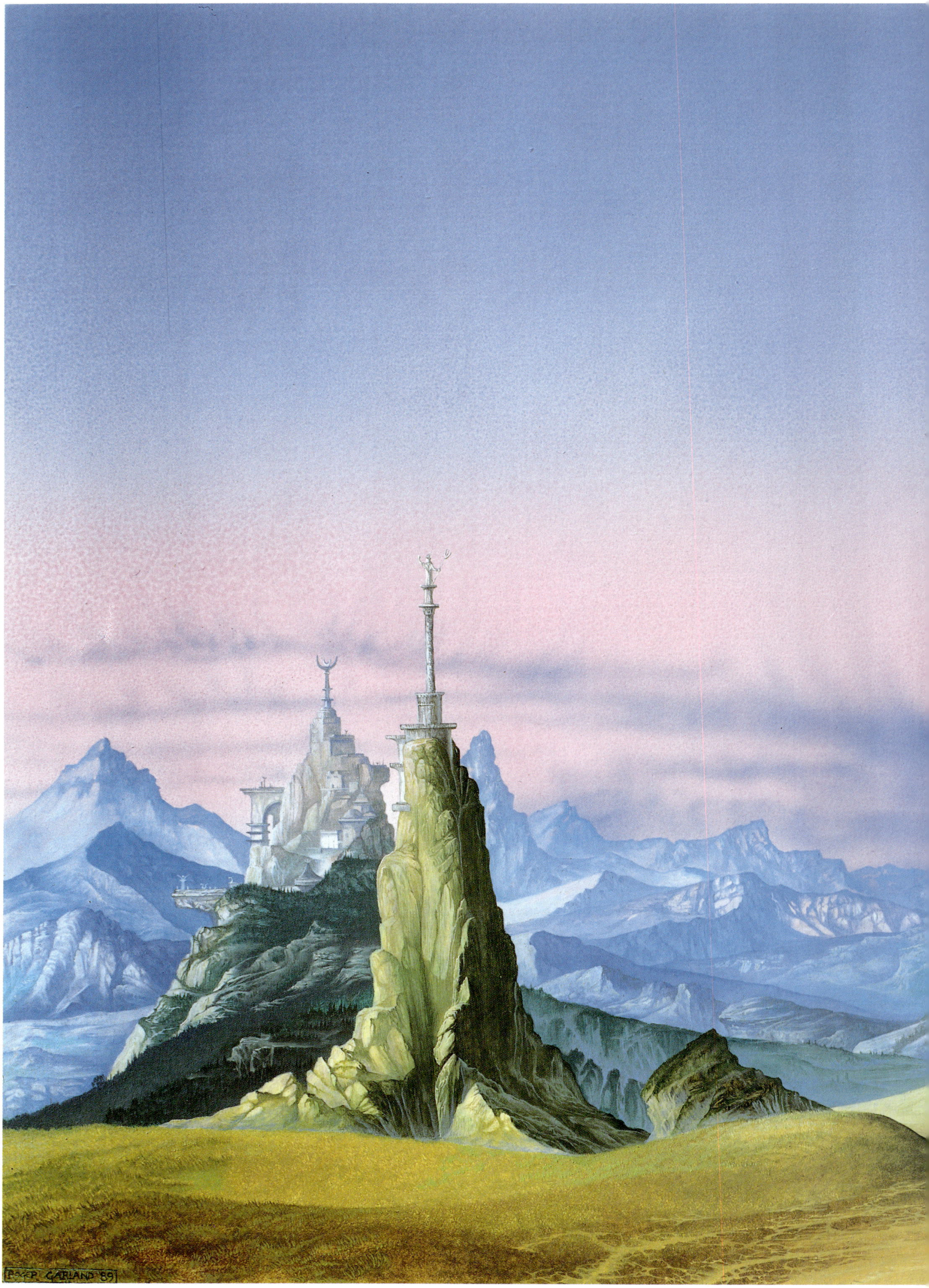

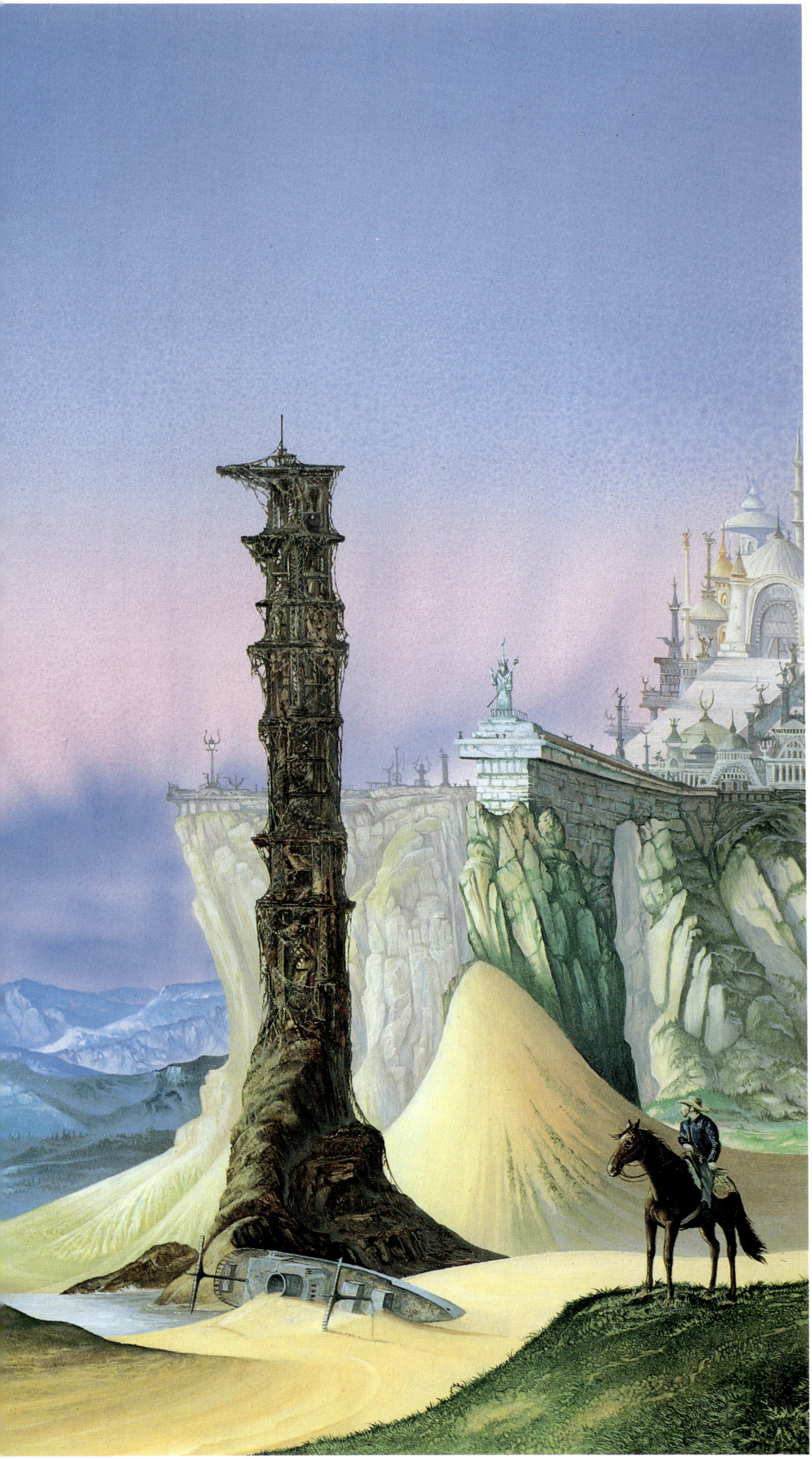

◁ Jerusalem Man
Roger 1989
Oils and Acrylic. 11 x 17in
Cover for a book by David
Gemmel, Century Hutchinson.

Continuing an earlier story, the man of the title is an officer upholding the law with a Bible in one hand and a gun in the other.

In the absence of real work, teaching beckoned. Linda trained while Roger jumped straight in, which came as a shock. As a novice he was given all the worst groups (memory flash of a syringe embedding itself in the blackboard by his head), plus other subjects like Drama, about which he knew nothing.

After a discouraging year or two in the capital they moved to the West Country and found jobs, he in St Austell, where they lived, she in Falmouth.

Did they enjoy teaching? Roger: 'I did on the shop floor level, but hated the bureaucracy.' Linda: 'The best part is the first few years when you are full of enthusiasm and still learning the ropes. It was satisfying also that one or two of my pupils went on to art college, but for much of the time the art classes felt like glorified babysitting. You felt children were dumped there when there was nothing better for them to do. Most didn't really want to be there. Without a sense of humour I don't think I could have coped. I knew I was winning when I overheard them say: "She's quite funny really once you get used to her."'

Meanwhile, they continued their own painting in the evening and at weekends, building up their portfolios for the day when some opening presented itself.

Linda was the first to get a break. A small exhibition in Falmouth resulted in an invitation to join a larger show in Bodmin. Here her paintings hung alongside those of Peter Blake, Graham Ovendon and, greatest thrill of all, right beside a picture by Ernst Fuchs, a member of the Viennese Realistic-Fantastic school who was one of the greatest inspirations of her college days.

Patrick Woodroffe also happened to catch the first exhibition, and was so enthusiastic that Linda was encouraged to approach, and be taken on the books of, the Young Artists (now called Arena) agency in London. This soon led to her first book jacket commission.

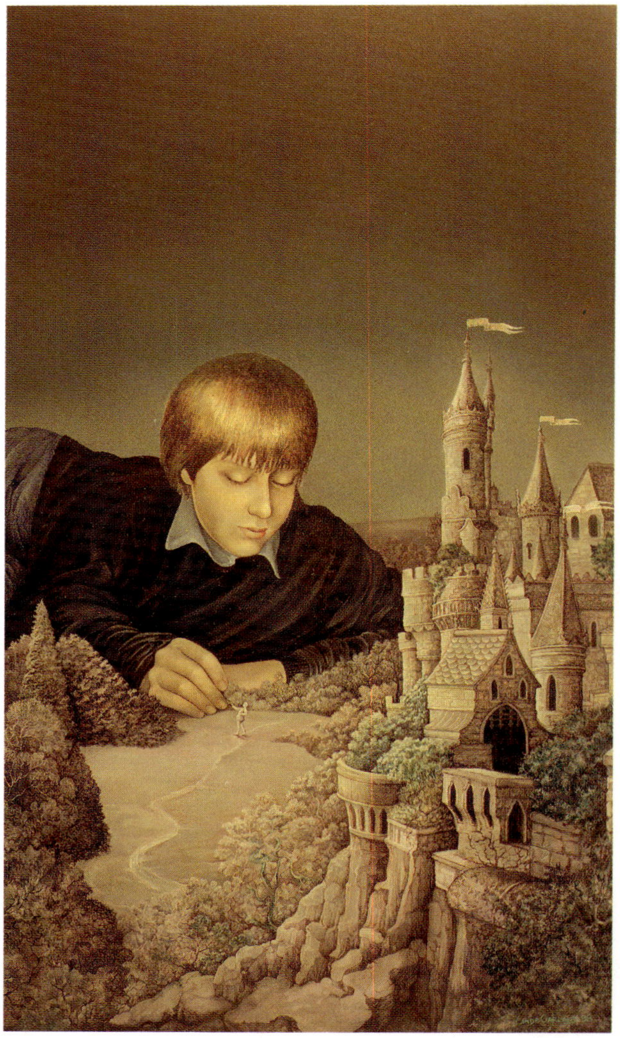

△ **Seth**
Linda 1988
Oils and Acrylic. 11 x 17in
Book cover, Corgi.

This illustration was for a young adults story (that is, aimed at the thirteen to seventeen year age group) in which the central character finds the key to enter a role-playing game. The Garlands' son, Seth, was the model, being aged a little to fit the part. He has since appeared in further pictures, along with other members of the family and their circle of friends.

▷ **Rainbow**
Linda 1988
Oils and Acrylic. 12 x 19in
(30 x 48cm)
Cover for *The Folk of the Air* by Peter S. Beagle, Headline.

'It's always a pleasure illustrating a well-crafted book like this,' says Linda, referring to this book by Beagle, whose most famous title, *The Last Unicorn,* remains something of a cult item. Motorbikes are outside Linda's usual territory, but as they feature in the story, which is a curious blend of the modern and medieval, she extended herself.

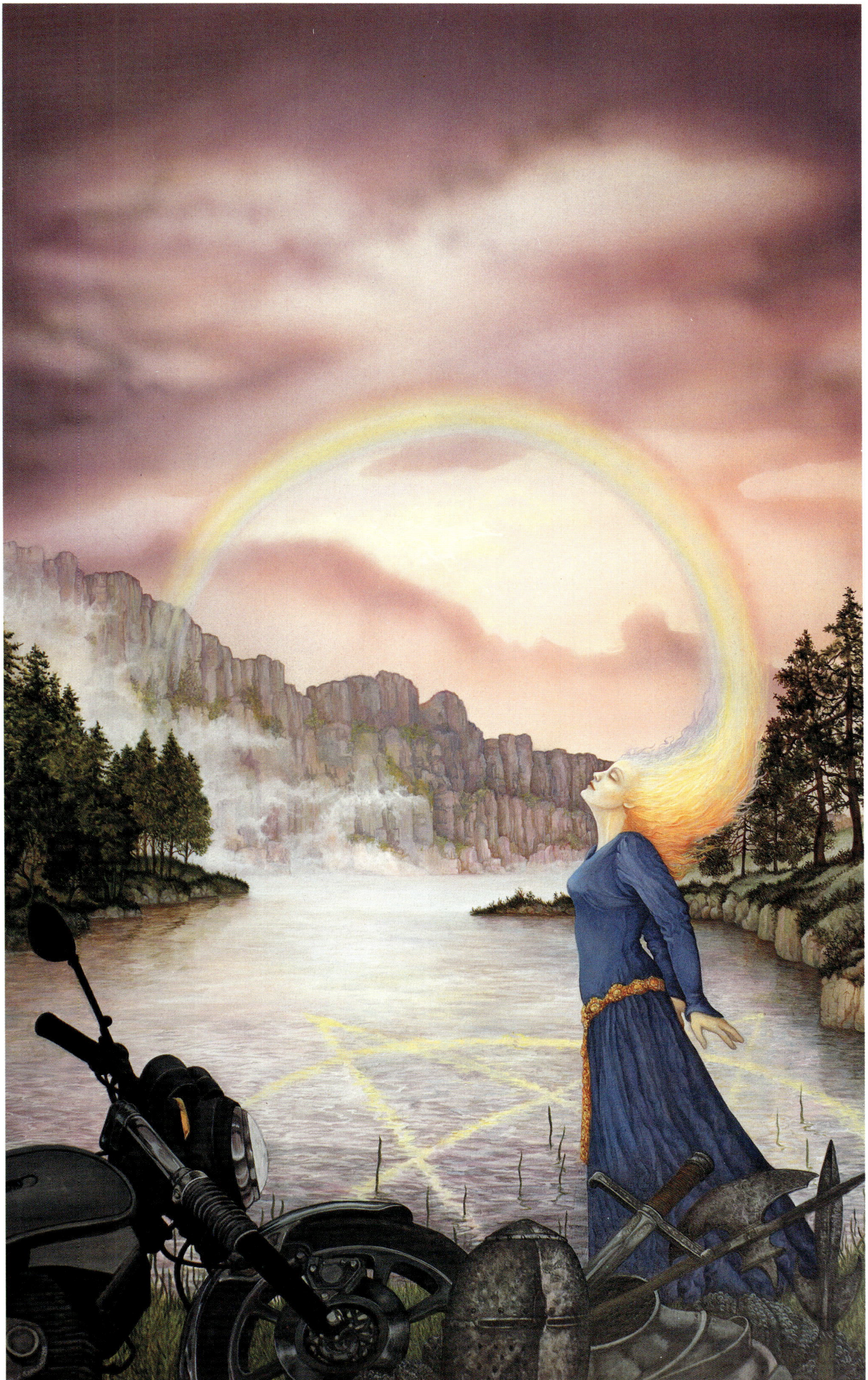

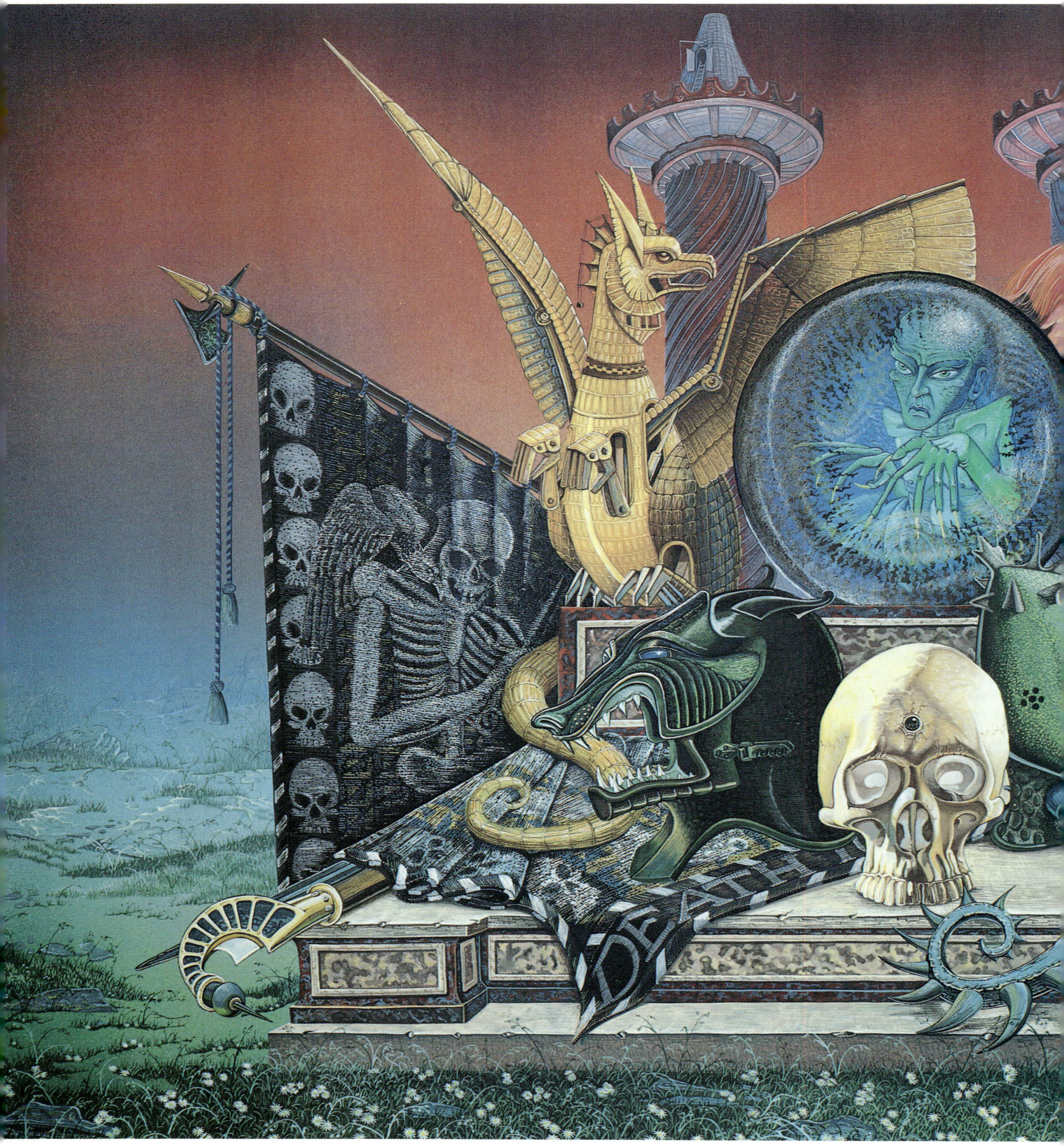
DEATH

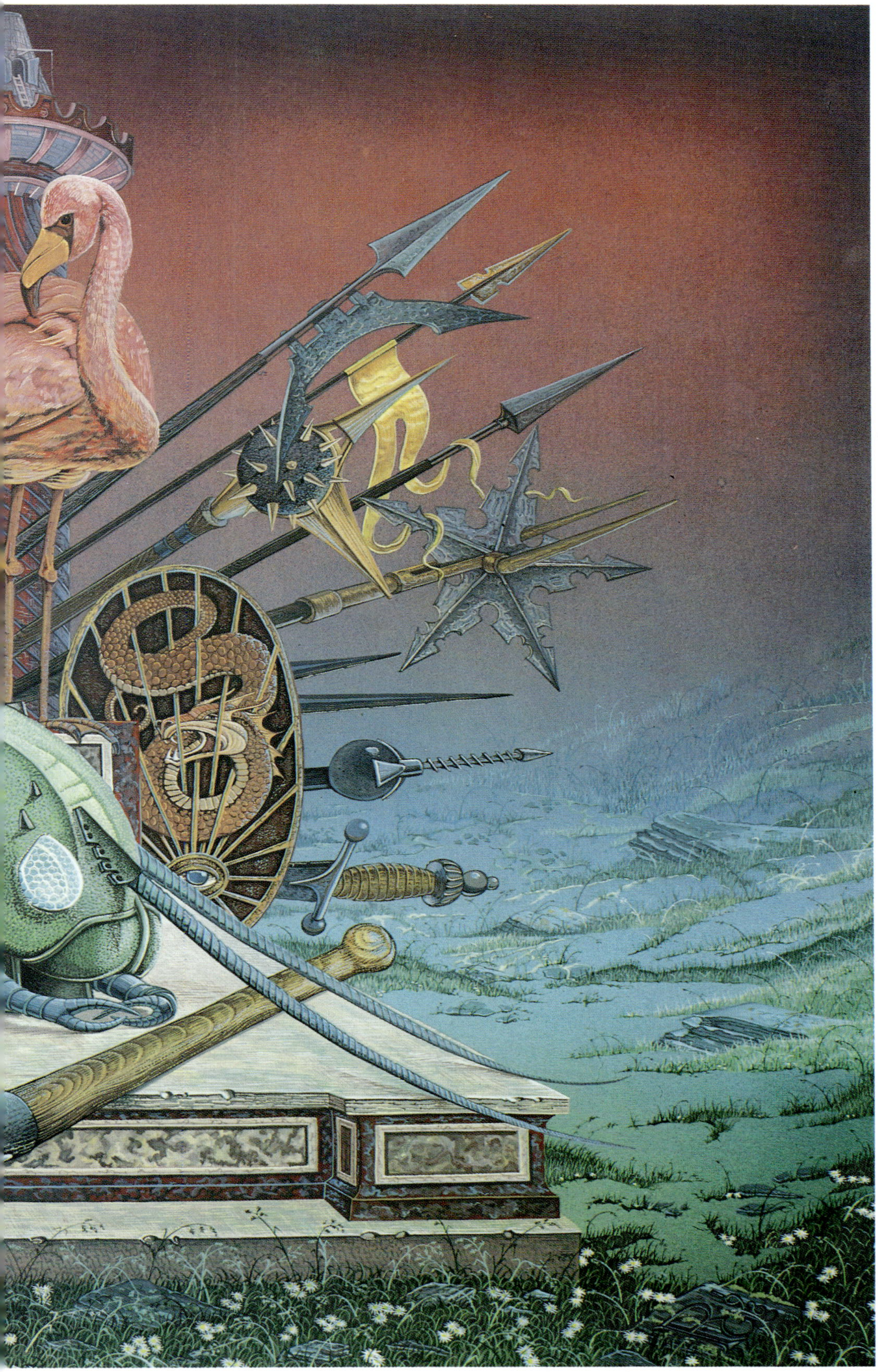

◁ **Jewel in the Skull**
Roger 1980
Gouache. 13 x 19in
(33 x 48cm)
Private work.

This began as a sample, in the early days of trying to drum up work as an illustrator, and drew on the imagery of Michael Moorcock's novel of the same name.

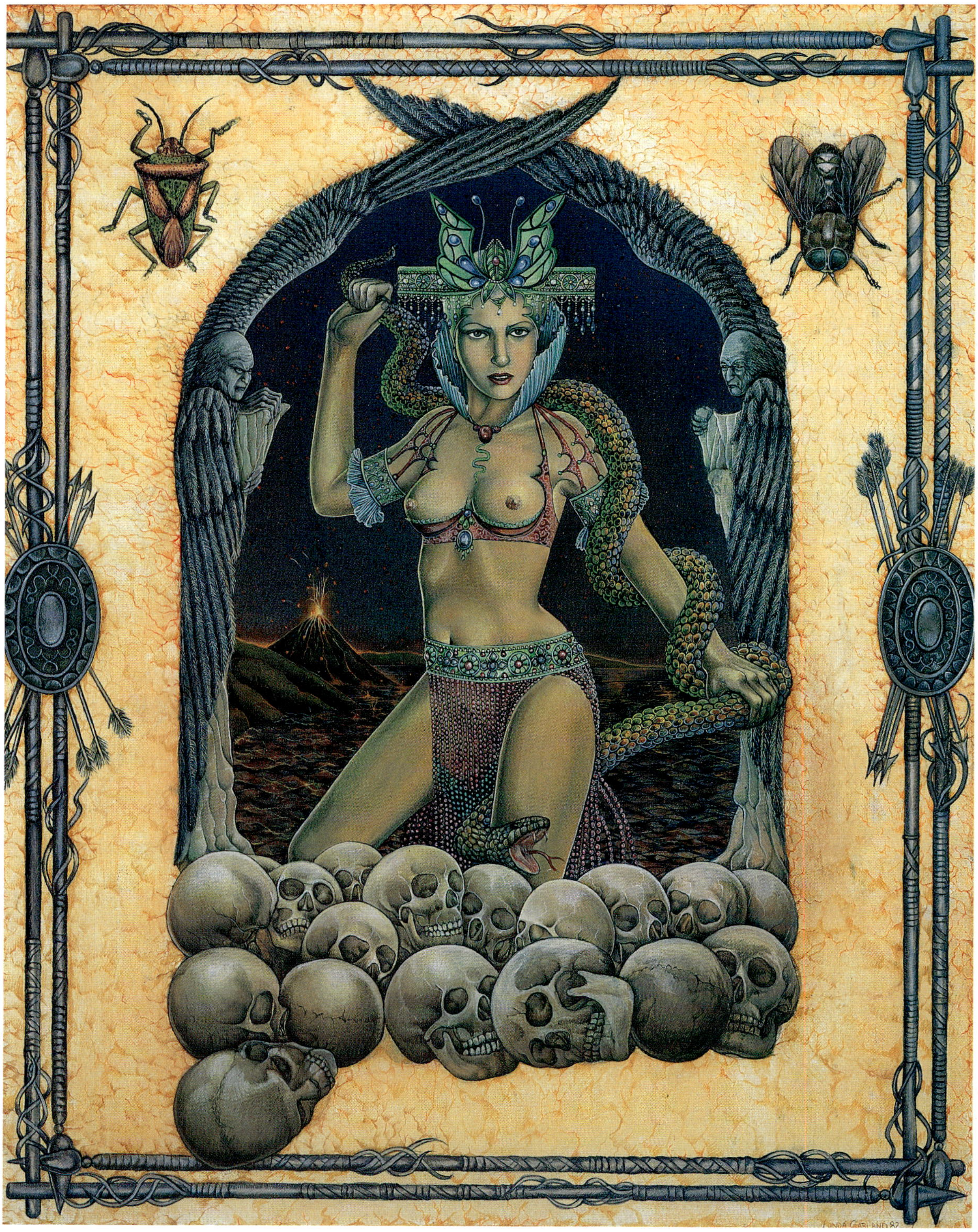

△ **Shamana**
Linda 1982
Oils and Acrylic.
11 x 13in (28 x 33cm)
Private work.

During a slack period, Linda was told by her agent at Young Artists (now Arena) to 'just do your own thing' and come up with some samples of what she could do. Unfortunately, the original of this was stolen during a break-in at the agency.

▷ **Serpentine**
Roger 1978
Gouache. 13 x 17in (33 x 43cm)
Cover for a book of the same name by Thomas Thompson, Jade/Futura.

This was Roger's first published book cover. The illustration was, in fact, first commissioned as a publicity poster before it was decided to use the same image on the cover, which happily meant being paid twice for the same work. The story was a true one of an Asian criminal genius, Charles Sobhraj, whose nefarious operations extended from India to Hong Kong, and included enticing Western hippies to the exotic East and bumping them off. It was made into a TV film starring Art Malik, famous amongst other things for his part in *Jewel in the Crown*.

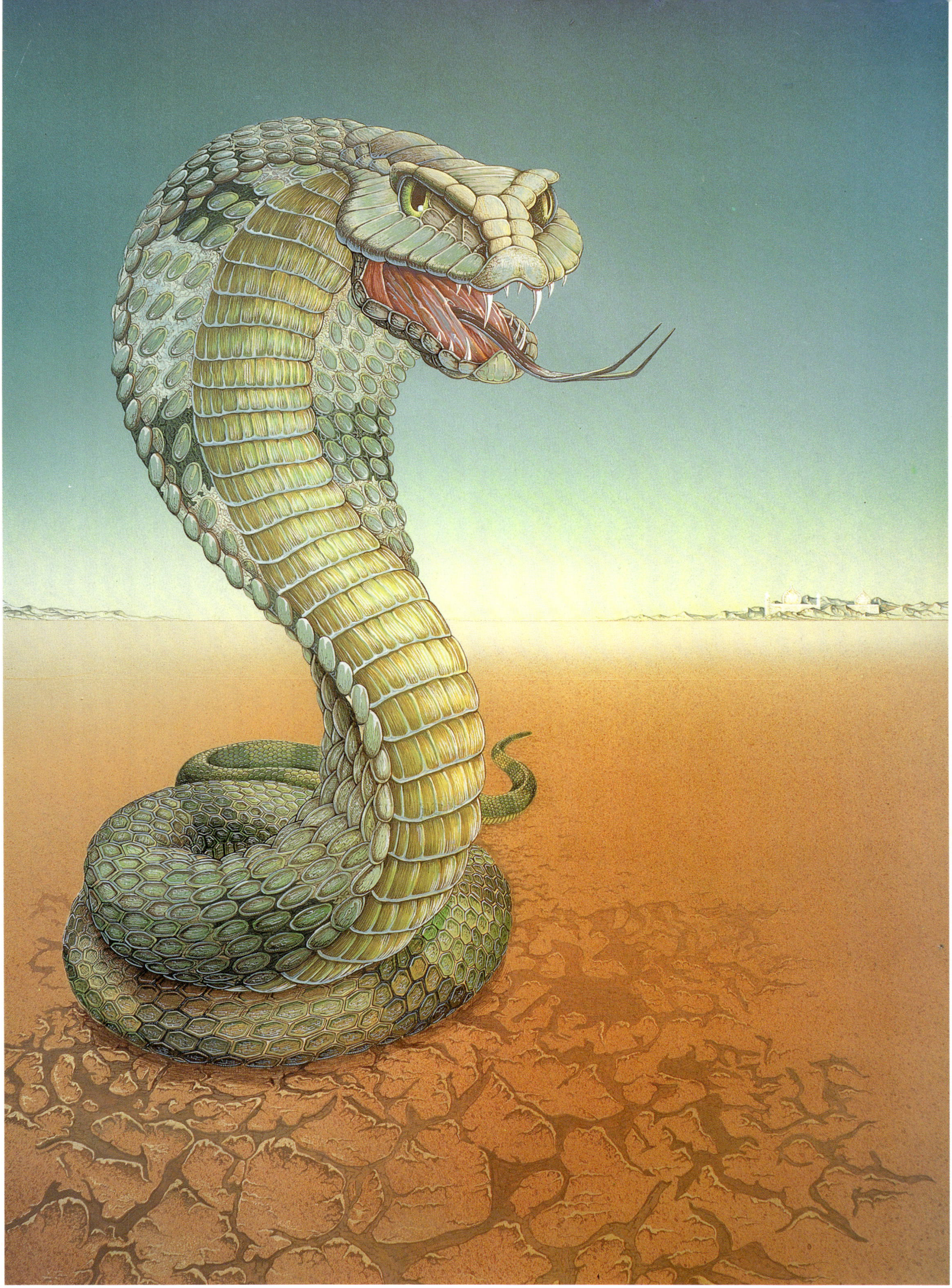

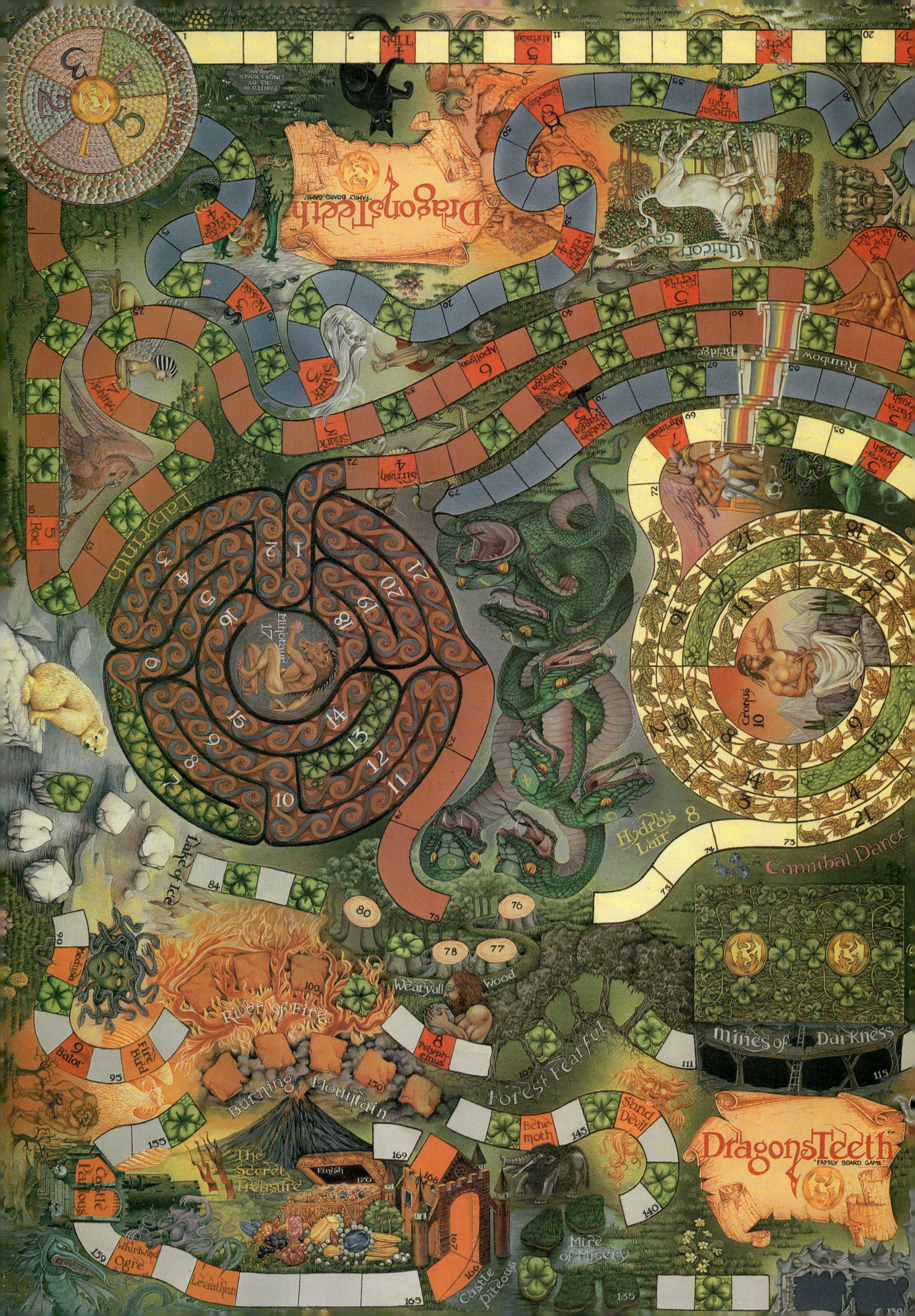
DragonsTeeth
FAMILY BOARD GAME
Start
Labyrinth
5 Roc
Minotaur 17
Hydra's Lair 8
Cannibal Dance
Cronus 10
Lake of Ice
Medusa
River of Fire
Wearyall Wood
8 Polyphemus
Forest Fearful
Mines of Darkness
Burning Mountain
9 Balor
Fire Bird
Sand Devil
Behemoth
The Secret Treasure
Finish
Castle Perilous
Whirlwind Ogre
Leviathan
Castle Piteous
Mire of Misery
Unicorn Grove
Rainbow Bridge
6 Apollyon
Sphinx
3 Shark
4 Siren
DragonsTeeth
FAMILY BOARD GAME

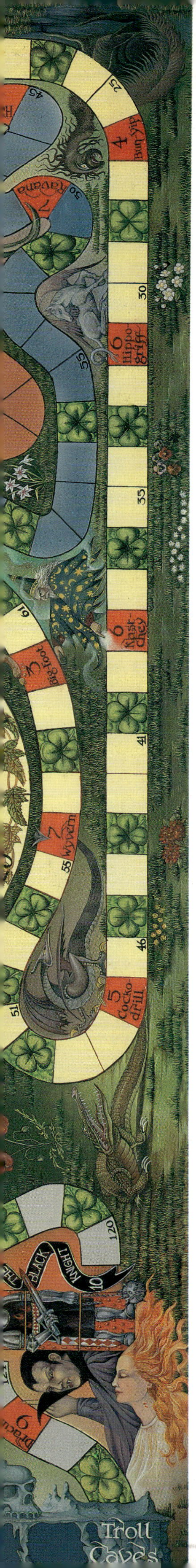


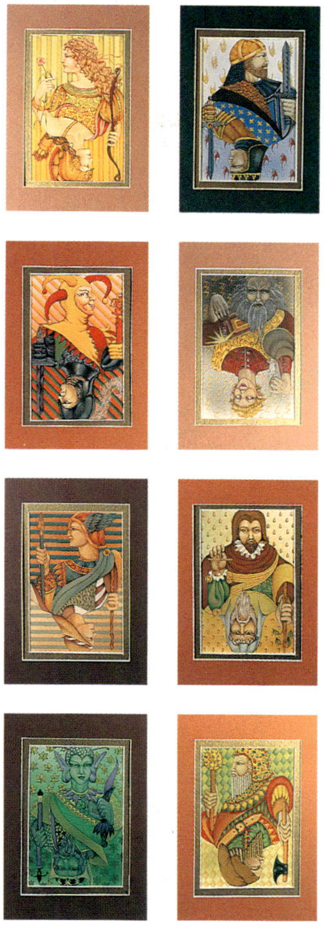

△ **Dragon's Teeth game cards** Linda and Roger 1982
Oils and Acrylic. 3 x 5in
(8 x 12cm)
Commissioned by TSR Games.

◁ **Dragon's Teeth Boardgame**
Linda and Roger 1982
Oils and Acrylic. 20 x 24in
(51 x 61cm)
Commissioned by TSR Games.

Sadly this game was sidelined by the boom in computer games and was never published by TSR, though the Garlands have heard rumours of it having been produced privately by publisher, Tom Kirby. It was basically an ingenious extension of the Dungeons and Dragons idea, with players throwing dice to determine their characteristics and strengths. The carefully thought out game included nice touches, such as the fact that the players ventured through it as a party, and all ended up on the same track for a final race for the treasure.

Linda and Roger worked on different corners of the picture simultaneously, which often led to them banging heads in the middle.

With this promising start the Garlands decided to try and launch Linda as a full-time illustrator. Looking back on it, the transition went very smoothly and was barely upset by the arrival of their son Seth. Gradually, work snowballed until commissions were rolling in at the gentle, but manageable, rate of about one a month.

Two essential factors, they believe, were having an agent in London and the cushioning steadiness of Roger's teaching. As for Linda's personal style, it somehow evolved quite naturally and she never felt forced to strain it by taking it somewhere she didn't want to. Linda: 'It was liberating living in Cornwall. It's such a backwater you feel you can do what you like.'

Roger continued teaching for twelve years, but he too joined Young Artists and began receiving commissions which he fitted around his job. Then, in 1983, he finally took the plunge and went freelance, partly prompted by the pressure of a full-time job on top of a healthy flow of illustration, but also because, he says: 'I couldn't face the prospect of ending up at sixty without ever having tried it. As you approach the age of thirty-five you get this feeling of being able to see to the end of your life and for me it felt time to do something new. My biggest fear was ending up teaching the kids of the kids I had first taught.'

The result was not a pleasant one. Work immediately dried up and for the next six months he went round feeling enormously guilty about not being in 'honest' employment: 'When out walking the dog I found myself hiding in the hedgerows to avoid meeting people who might wonder why I was not at work. To make things worse, Linda was carrying our daughter Amy then. I felt incredibly irresponsible.'

However, in due course business picked up, and although it has sometimes been a precarious ride, both Garlands have remained freelance artists since.

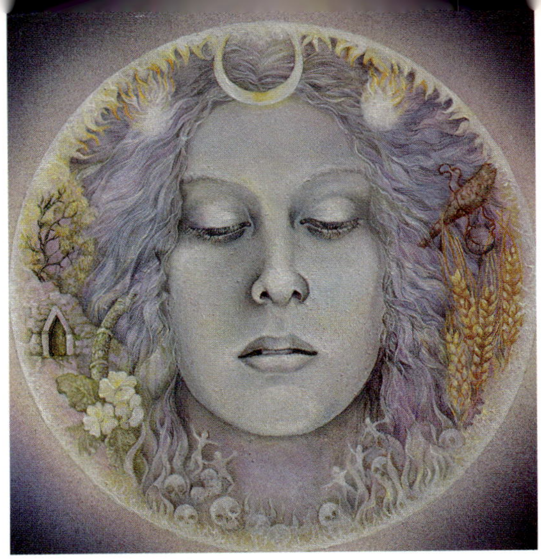

# REFLECTIONS OF THE GODDESS

*" The Celtic myths are still shrouded in mystery, more open to interpretation and on the whole more earthy, more instinctive and, therefore, more associated with witchcraft."*

People get curious ideas about artists from seeing their work. At exhibitions both Garlands have often been greeted with: 'You're not at all like I imagined.' Which leaves them wondering what the person did have in mind.

Linda's Goddess pictures have led many to suppose that she is some kind of a white witch. Her son, while working at a place where her cards were being printed, was once asked 'what she was on', and whether she was very strange to live with. To which Seth could only reply that she sometimes went a bit peculiar after a few glasses of wine, but that was about it.

The strength of these pictures comes simply from a vivid imagination tied to a deep interest in mythology, which is not always the same thing as magic. One of the few valuable pointers Linda received on her degree course (and the only thing this particular tutor ever said to her, on seeing one of her 'Medieval' drawings) was: 'You must read Robert Graves' *The White Goddess*.' It changed my life,' says Linda, 'and I've taken it with me everywhere since.'

Perhaps part of the assumption of witchiness comes from Linda being drawn more naturally to Celtic mythology than to the classical kind, although that does have its own fascination. Linda: 'I think art in the past, particularly since the Renaissance, perhaps sanitized classical mythology. It became very intellectualized, whereas the Celtic myths are still shrouded in mystery, more open to interpretation and on the whole more earthy, more instinctive and, therefore, more associated with witchcraft.'

From the beginning Linda wanted to use Celtic themes and motifs in her paintings, but for a while had no idea how: 'I kept reading other people's concepts of Celtic art and finding I could not agree. If you mention the subject most people think of the *Book of Kells* and the *Lindisfarne Gospels*, which are fantastic but also full of Viking and Anglo-Saxon designs. What I was interested in was the earlier, purer Celtic style associated with their wonderful myths.'

△ **Way of the Goddess**
Linda 1986
Oils. 5 x 5in (13 x 13cm)
Book cover, Prism Press.

The subject of this book is the role of White Witches in society, so the picture is bordered by various symbols associated with the Goddess, such as the well, moon and corn (for rebirth). The original was purchased by a lady visitor to the Lakeside Gallery who just could not resist it, even though she had never bought a picture before in her life.

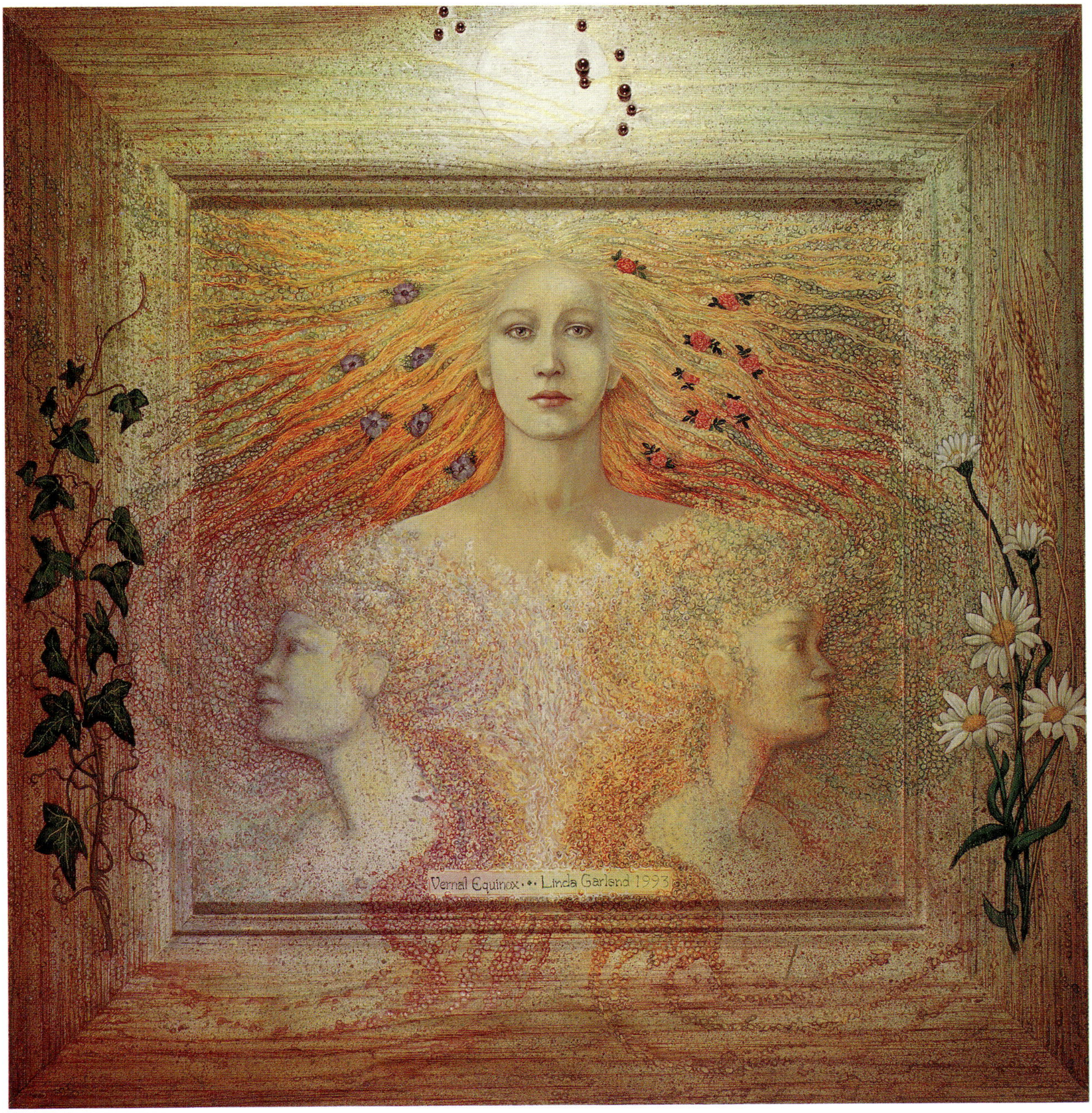


△ **Vernal Equinox**
Linda 1993
Oils. 15 x 15in (38 x 38cm)
Private commission,
Nick Roberts.

The flowers in the central figure's hair were chosen by the commissioner for private reasons, but the composition is otherwise Linda's. The figures on either side look forward to summer and back to the winter past.
The metal studs, set into the painted frame at the top, are in the configuration of Aries, the constellation of spring, through which the rejuvenated sun is emerging.

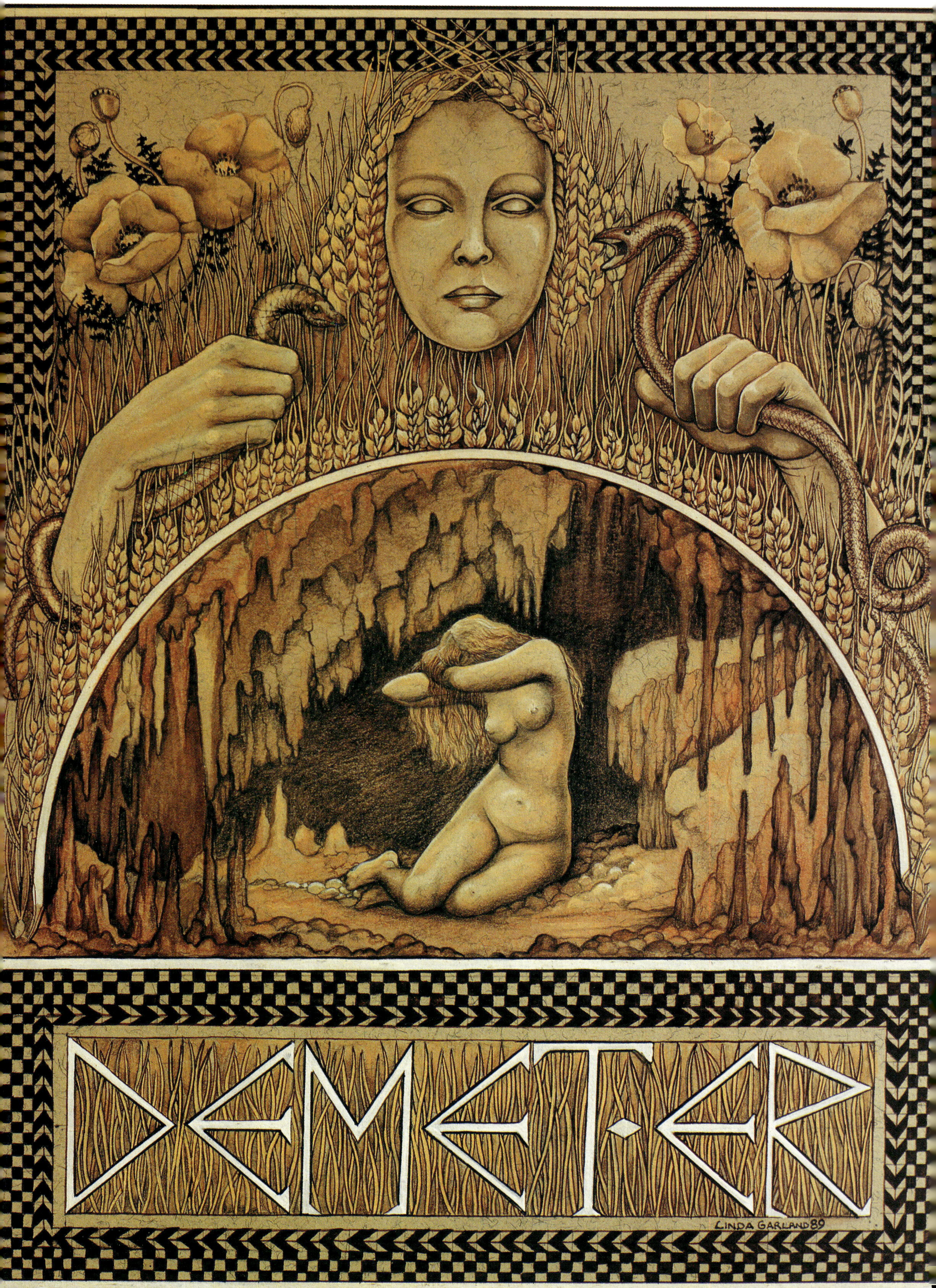
DEMETER
LINDA GARLAND 89

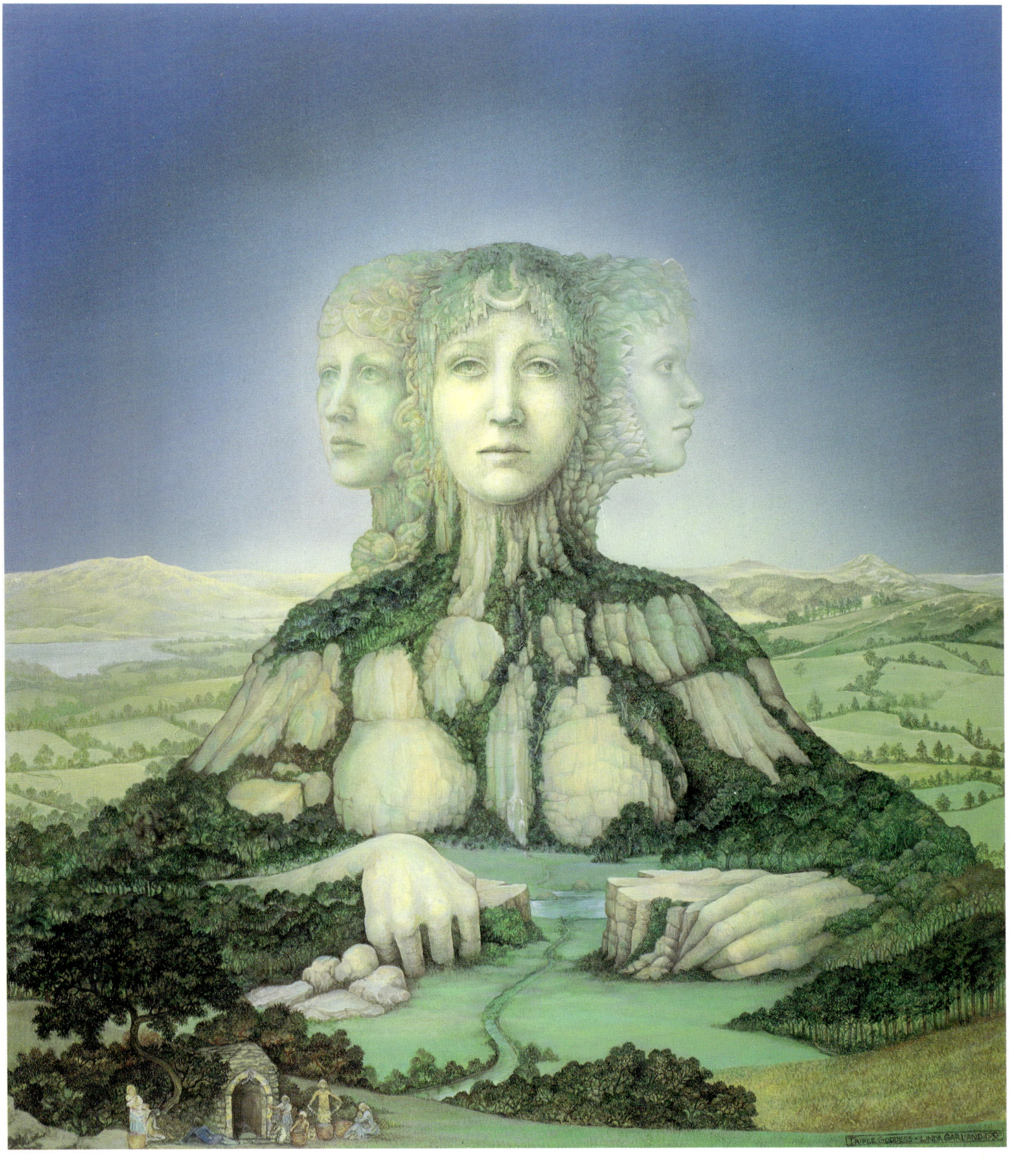


◁ **Demeter**
Linda 1989
Mixed media. 8 x 10in
Private work.

In Greek mythology, Demeter was the sister of Zeus. Amongst her symbols were the snake and poppy and she presided over agriculture, making her one of the principal deities of early civilization.

△ **Brigit**
Linda 1992
Oils. 12 x 14in (30 x 35cm)
Private work.

Three aspects of the Goddess are illustrated here – the goddess of water, hence the wells; the goddess of very fine metalwork; the goddess of fertility. Otherwise, it is a pure English landscape.

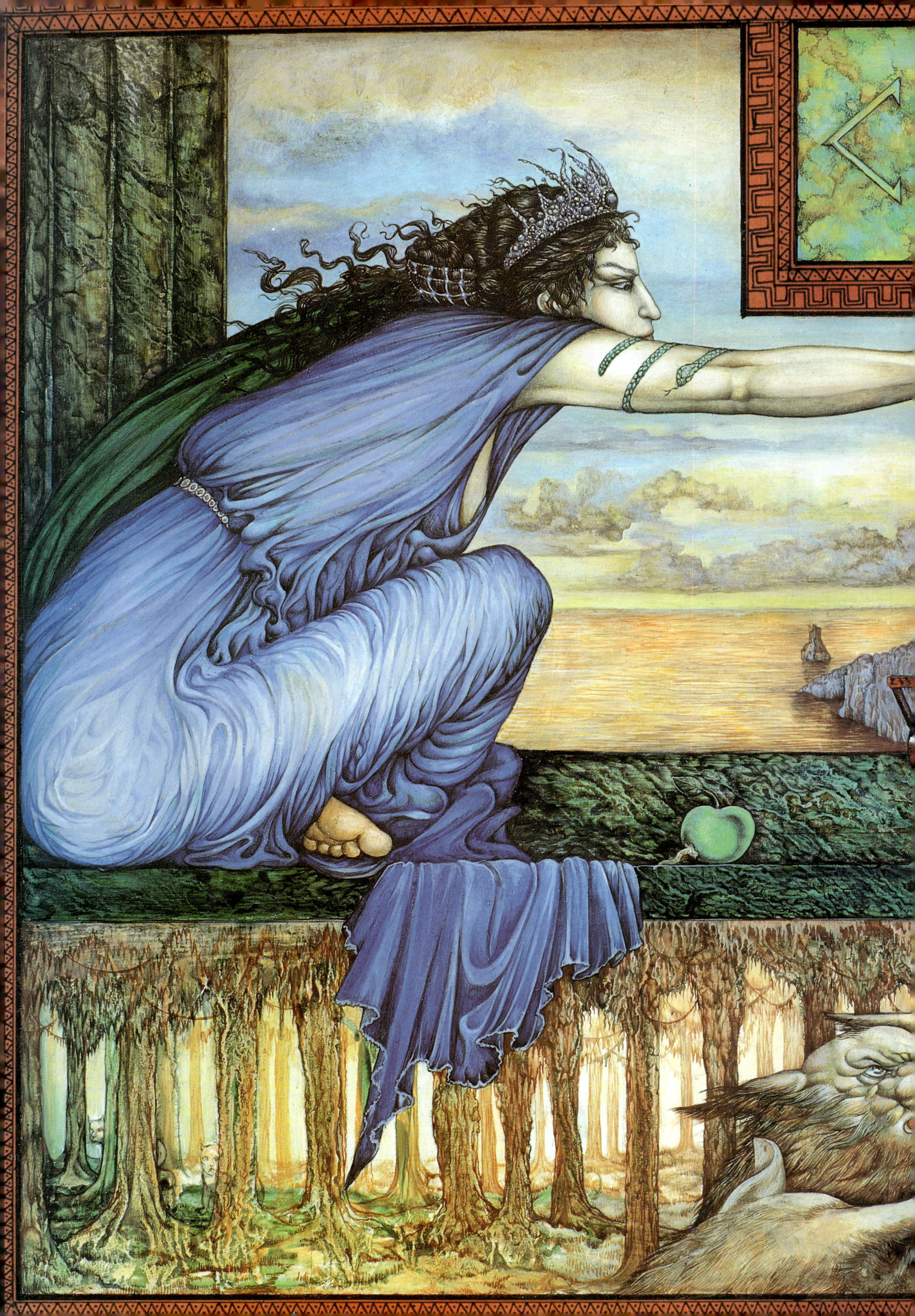

Her first serious attempt in this line was *Triptych* (see pages 30-31), which avoids the overt use of Celtic motifs, but is steeped in that feeling and was an attempt to capture her impressions of the Cornish landscape, the profusion of growth there compared with her native Yorkshire, and its distinct, otherworldly feel. Since then she has returned repeatedly to the seam, and it shows no sign of becoming exhausted.

It is also often assumed that Linda is a feminist, and in practice she fits most of the definitions, but where it veers towards aggression she distances herself from the movement completely: 'Perhaps I've led a charmed life, but I've never met any obstacle because of gender. From school I went to college and from there into teaching and illustration. In none of this has being female mattered either way. Maybe it helps also being married to a man whose family has a tradition of strong females, Roger's grandmother in particular. With the Garlands there is no question of a woman being expected to be her husband's submissive shadow.'

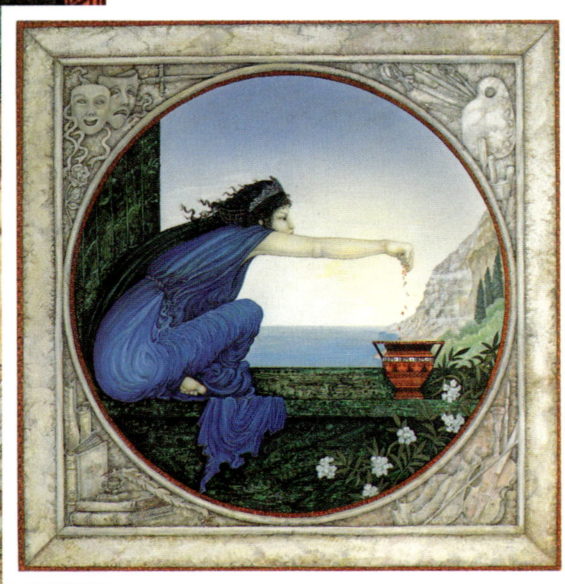

◁ **Circe**
Linda 1986
Oils. 10 x 10in (26 x 26cm)
Private work.

This was the first of Linda's goddess pictures. It was included as a sample in the Young Artists brochure, where it caught the eye of an Art Director who commissioned something very similar as an advertisement for IBM computers (see *Circe II*), with Circe sprinkling microchips, instead of herbs, into the crater.

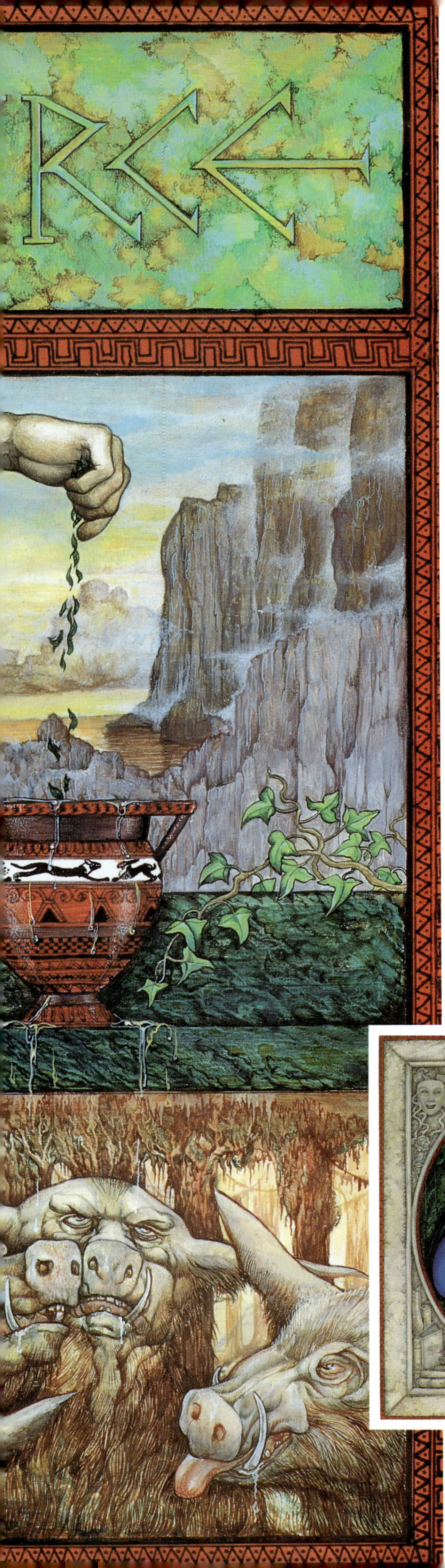

◁ Circe II
Linda 1989
Oils. 10 x 10in (26 x 26cm)
Advertisement, IBM.

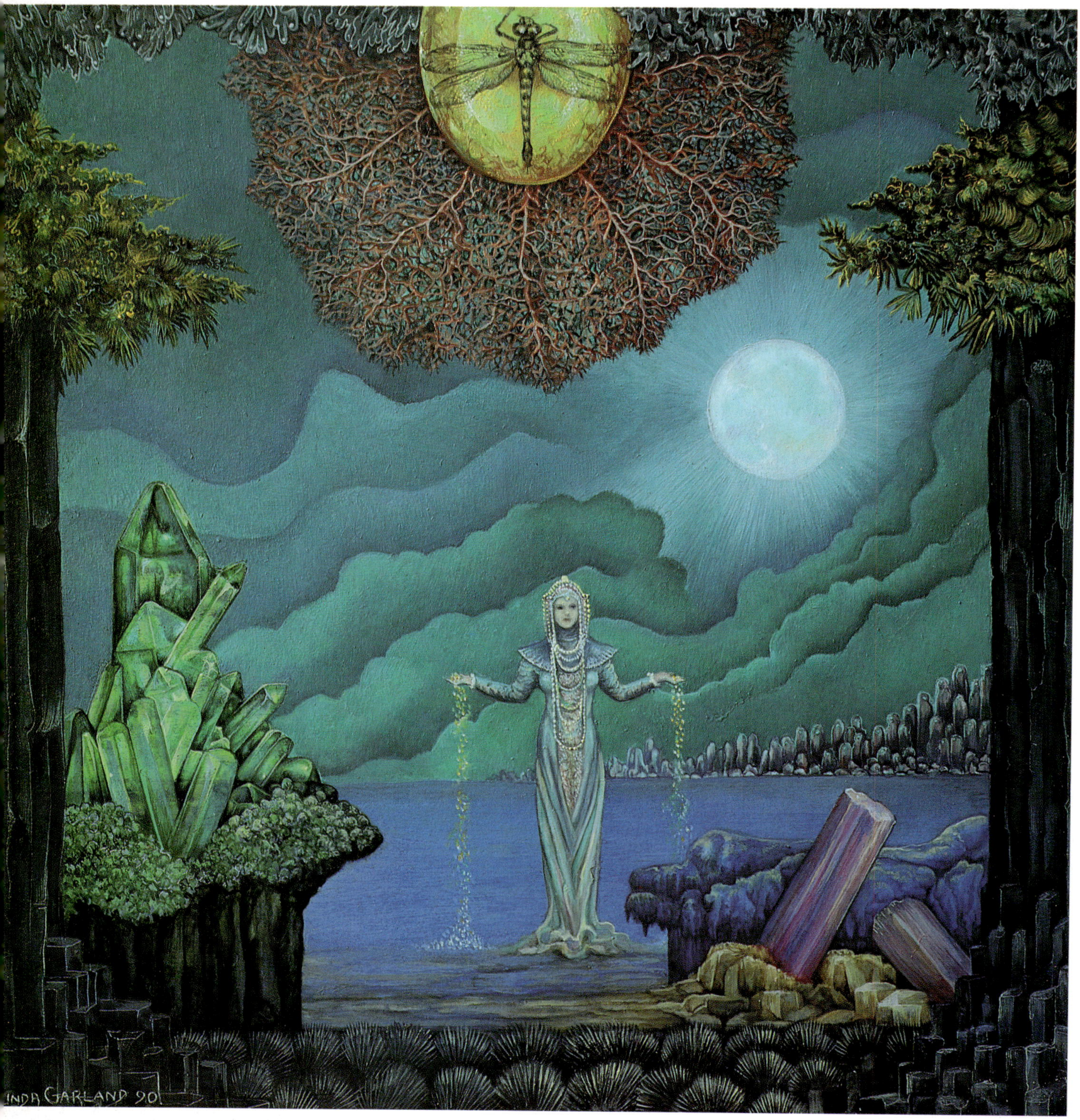


△ Crystal Goddess
Linda 1990
Oils. 7 x 7in (18 x 18cm)
Book cover, Prism Press.

This composition aimed to include as many different crystals as possible, using the term in its broadest sense to include amber, coral and silver. The pattern of the sky is taken from malachite.

▷ Ice Goddess
Linda 1992
Oils. 12 x 14in (30 x 35cm)
Calendar illustration, Visionary Publishing.

Linda is particularly pleased with the radiating iced hair effect.

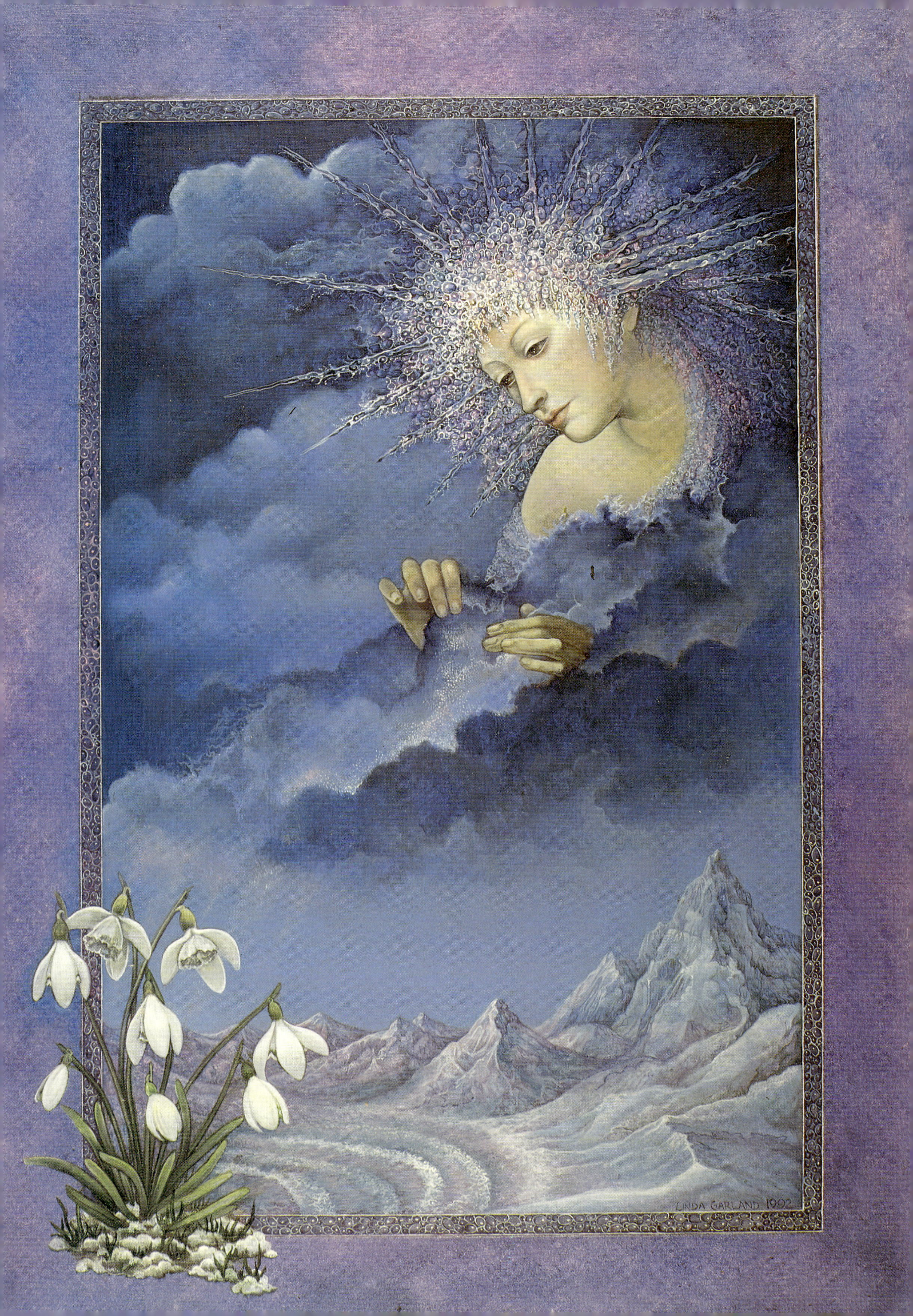
LINDA GARLAND 1992

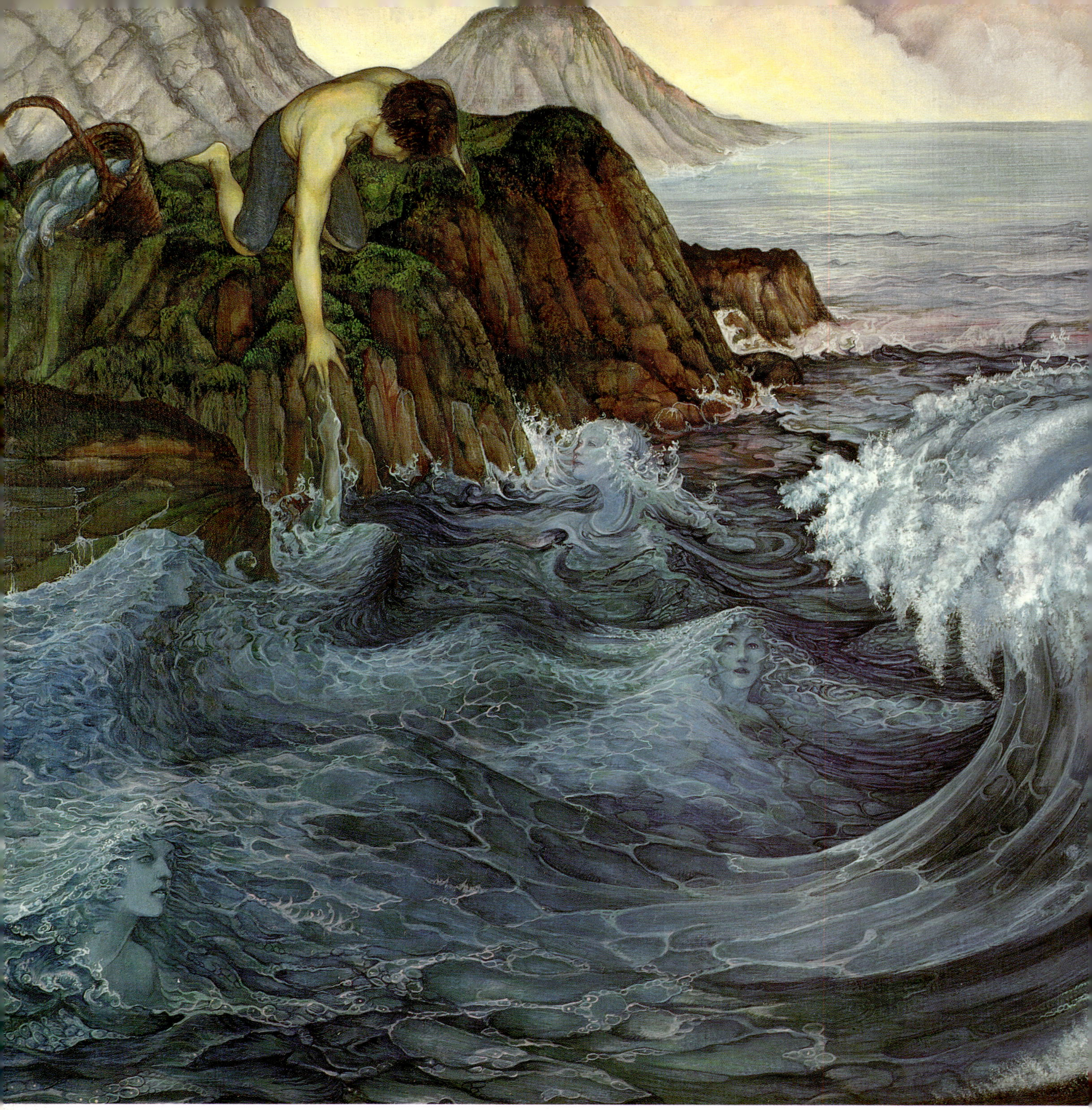

Many of Linda's paintings celebrate the female side, but they are neither defensive nor aggressive about it.

Linda grew up in Scarborough and had a 'lovely childhood'. Her earliest clear ambition was to go to art college and, once decided, she never deviated from this. As far as she can remember, the moment of inspiration came on a family visit to Liverpool when she was thirteen. Her parents took her to the Lady Lever Gallery in Port Sunlight and there, amid the Pre-Raphaelite collection, Linda realized that what she wanted, above

△ **Sirens**
Linda 1993
Oils. 12 x 18in (30 x 45cm)
Calendar illustration, Visionary Publishing.

This work represented the chance to illustrate a classic theme.

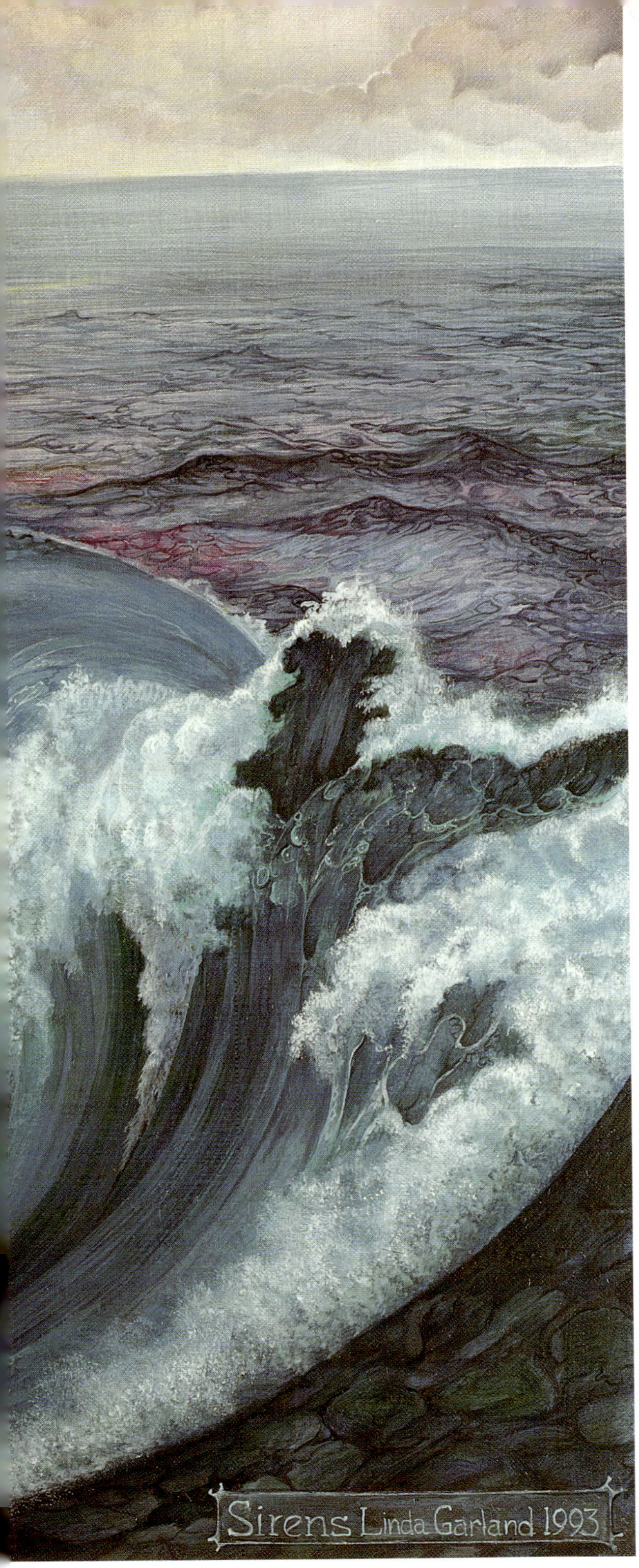


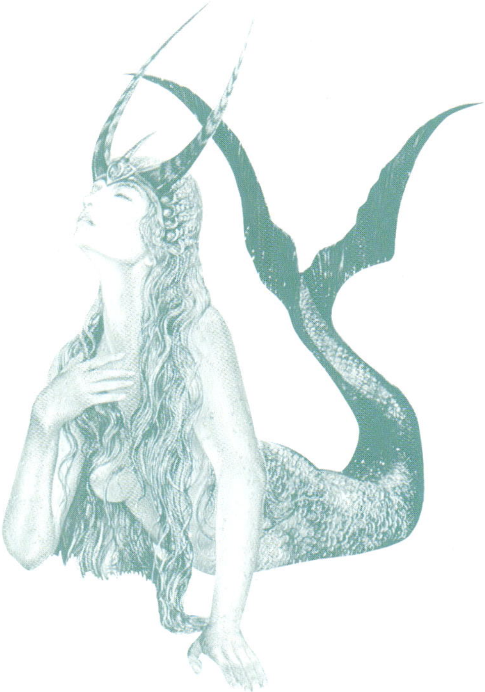

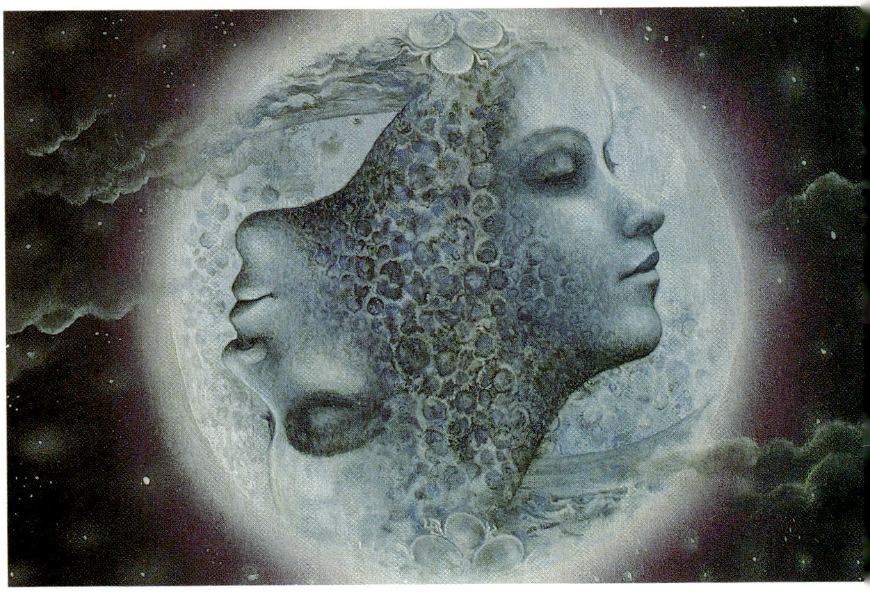

all else, was to paint in a similar vein. They went on to the Walker Gallery in Liverpool, where further Pre-Raphaelites confirmed the feeling, particularly work by Rossetti.

This was the first real spark, although Linda had always previously painted, and her family had a strong general interest in art and culture. Her grandmother, in particular, was obsessed with music and insisted everyone learn to play an instrument. Linda's grandfather too, a builder by trade, produced some 'fantastic' drawings of architecture and plant life.

△ Moon Goddess
Linda 1987
Oils. 3.5in diam. (9cm)
Card illustration, Karma Cards.

This is the central insert for one of a pack of fifty fortune-telling cards, which Linda produced at a breakneck pace. One of four border designs completed each card, with spaces for the relevant attributes, hints, or whatever.

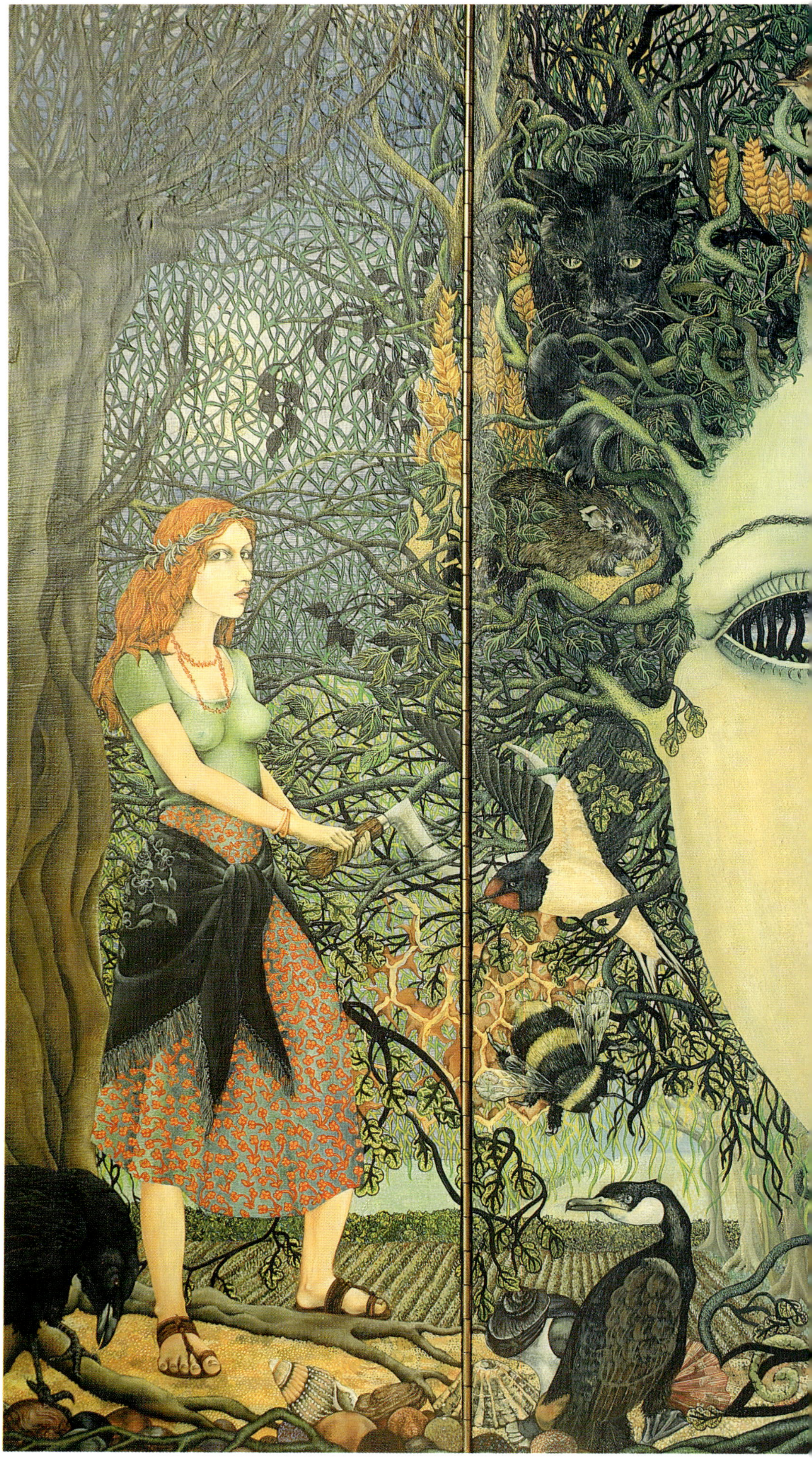

▷ Triptych
Linda 1975
Oils. 26 x 34in (66 x 86cm)
Private work.

One of the largest and earliest of Linda's paintings, this was a labour of love which led to many commissions for work in the same vein. The picture represents the Seasonal Chase and relates the turning of the year to the moon's cycle and the three ages of woman. Among the details woven into the scene are the prophetic raven on the left; a sickle representing the new moon; a ploughed field ready for growth; a bee and a swallow signalling the arrival of summer; a hare chased by a greyhound indicating winter and the coursing season; and thence, by way of the absent moon and winter, one returns to spring.

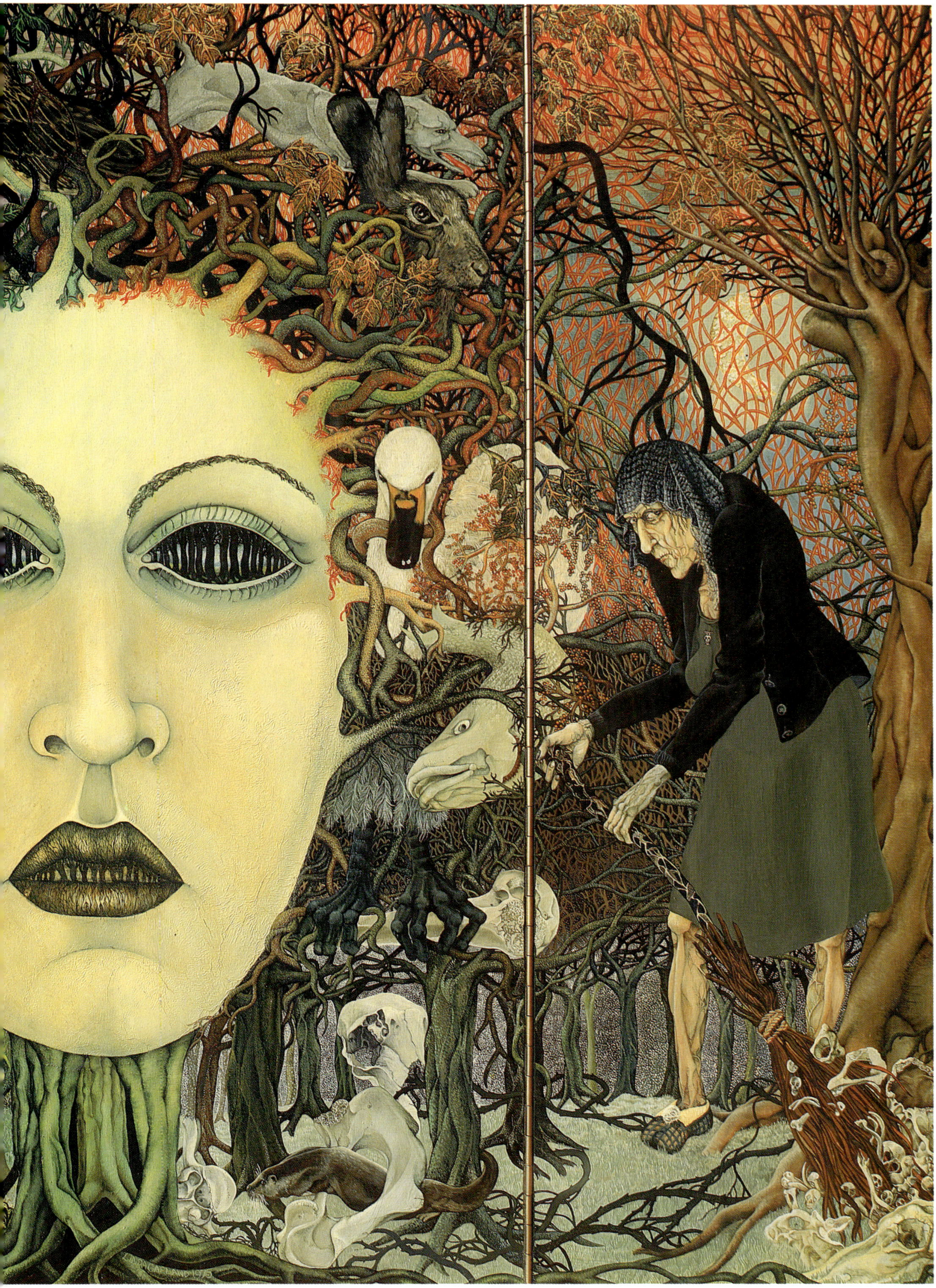

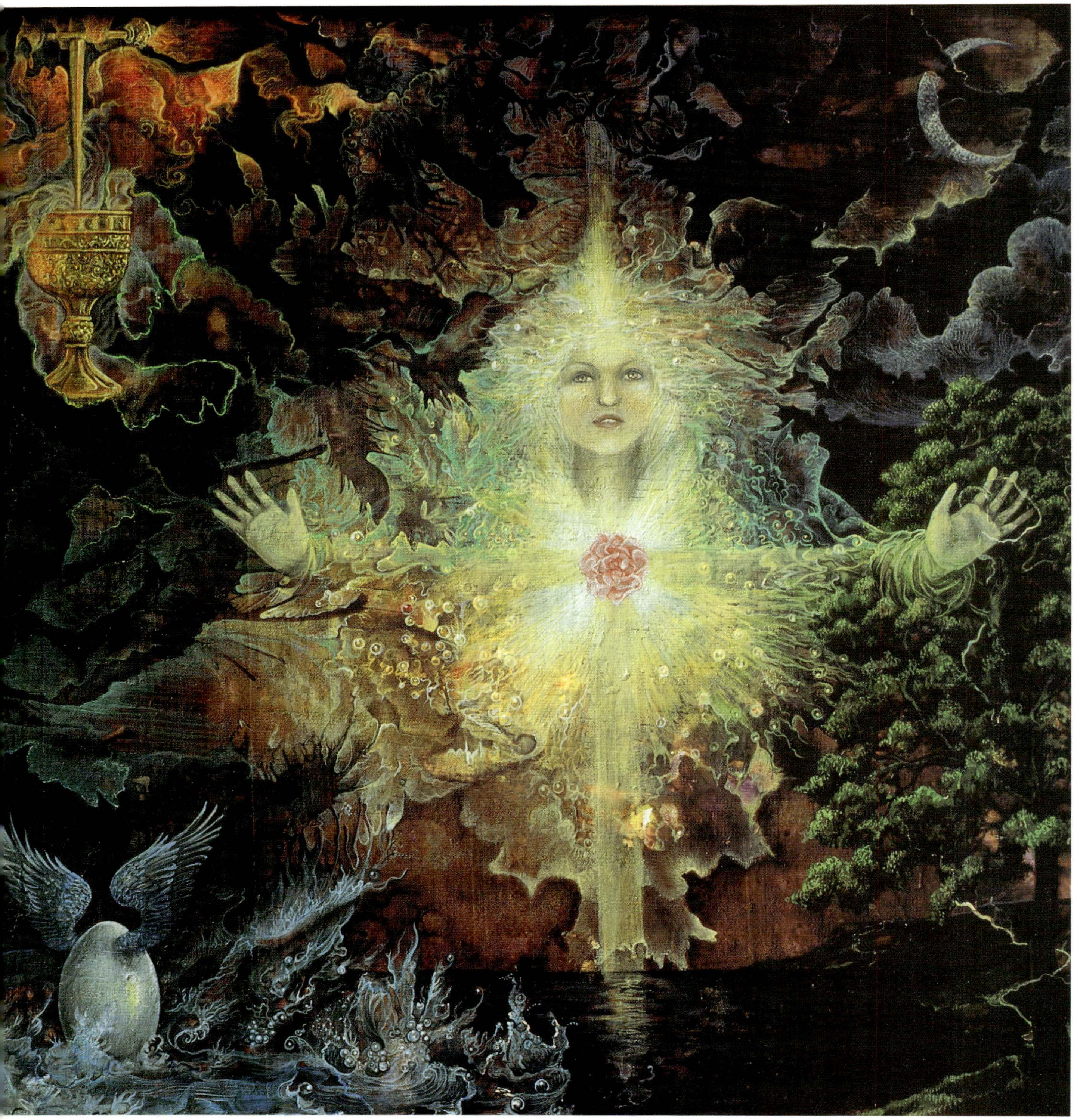

△ **Starchild**
Linda 1989
Oils. 7 x 7in (18 x 18cm)
Cover for *Modern Ritual Magic*, Prism Press.

The theme of this book was spiritual hallucination, which allowed a very free hand with the imagery. It was tackled by splashing paint, more or less randomly, on to the panel and elaborating whatever was suggested. Note the hint of Rosicrucianism in the main figure and the Holy Grail in the top left. The beauty of this series of covers for Prism, was that no allowance had to be made for lettering, as the square panels were inset.

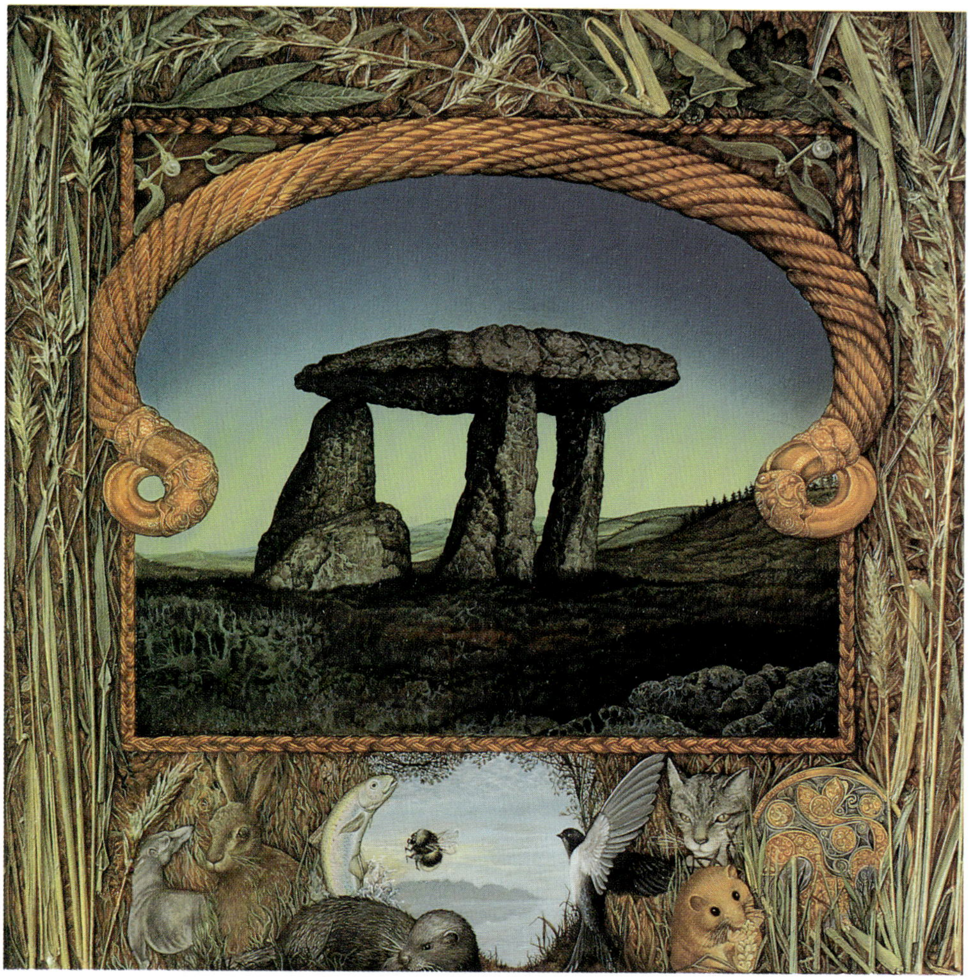

◁ **Celtic Twilight**
Linda 1989
Oils and collage. 12 x 12in (30 x 30cm)
Book cover, Prism Press.

The scene is Lanyon Quoit in Cornwall, framed by the famous Snettisham Torc and a collage of mistletoe, willow and oak, plus various wild grasses. These collages are made by soaking the items in PVA glue before sticking them to the surface. Once dry, they are painted back to their original colours with oils. At the base is a miniature Seasonal Chase scene using some of the elements in *Triptych*.

From school, Linda took an art foundation course in Scarborough, before going on to study Fine Art in Wolverhampton. Her ambition was achieved, but it was not quite the heaven she had anticipated: 'College for me was a terrible experience. I wanted to be taught how to paint like Leonardo but we ended up climbing through boxes and sucking oranges because John Cage said it was the thing to do. "Happenings" were all the rage then and representational art was considered below what any polite word could describe.'

The course began with the students going to a life drawing class, which to Linda seemed encouraging. However, afterwards a line of tutors marched in like storm-troopers, tore up the drawings without looking at them, and announced that it was the last life drawing the students would do for the next three years.

From then on she kept her head down and toed the line, surreptitiously drawing under the desk and not daring admit how much she admired the Pre-Raphaelites for fear of being laughed off the course. A flash of defiance, or subversion, came at the end when she chose *Rossetti's Women* as the title of her thesis, but that was about it.

Apart from gaining her a degree, the course gave Linda few direct benefits; in fact, it left her feeling decidedly useless and unlikely to make the grade in art. However, there were indirect benefits: if it did not teach her any way of applying her talents, the course did at least sharpen her ideas about the kind of art she believed in.

The pessimism did not last, and before very long, following the move to Cornwall, she was launched as a freelance illustrator.

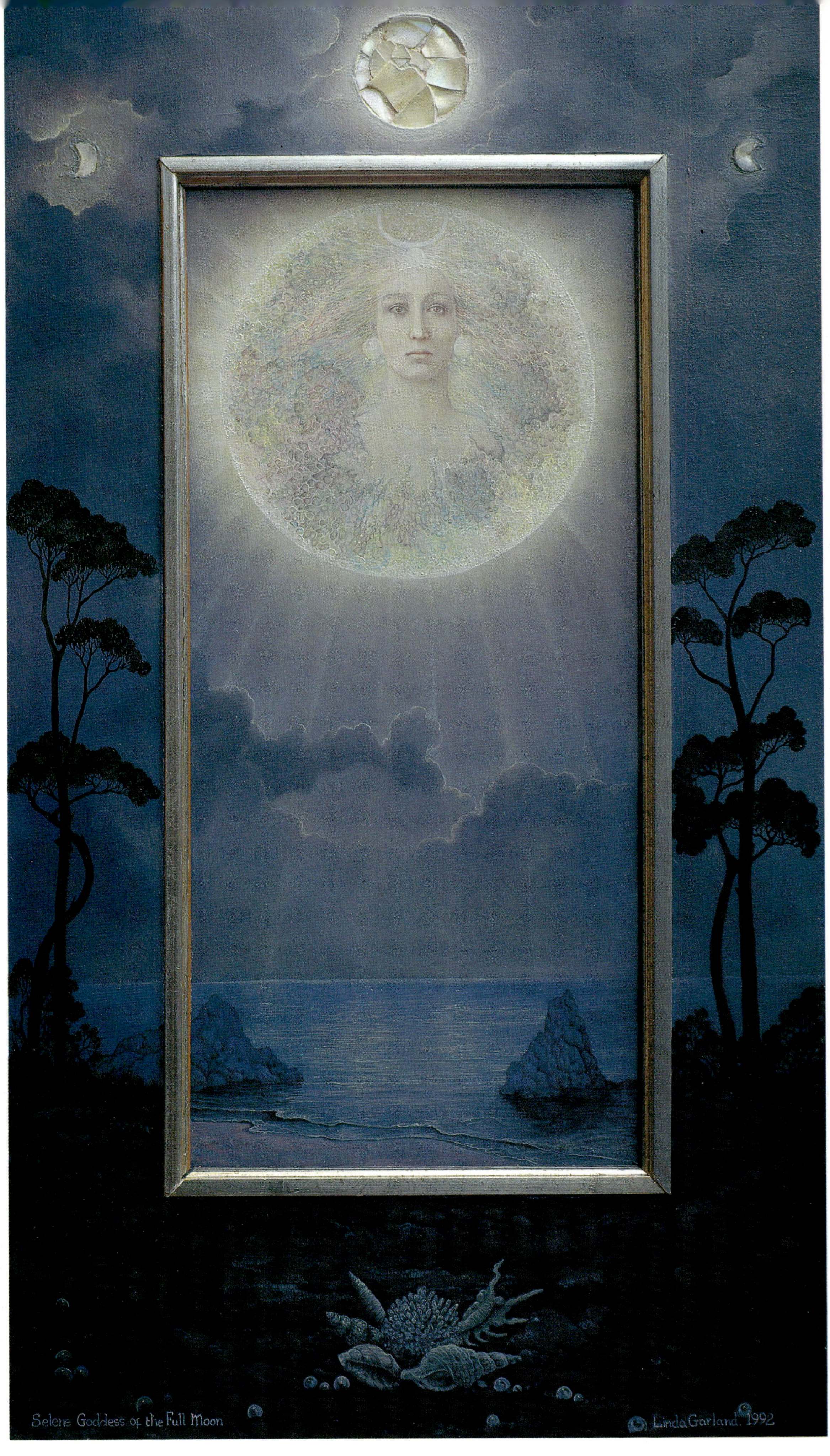
Selene Goddess of the Full Moon
Linda Garland. 1992

◁ **Selene: Goddess of the Full Moon**
Linda 1992
Oils. 11 x 16in (28 x 41cm)
Private commission,
Barbra Brannon.

The picture border contains inlaid mother-of-pearl.

For a while the commissions were for book covers, but then came the chance to illustrate one throughout, *The Countryside Cook Book* by Gail Duff, Linda's first commission from Prism Press with whom she has had a long and fruitful association.

The book was a collection of folk recipes using plants and herbs that grow wild in the countryside, with a view to their medicinal as well as their nutritional value. Care was taken not to include any rare species and the recipes were, apparently, delicious, particularly the nettle soup.

Both Garlands worked on the project, Roger doing the line drawings, Linda the paintings of featured plants against rural backgrounds. It was, she says: 'Very enjoyable work, if not greatly taxing on the imagination, a bit like knitting really.' Unlike strict botanical illustration, the subjects show the same blemishes and variation in number of leaves and petals that one finds in the wild.

The book was very successful and led to many spin-offs which, while being a bit of a sidetrack, were nevertheless welcome. Most exciting of these was a call from Milan a few years later, from a lady who had come across the book on a stall. Would Linda be interested in producing similar paintings for the first ever gardening magazine in Italy?

The magazine, called *Gardenia*, was given an extravagant launch in 1984, for which Linda was flown over and put up in a first-class hotel. Roger, as technical assistant and photographer, had to make his own way there, but otherwise received the same treatment. Nearly 2,000 guests were invited to a lavish banquet to the accompaniment of a string quartet. The centrepiece was a giant cake made of gardenias, and at the end each guest was presented with a set of gardening tools, which caused not a little curiosity at customs on the Garlands' return. Before this, they were indulged with an all-expenses-paid tour of Italy to get a 'feel' of the landscape, an experience which left Linda with a passion for that country.

Such adventures are not common for illustrators, but they do happen and are part of the appeal: you never really know what will happen next.

What did happen for Linda was that the magazine kept her occupied for a well-rewarded year, during which she also managed a fair number of other covers. It led to more horticultural spin-offs too, but when these dropped to the level of seed packets Linda posted word with her agent that she was going back to fantasy full time.

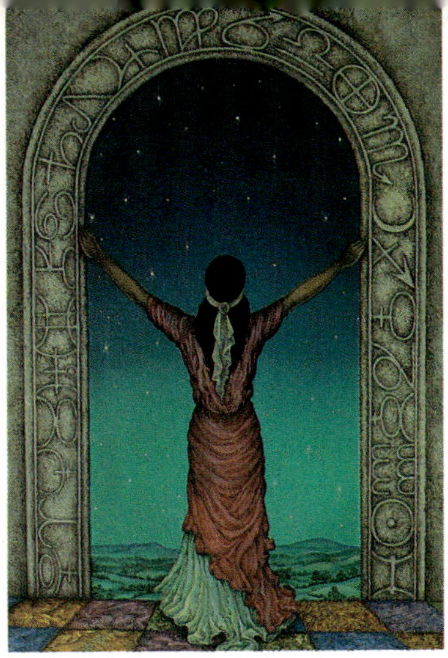

# THE LIVING ZODIAC

*"Canadian astrologer, Patricia Sereno . . . offered to barter for a painting by drawing up the Garland's birth charts. Out of curiosity they accepted, knowing nothing at all about the subject beyond what mythology has to say about the gods associated with the planets."*

'One advantage of giving up teaching', says Roger, 'was being able to choose where we liked to live.'

What they had in mind was a barn, ripe for conversion, somewhere in the West Country. And it so happened, after they had been looking for a while, that Roger's parents retired to a farm in Cornwall which had just the thing – a redundant and collapsing ninety-five foot granite and brick banked barn, meaning that one side was half buried in the hillside.

Resisting the offer of a local builder to have it 'all straightened up and looking just like a Wimpey home in four months', the Garlands set about restoring it in a more sympathetic way which, over the next decade, cost about twice as much as building a new house; but they feel it was money well spent and the whole project far more interesting than simply having somewhere comfortable and warm to live.

Like the night they heard scrabbling sounds in the studio behind the bedroom. Paranoid about rats tunnelling through from the adjoining farm buildings, Roger leaped into action, snatched open the studio door, and was bowled over by a big, beautiful barn owl which came sailing into the room and then flapped about in panic trying to get out. It lives still there, though not in the bedroom of course, and is having its own house built in the rafters by the RSPB.

In 1988, they opened part of the building as the Lakeside Gallery, housing a permanent exhibition of Roger's Tolkien paintings, plus a rotating display of others, including work by other artists.

The Garlands believe it was one of their best moves. There is, of course, a downside to running a gallery, such as being tied to the place in summer. There was also the occasion when, investigating a noise downstairs one day, they found a party of tourists wandering around inspecting the pictures. Whether they thought the bed in one room was a piece of installation art goes unrecorded, but the front door has been kept locked since.

△ Astrology
Linda and Roger 1989
Oils. 6 x 10in (15 x 25cm)
Private work.

This was a cover design for the ongoing *Secrets of Astrology* project, and was intended to be reduced and inset on the front of the book.

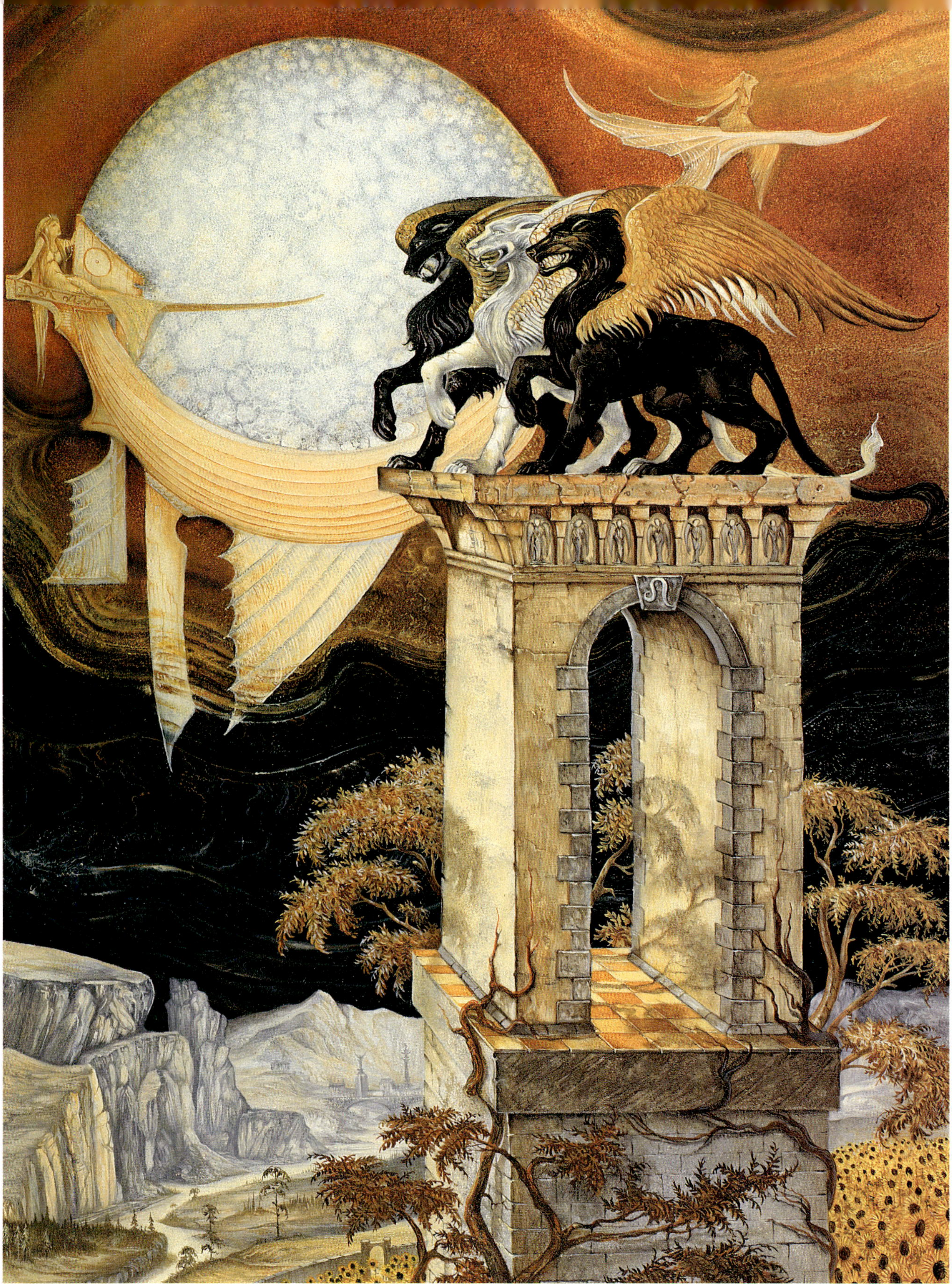

△ **Onyx**
Roger 1993
Oils. 8 x 11in (20 x 28cm)
Private work.

Zodiacal sign: Leo.
Associated planet: sun.
Stone hardness: 7 on the Mohs scale.

Associated angel: Gabriel. The winged lions and carved symbol in the Roman arch, reflect onyx's relation to Leo. The seven angels represent the stone's hardness, and on the boat is a symbol of the sun, Leo's planet.

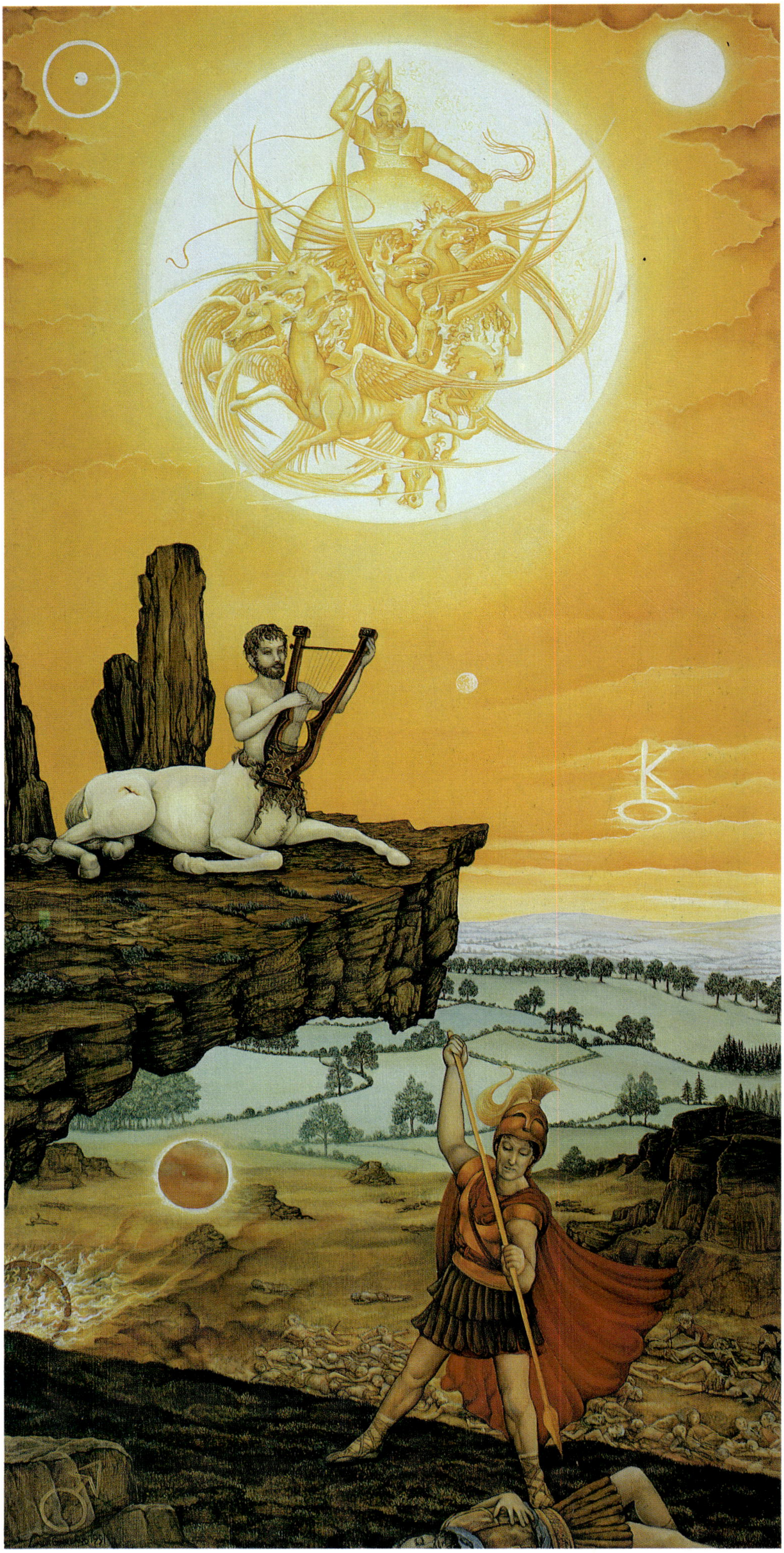

▷ **Ruling Planets: Fire**
Linda and Roger 1991
Oils. 10 x 21in (25 x 53cm)
Private work.

The challenge in this set of pictures was how to fit three separate elements into the same composition. The overall colouring of the picture was decided by the element in question, and on each level is shown the planet's symbol, mythological form and physical appearance. The planet in the centre is Chiron, the Healer, only recently discovered and given a place in astrology. The Garlands' individual contributions to these joint pictures vary. Here, Roger drew and Linda painted.

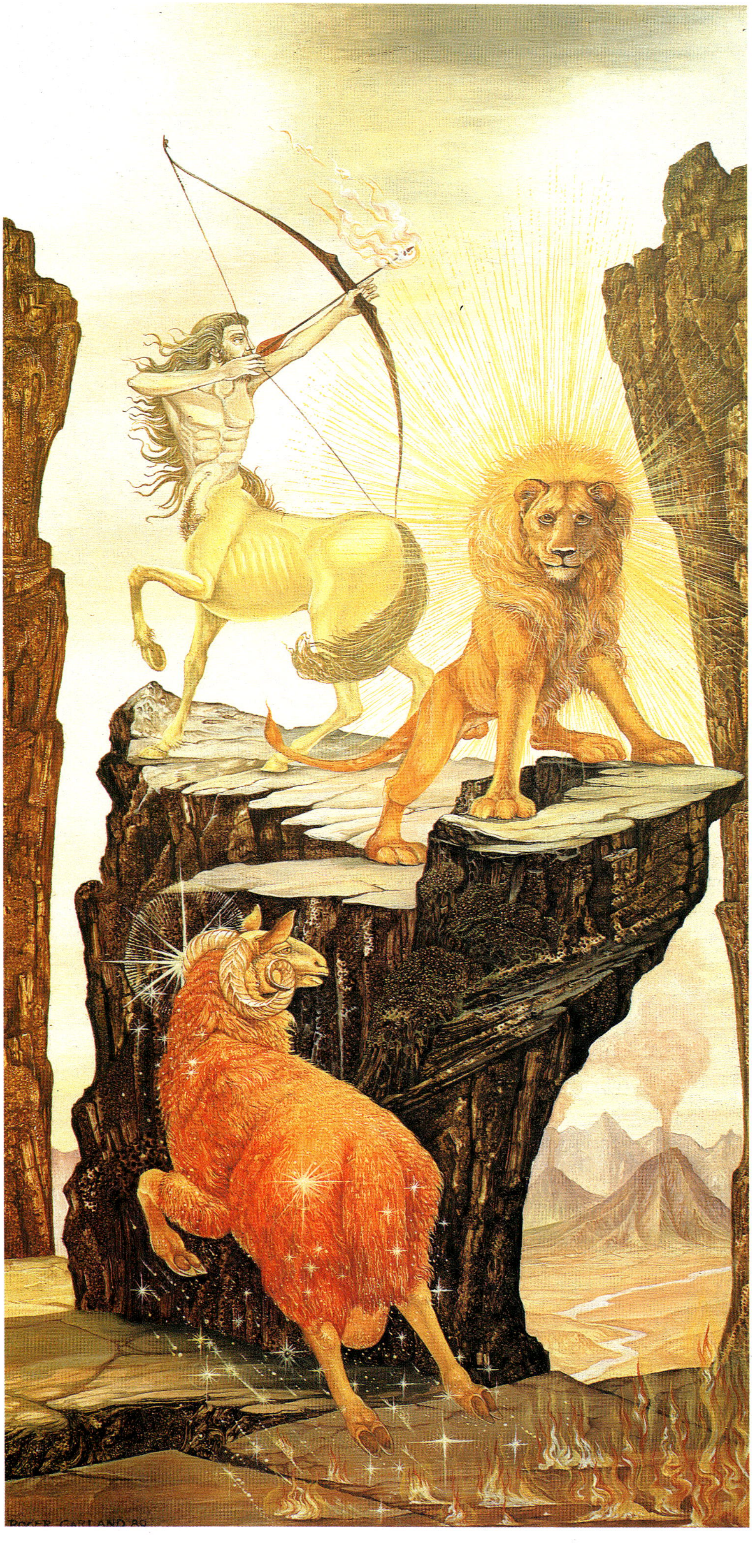

◁ **The Elements: Fire**
Linda and Roger 1989
Oils. 6 x 12in (15 x 31cm)
Private work.

The three signs shown here have basically the same fiery colouring, but its strength depends on whether, in astrological terms, the sign is Mutable, Fixed or Cardinal (or active). Their stance is similarly affected – note the fire-spreading sparks struck by the ram's hooves.

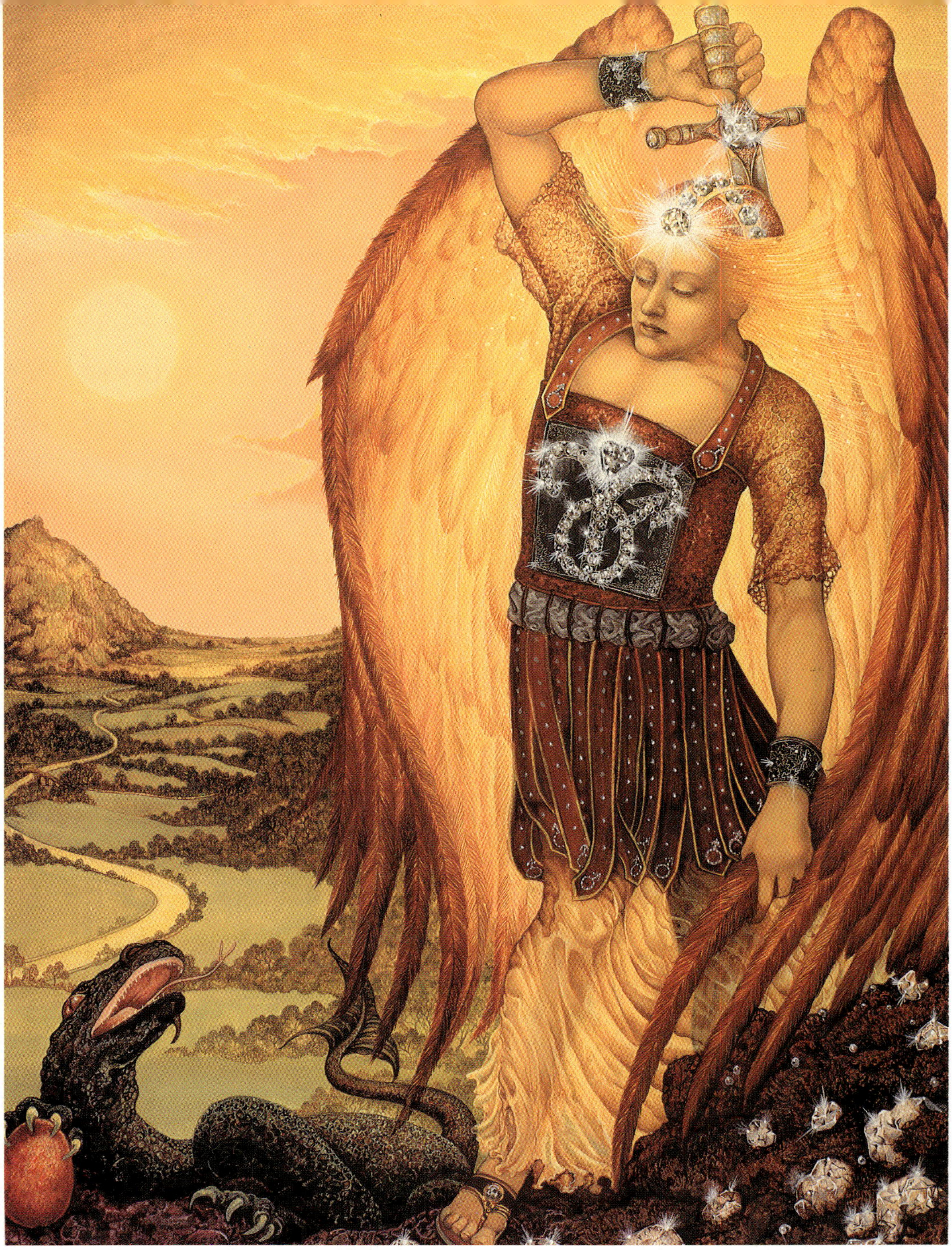

▷ **Diamond**
Linda 1992
Oils. 8 x 11in (20 x 28cm)
Private work.

Zodiacal sign: Aries. Associated planet: Mars. Stone hardness: 10 on the Mohs scale. Associated angel: Humatiel. The diamond is given, traditionally, as a love token because of its durability. It is also supposed to ward off evil, hence the angel attacking the dragon.

But such drawbacks are more than balanced by the benefits, not least of which is that rainy summer days are now welcomed, because they bring in visitors. Also, the gallery gives Linda and Roger a place in the local community which they had previously lacked, being locked away in their studio most of the time, and there is a local pride in it.

The most enjoyable part is meeting people. Linda: 'It feels a bit like opening our home to the public and I think both Roger and I have got to like people a lot more since doing it. Illustration is a very inside occupation. You only communicate with the world by telephone and then usually only at the beginning and end of a job. It's refreshing to hear the views of complete strangers.'

It can also be a bit disconcerting, as when a little girl pointed to an angel in the background of a picture and said: 'Look Mummy, a squashed fly', a comment

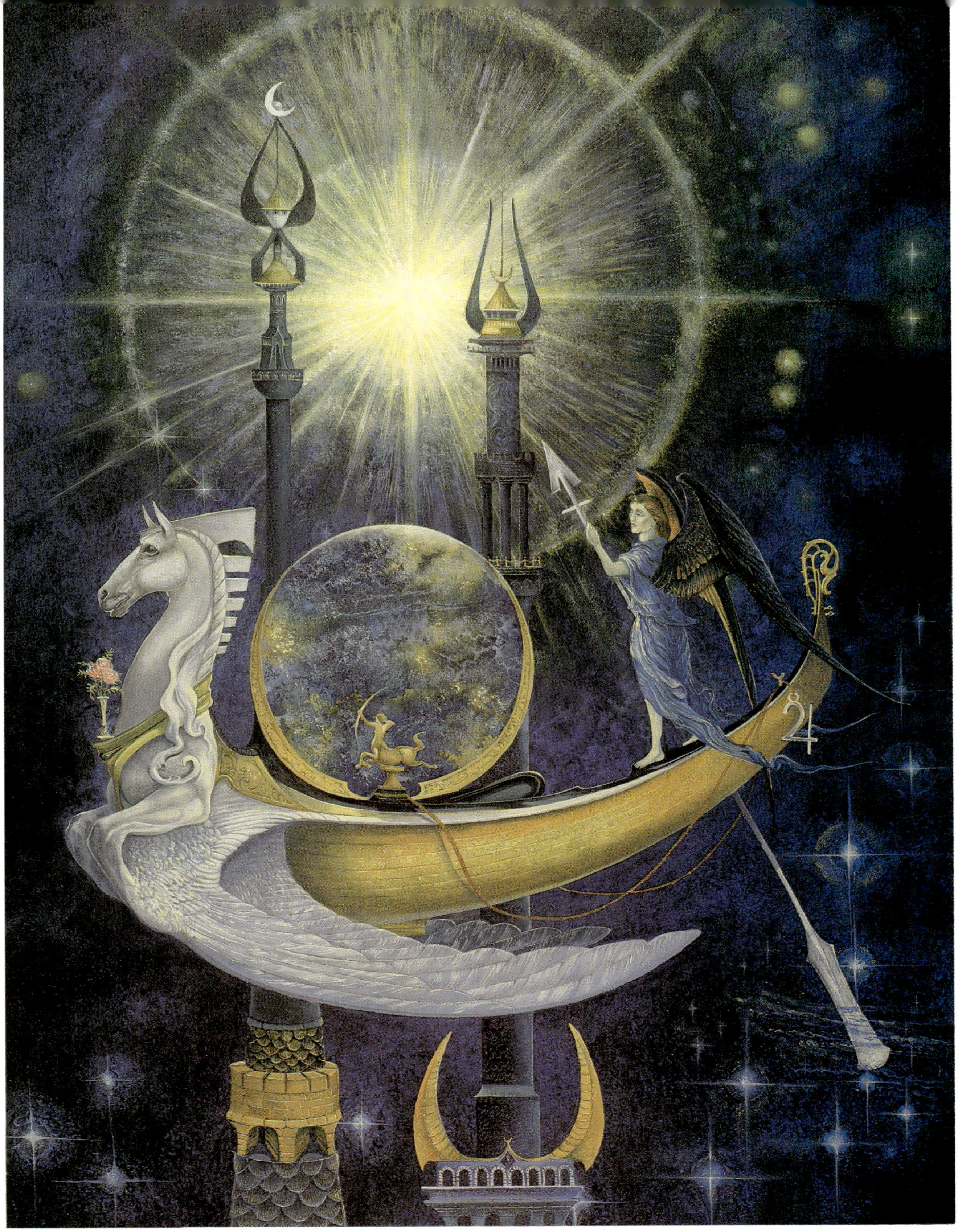

△ **Lapis Lazuli**
Roger 1993
Oils 8 x 11in (20 x 28cm)
Private work.

Zodiacal sign: Sagittarius. Associated planet: Jupiter. Stone hardness: 6 on the Mohs scale. The silver flecks and streaks in Lapis Lazuli often make it a picture of the night sky, and it is also said to be the material of the City of the Gods – whose spires the angel is gliding above in the picture, steering with the arrow of Sagittarius.

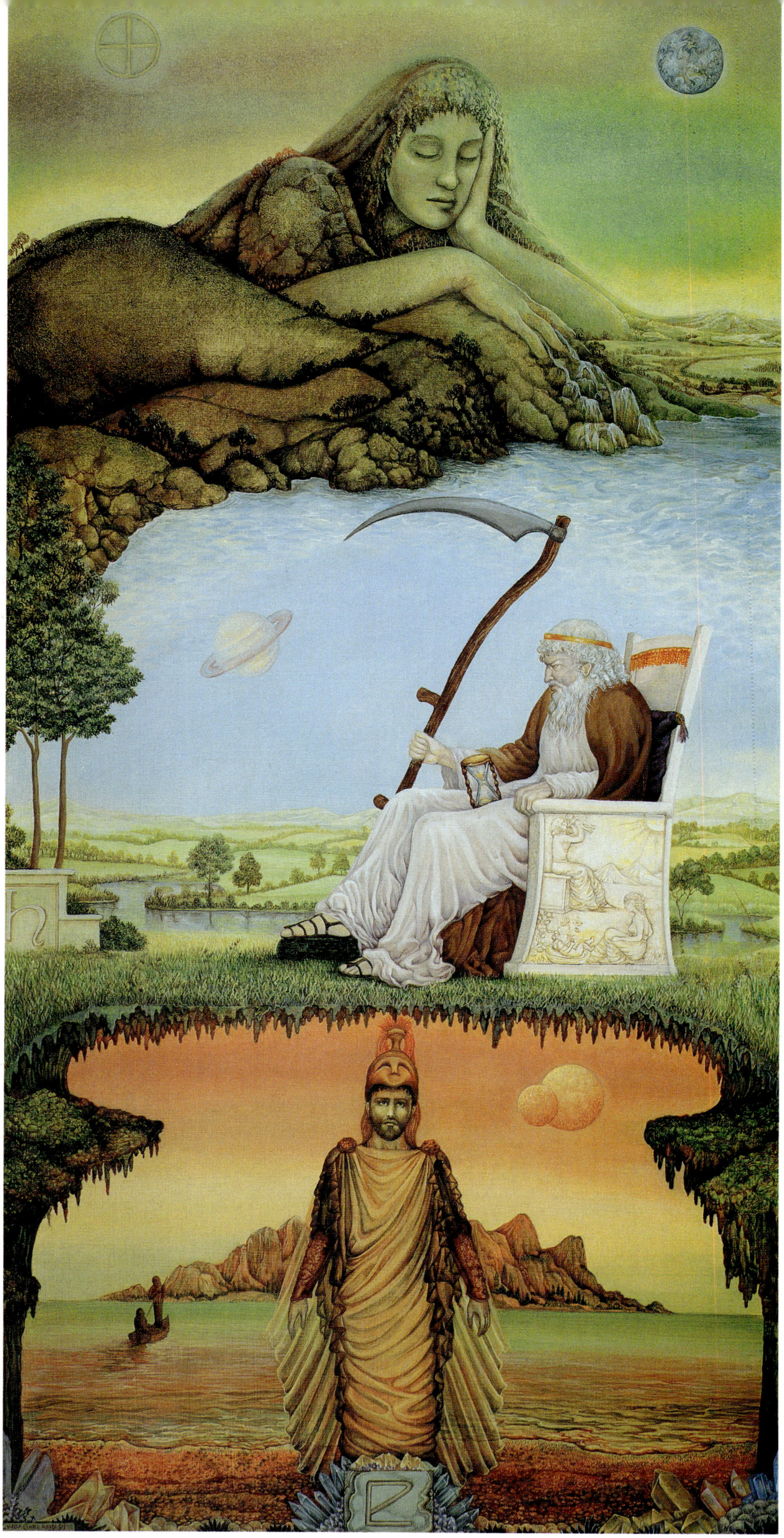

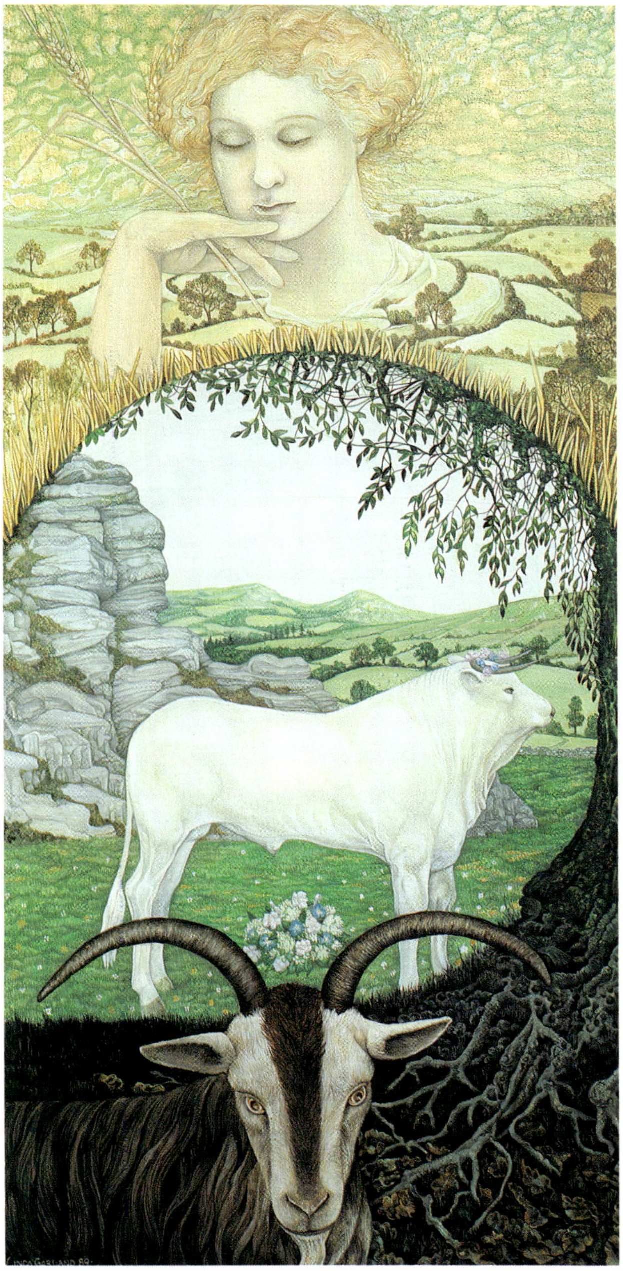

◁ **Ruling Planets: Earth, Saturn, Pluto**
Linda and Roger 1991
Oils. 10 x 21in (25 x 53cm)
Private work.

In descending order: Earth, Saturn and Pluto, god of the underworld. Behind Saturn lie the Elysian fields, scene of the Golden Age over which he presided.

△ The Elements: Earth
Linda and Roger 1989
Oils. 6 x 12in (15 x 31cm)
Private work.

The three signs depicted here are Virgo, Taurus and Capricorn. These signs proved the hardest to unite happily, so clear divisions were introduced.

Linda is unable to forget every time she now sees it. Or: 'Of course it's only imagination after all. Why don't you paint something real that people will want to buy, like scenes of Dartmoor?' It is surprising, though, how many people come into the gallery looking slightly bewildered and leave as converts.

An early surprise after opening the gallery, was the range of people who came in. The Garlands expected mainly fantasy buffs but, in fact, got a complete cross-section of the public, including many who had never bought a picture in their lives, but who did so on the spur of the moment.

The timing was also right, for just as the gallery took off a recession hit publishing, so even if they had not been thinking of moving away from book covers, the demand was about to drop anyway. The gallery took over as an outlet, with the added advantage of allowing them to follow their own inclinations more than was possible with commissioned work.

Much of the discipline the Garlands acquired through illustration, continues to apply in their own work. They tend to work in sets as, for example, with the Crystal paintings in this chapter, although it is obviously more satisfying to explore their own chosen themes. The scale of their pictures has tended to shrink to the size they are most naturally suited to, while the compositions have become more adventurous. But overall they feel that book cover illustration was the best possible foundation for what they want to do in painting.

One reason for setting up the Lakeside Gallery was to promote illustration as art and, judging by the response, it seems to be succeeding. 'It would almost certainly do better in a city,' says Linda, 'but as we don't want to live in Hampstead we have to make the best of things as they are.'

An advantage of Cornwall is that in summer there are passing visitors from around the world, such as Canadian astrologer, Patricia Sereno.

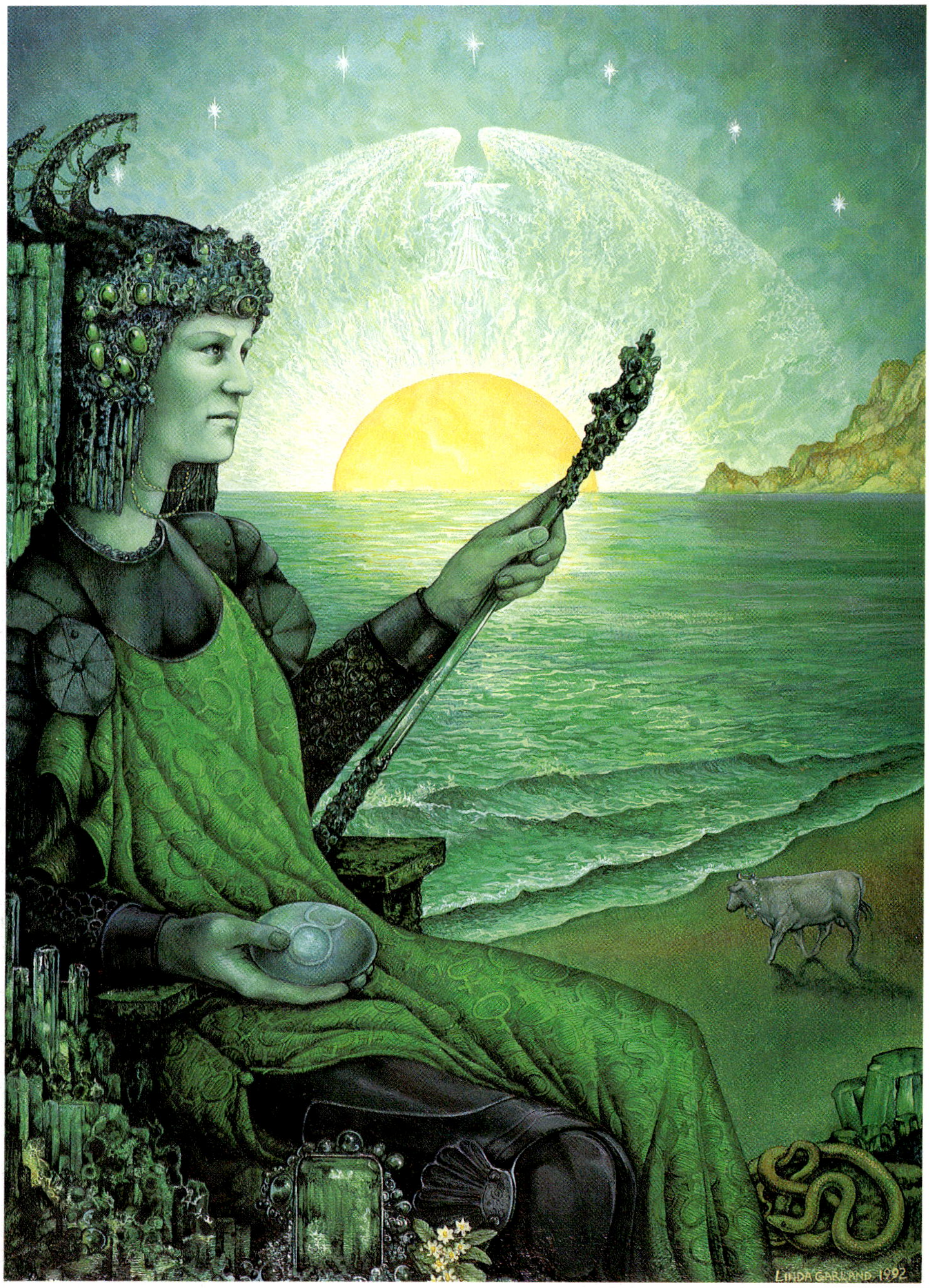


◁ **Emerald**
Linda 1992
Oils. 8 x 11in (20 x 28cm)
Private work.

Zodiacal sign: Taurus. Associated planet: Venus. Stone hardness: 8 on the Mohs scale. Associated angel: Muriel. Emerald is said to have a calming effect on the wearer, is good for the eyes, and sharpens the memory. It is also a talisman against snakes and evil.

▷ **Sapphire**
Linda 1992
Oils. 8 x 11in (20 x 28cm)
Private work.

Zodiacal sign: Virgo. Associated planet: Mercury. Stone hardness: 9 on the Mohs scale. Associated angel: Herschel. Sapphire is reputed to clear the mind and lengthen one's life.

This lady offered to barter for a painting by drawing up the Garlands' birth charts and giving them a reading. Out of curiosity they accepted, knowing nothing at all about the subject beyond what mythology has to say about the gods associated with the planets.

In due course they received their readings and were impressed by their accuracy and relevance. Complications arose, though, when it came to explanations of how the readings derived from the charts. Thus emerged the idea of doing a book explaining astrology to the complete novice, in plain language that aimed to inform the readers without baffling them with science – the fault, however unintentional, of so many guides. Patricia Sereno was to write the text using the Garlands as a sounding board. Meanwhile, they would produce a set of full colour illustrations of the ruling planets and zodiacal signs grouped according to the elements with which they are associated: Fire, Earth, Air or Water.

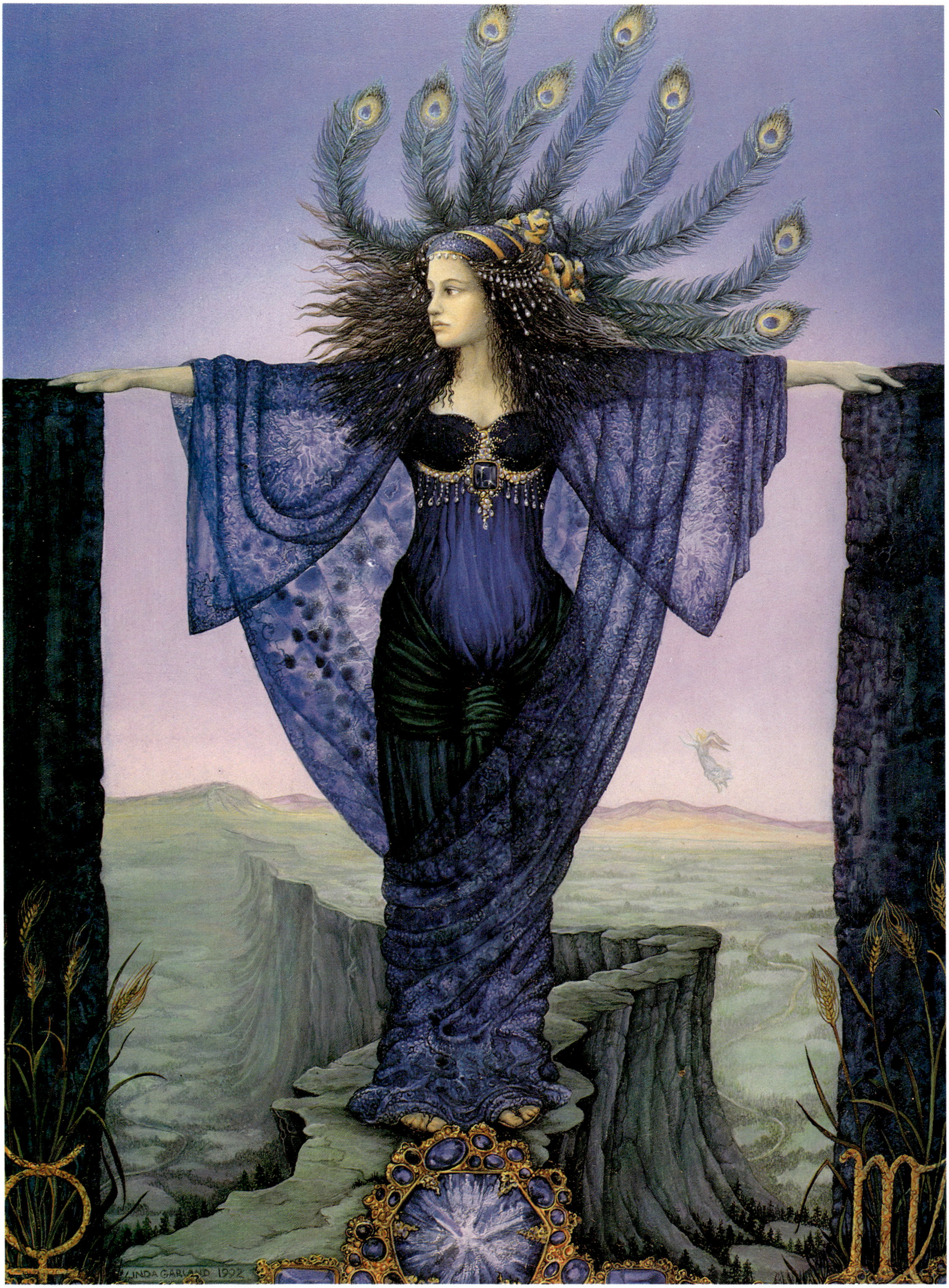
LINDA GARLAND 1992

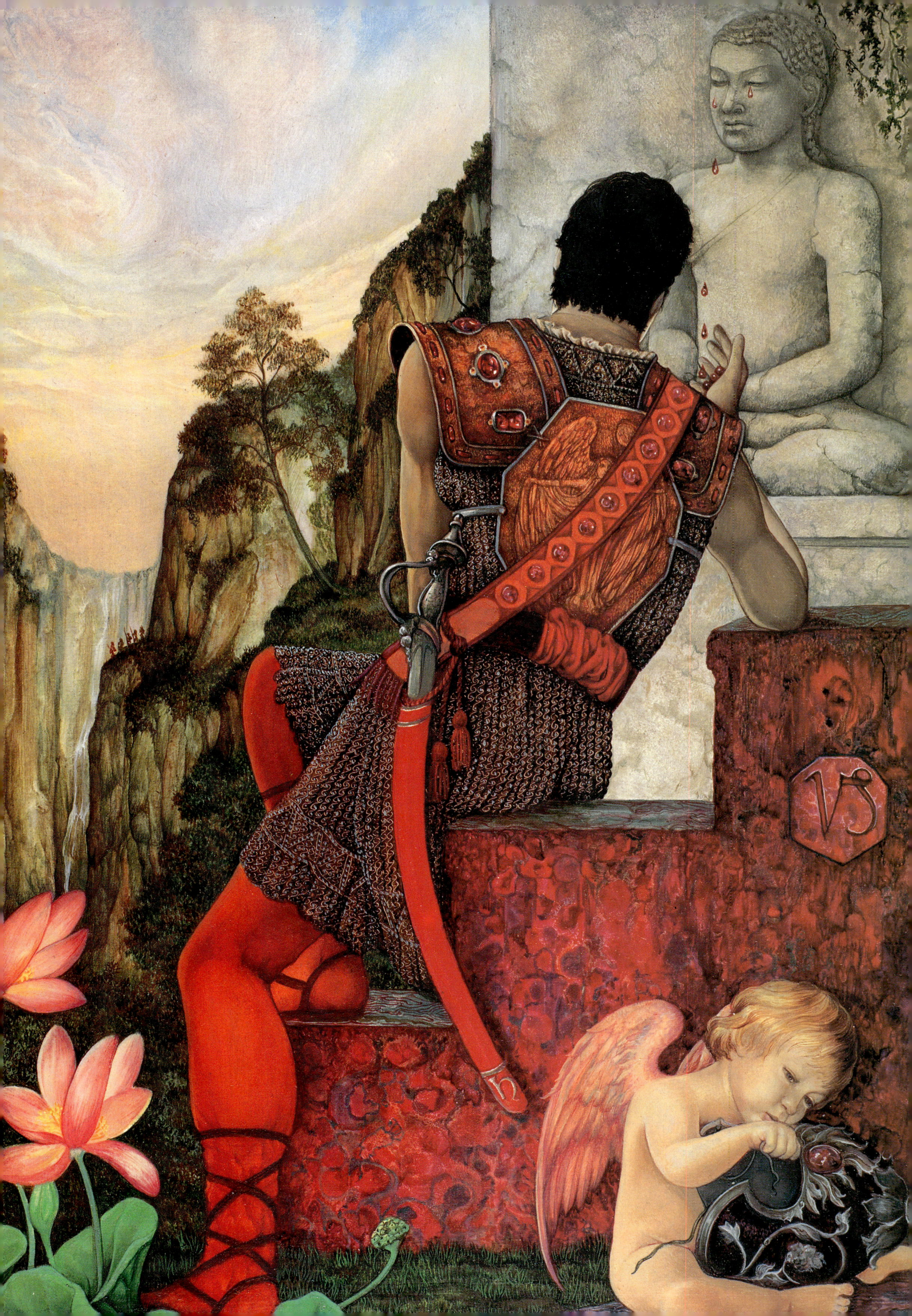

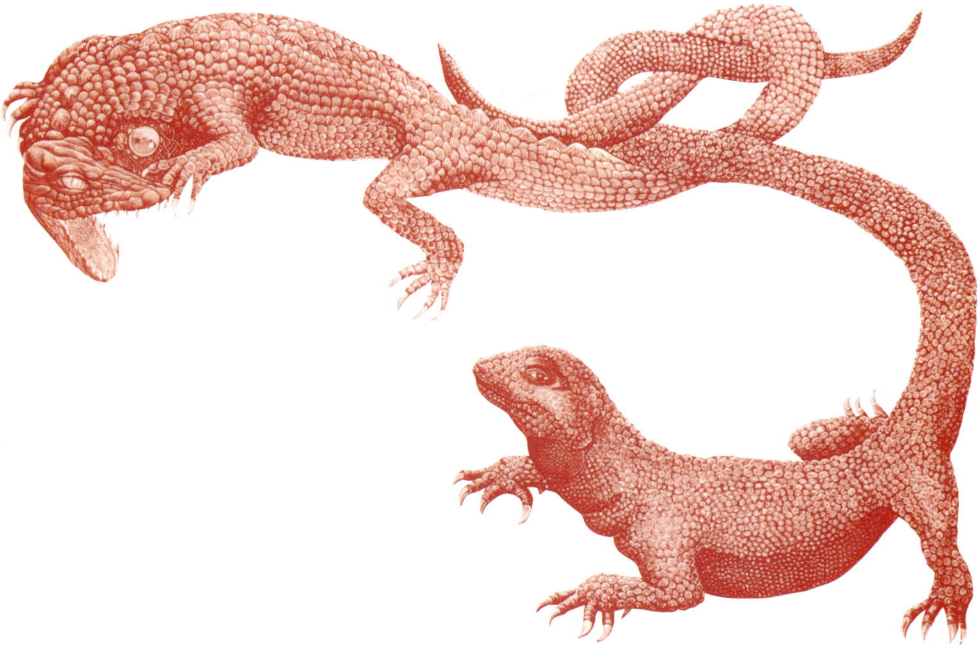

◁ Ruby
Linda 1993
Oils. 8 x 11in (20 x 28cm)
Private work.

Zodiacal sign: Capricorn. Associated planet: Saturn. Stone hardness: 9 on the Mohs scale. Associated angel: Malchediel. Rubies worn in battle stem bleeding. The best stones come from Sri Lanka, which is the setting of the picture. They are also believed to be the tears of Buddha.

The eight resulting paintings, plus a cover, were commissioned by an interested publisher, but sadly recession struck and the book was shelved. This was naturally disappointing, but it gave the Garlands an idea. Being left with a set of paintings they had expected to see in print, suggested that perhaps it was something they should do themselves. They had often been asked for card reproductions in the gallery, so they knew there was a market. But, as approaches to established card companies had revealed, the only worthwhile way was to do it alone.

Setting up the card business was a far bolder venture than opening the gallery, because of the outlay. It was a decision born, according to Linda, 'of pure necessity and panic'. Recession had not only hit the astrology book, work all round was scarce, and paying for the first batch of cards meant drawing all but a month's mortgage out of their building society.

When the delivery came, the first shock was appreciating just how much space is taken up by 24,000 cards; they couldn't believe the number of stacks that kept coming coming out of the van. The next was the duller one of realizing, after the van had left, that all their security was piled up before them. On 6 January 1991 (the date is engraved on his mind), after a rather fraught Christmas, Roger went out on the road to sell the cards with little hope in his heart. However, a tour of shops in north Devon netted seventy pounds worth of sales, and he arrived home to a burnt dinner in a state of elation, thinking it was not going to be so bad after all.

His next outing was a disaster. A round of six shops prompted only one sale. He fell into the last shop at closing time and at the end of his tether confessed to the owner that he really could not see himself doing this for the rest of his life.

'What you need', said the man sympathetically, 'is an agent.' And he gave Roger the name of one who turned out to be ideal, having a large round of New Age and quality gift shops which welcomed the cards.

Since then, the business has grown beyond recognition, which the Garlands attribute to luck in meeting the right people, rather than skill or acumen. The original range of twelve images has grown to about seventy and they have eight agents distributing nationally and to countries like Switzerland, Germany, America and Australia.

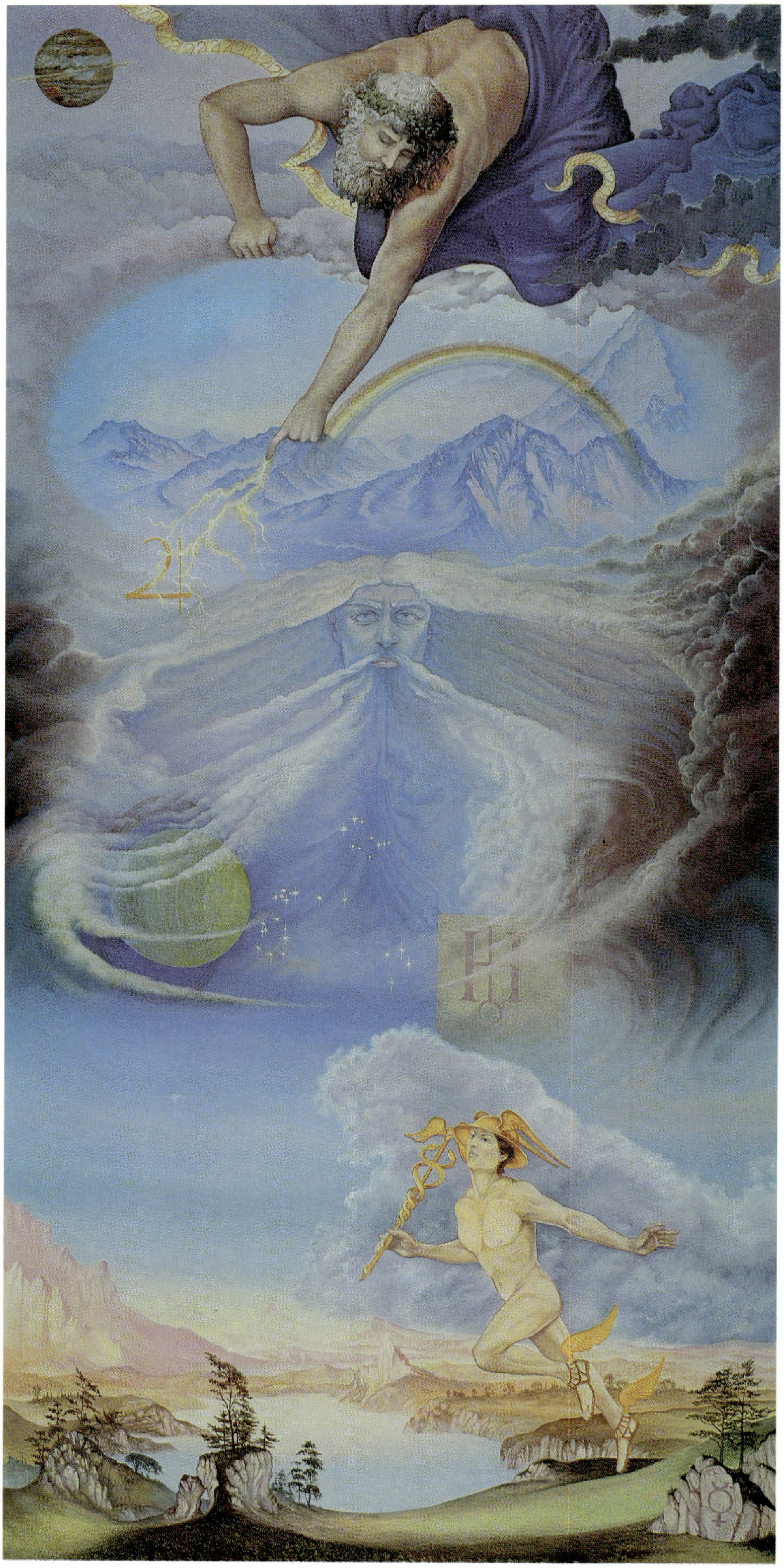

▷ **Ruling Planets: Air**
Linda and Roger 1991
Oils. 10 x 21in (25 x 53cm)
Private work.

The three signs shown in this work are Jupiter, Uranus and Mercury, whose staff, with its two serpents, represents the riddle of life.

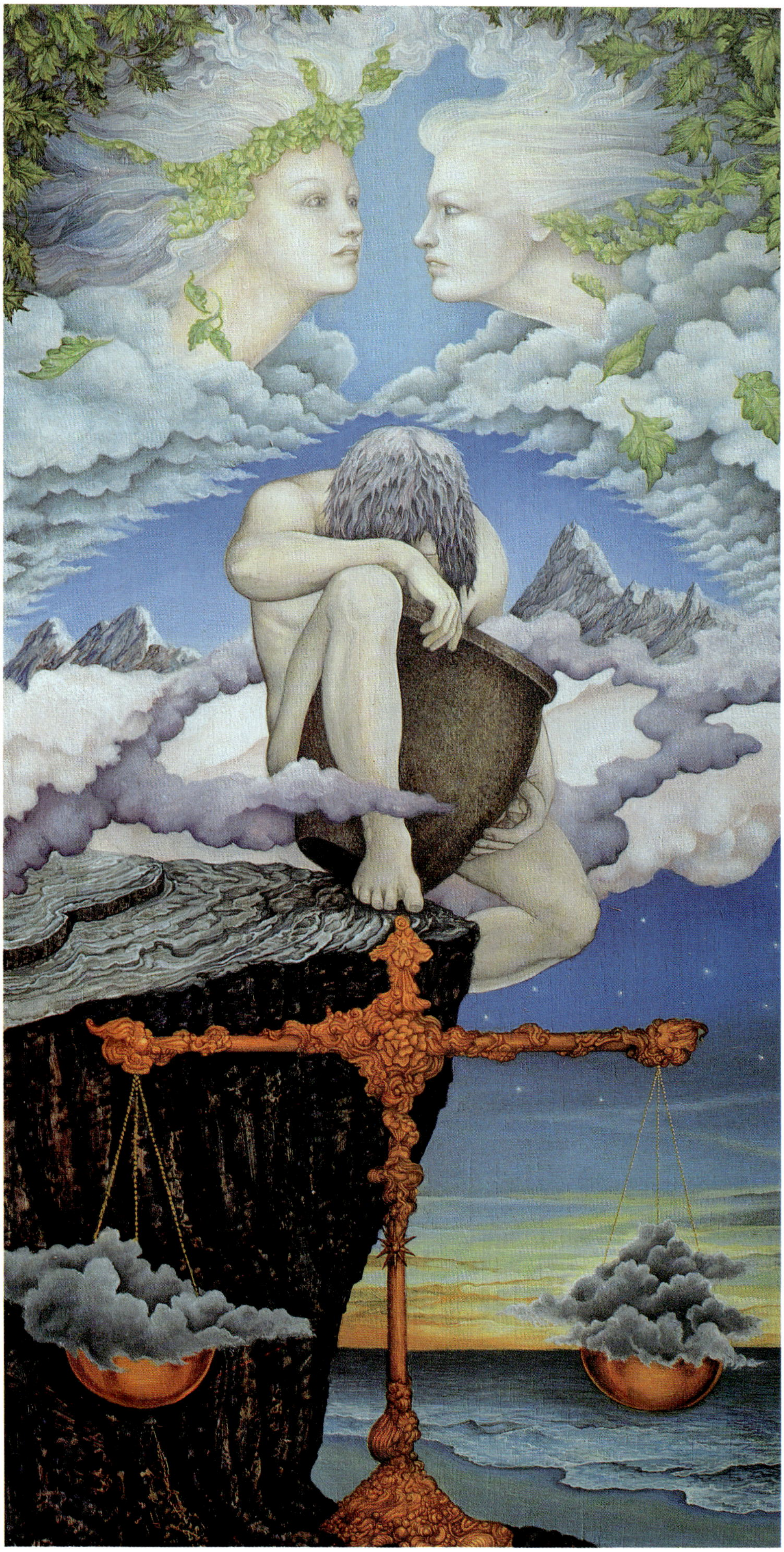

◁ The Elements: Air
Linda and Roger 1989
Oils. 6 x 12in (15 x 31cm)
Private work.

This painting depicts Gemini, Aquarius and Libra. Why Aquarius, the water-bearer, should be an air sign, is one of astrology's little mysteries.

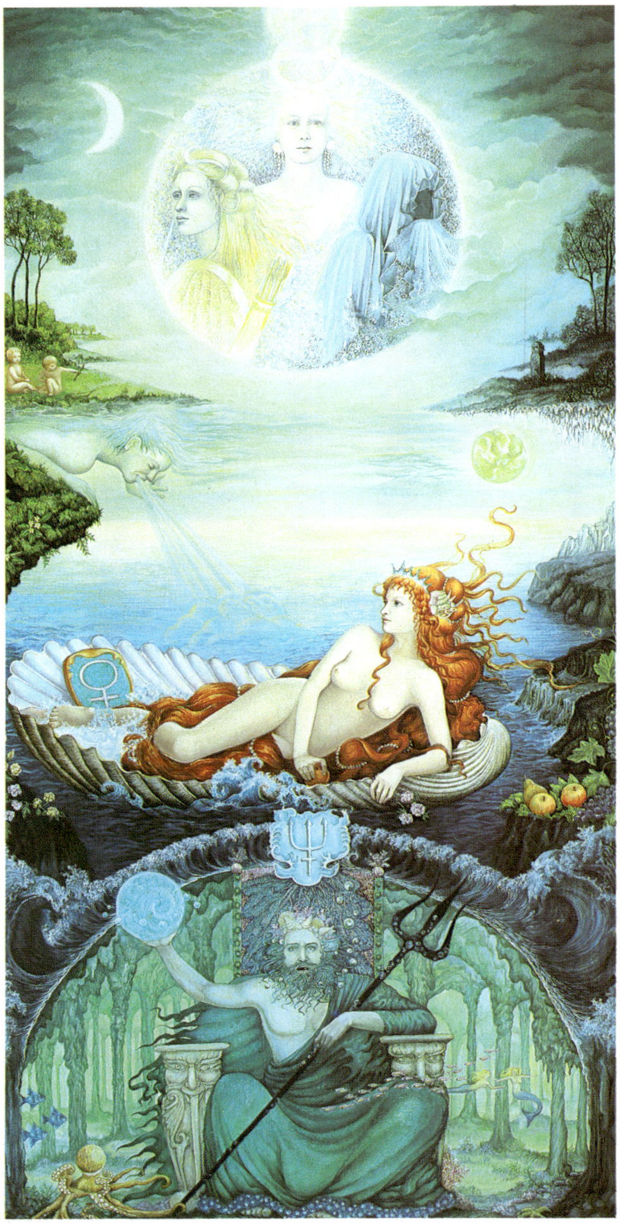

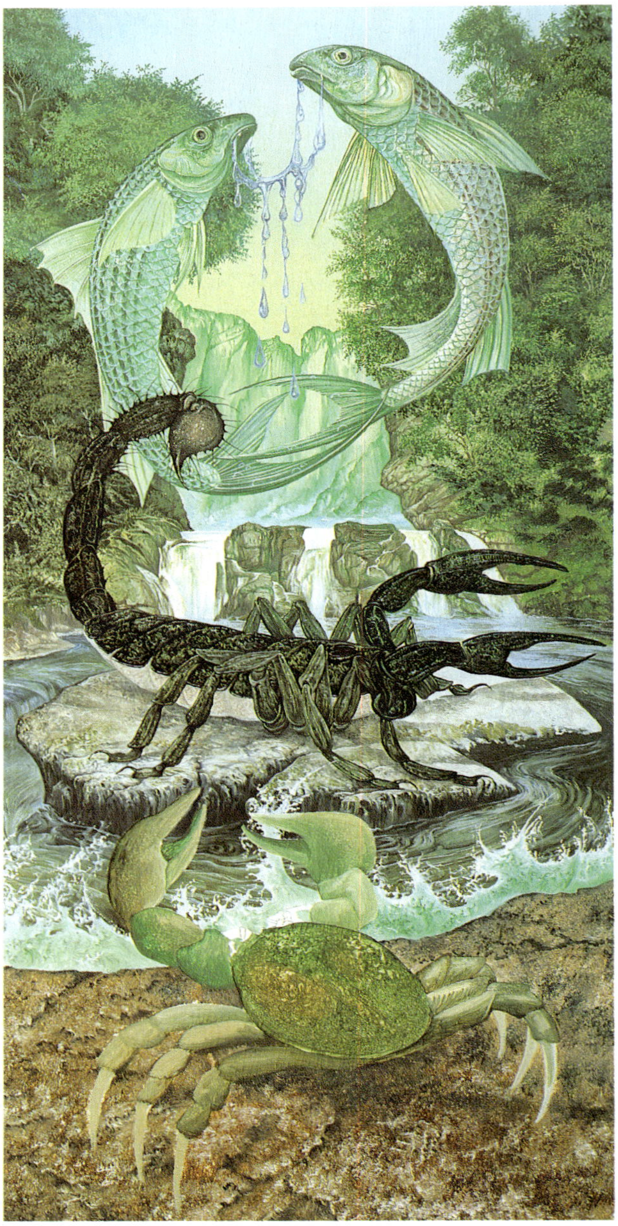

△ **Ruling Planets: Water**
Linda and Roger 1991
Oils. 10 x 21in (25 x 53cm)
Private work.

Shown here are the Moon, Venus and Neptune.

△ **The Elements: Water**
Linda and Roger 1990
Oils. 6 x 12in (15 x 31cm)
Private work.

As a card, this scene of Pisces, Scorpio and Cancer is enormously popular, perhaps because it is so realistic.

▷ **Pearl**
Linda 1993
Oils. 8 x 11in (20 x 28cm)
Private work.

Zodiacal sign: Gemini. Associated planet: Mercury. In antiquity, pearls were a symbol of chastity.

Much has been learned along the way, not least how exciting it all can get. Roger: 'In some ways the card business feels as creative as painting because there are so many different ways of presenting images. Standard cards lead on to notelets, notebooks, prints of various sizes, the possibilities are endless.'

How profitable the business is remains debatable. Sales are healthy, but as stock constantly has to be maintained and the range expanded, the Garlands prefer not to work out how much actually ends up in their pockets. If nothing else, however, it keeps them busy, brings visitors into the gallery from far afield, and has the incidental benefit of making their studio far easier to heat than before, the high rafters having become a card warehouse. No more huddling round the wood-burning stove in winter, and painting with blue fingers.

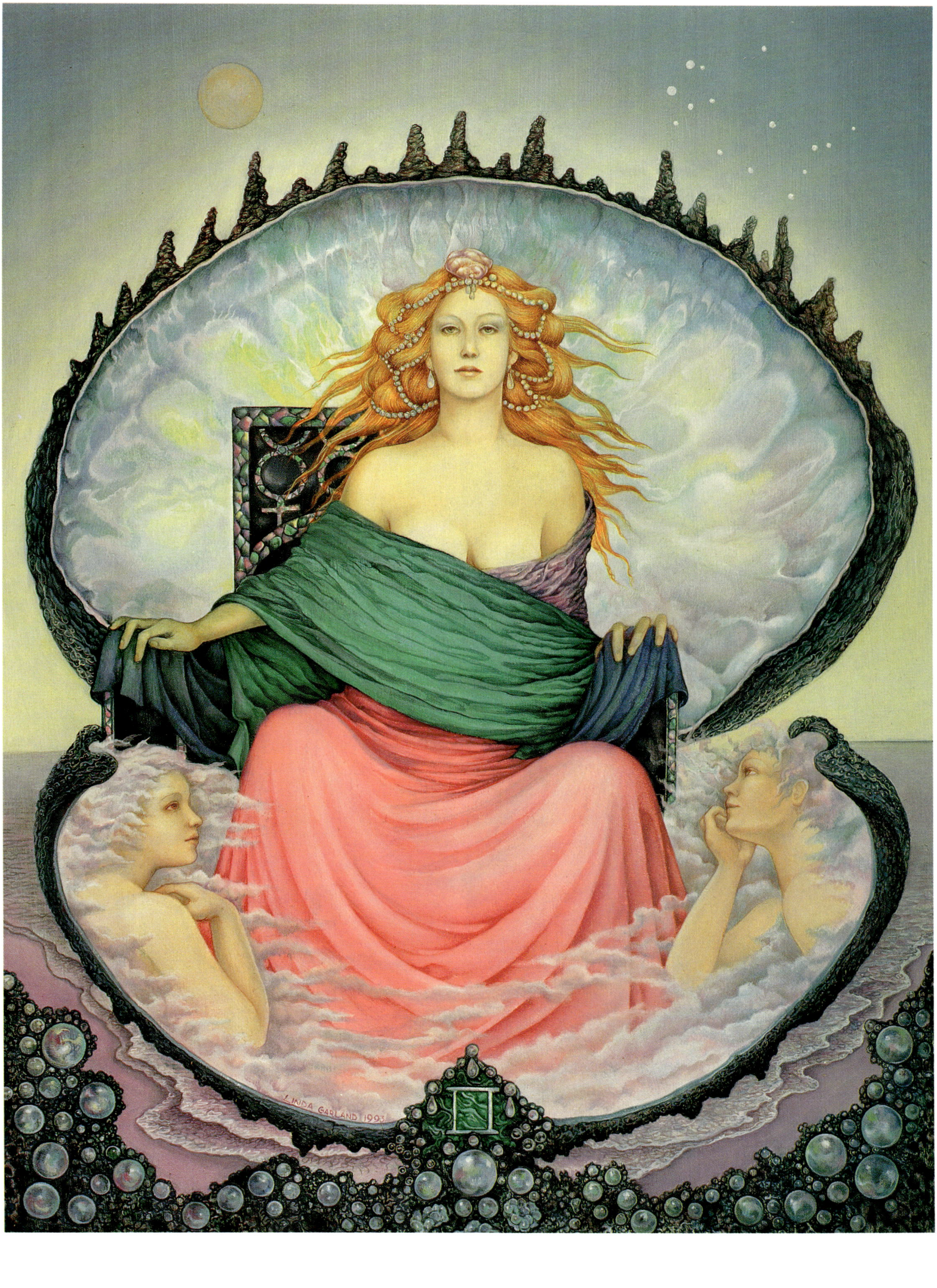
LINDA GARLAND 1993

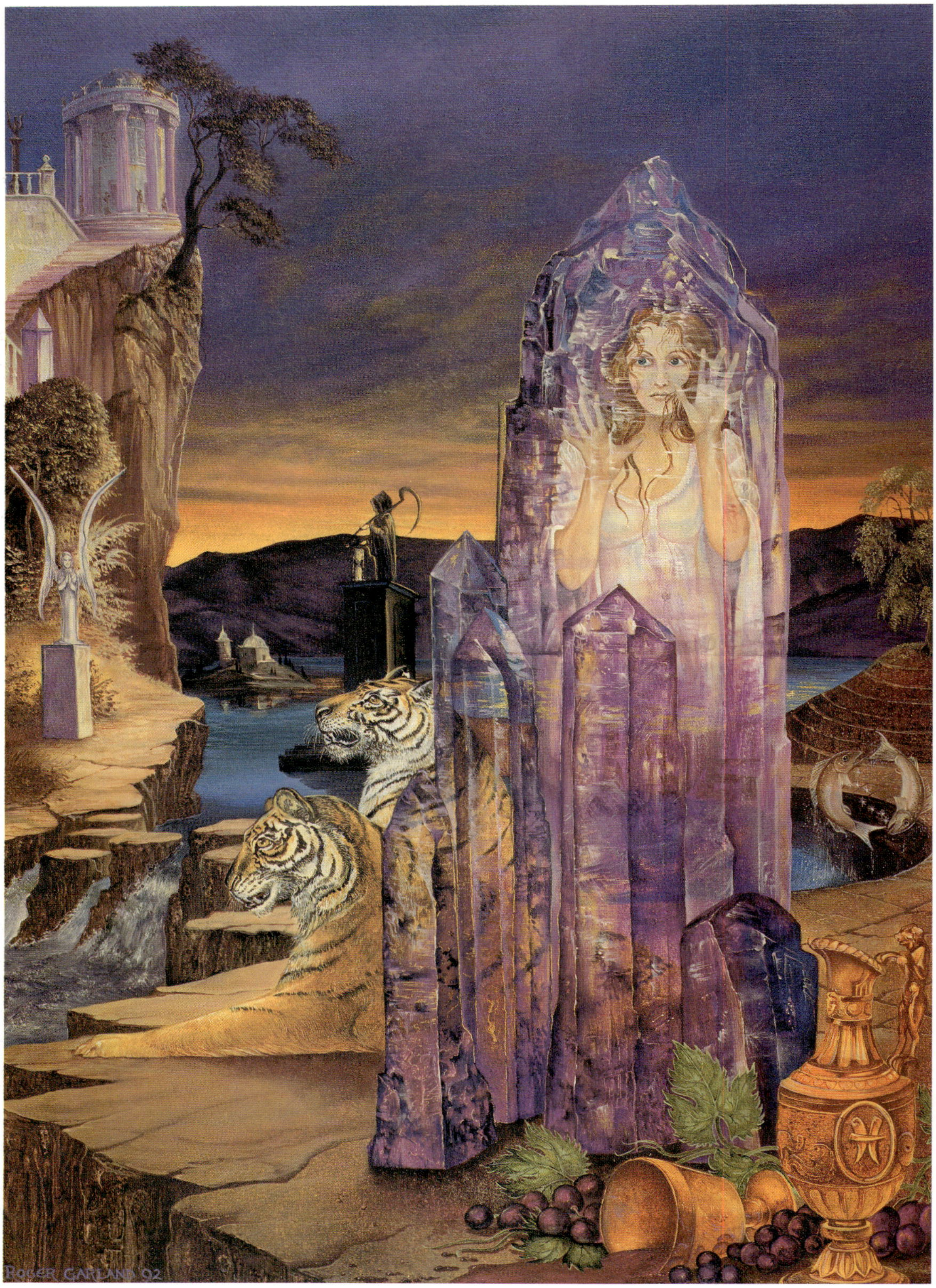


△ **Amethyst**
Roger 1992
Oils. 8 x 11in (20 x 28cm)
Private work.

Zodiacal sign: Pisces. Associated planet: Neptune. Stone hardness: 7 on the Mohs scale. Associated angel: Adnachiel. Believed to be an antidote to drunkenness, Amethyst was originally a nymph whom Bacchus, god of wine, fell in love with. He set his tigers to catch her, but Diana (whose temple is on the cliff) turned her into crystal to save her. The colour of the stone comes from wine which Bacchus spilt over it.

▷ **Moonstone**
Roger 1993
Oils. 8 x 11in (20 x 28cm)
Private work.

Zodiacal sign: Cancer. Associated planet: Moon. Stone hardness: 6 on the Mohs scale. In antiquity, moonstone was used to curb lunacy and epilepsy.

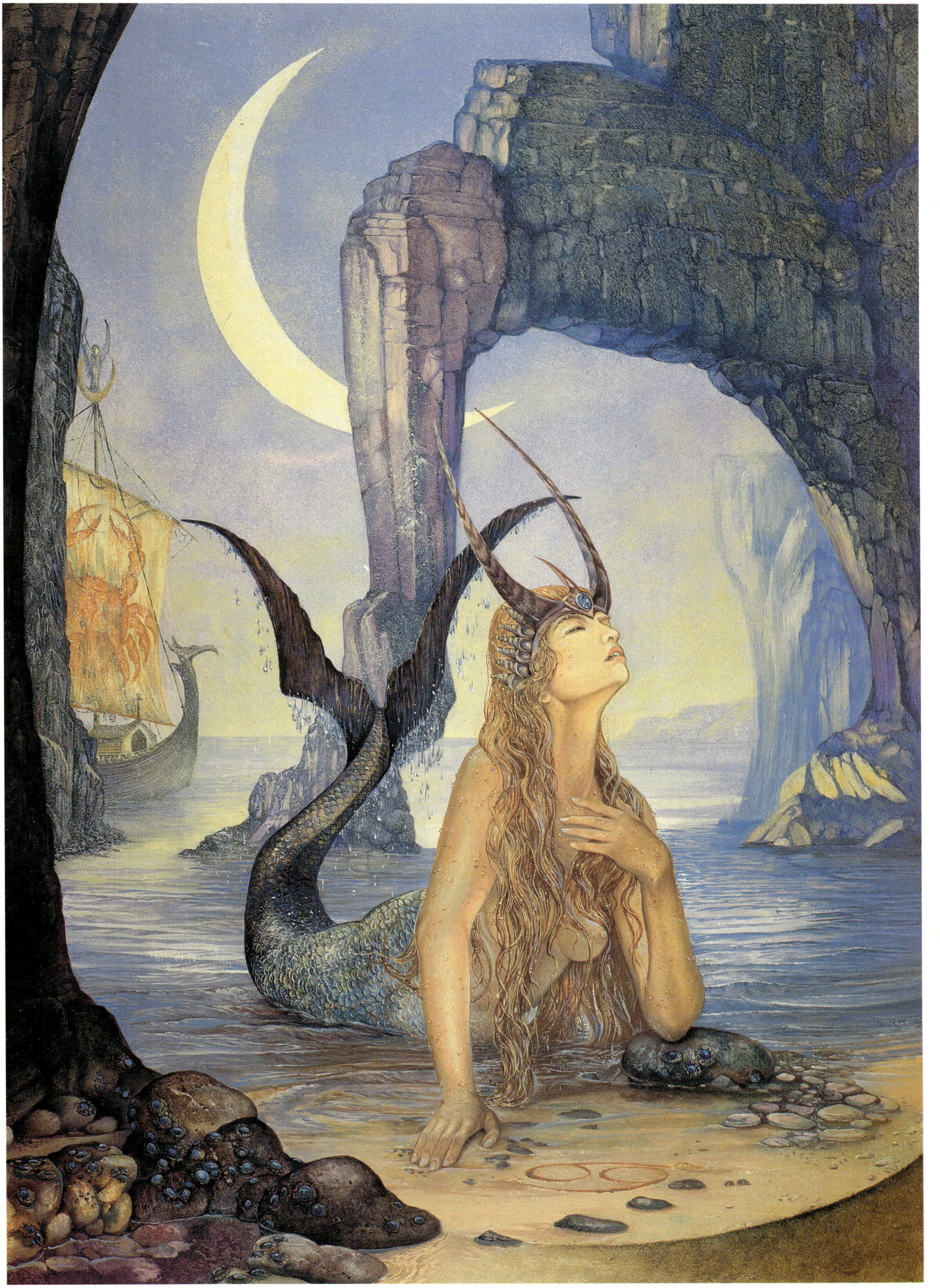

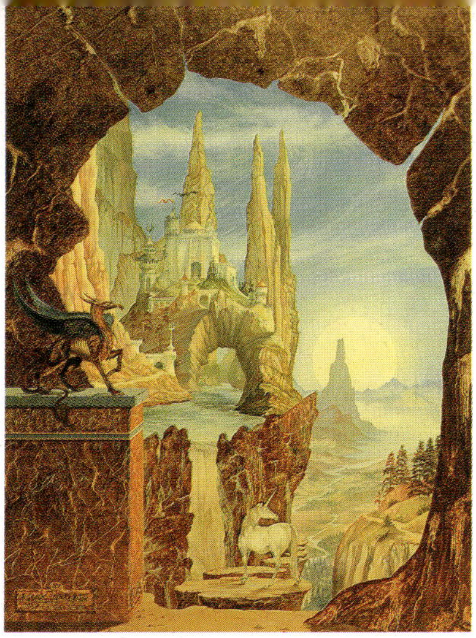

# MARVELLOUS CREATURES

*"It's almost like there is another world you can just sometimes catch out of the corner of your eye. The spirits are there if you can only open your mind to see."*

Roger Garland grew up on the Somerset Levels – those flatlands which were once a tidal swamp blending imperceptibly into the Bristol Channel, and from which the hills still rise as abruptly as islands. Much of the area is now drained, but there are still places which get submerged for nearly half the year, such as the fields around the Isle of Athelny, where the Garlands have farmed for hundreds of years.

There was little in his childhood to suggest that Roger would become a fantasy painter, though his grandfather was a signwriter who also painted animal portraits and pub signs – a craft Roger admires, not least for the speed and confidence with which such artists work. His father, too, has a habit of carrying around a piece of chalk for dashing off portraits and still lifes on bits of farm machinery. Roger, though, showed no such inclinations, and his taste for the fantastic certainly wasn't nurtured by books – the only literature in the house was *Farmer's Weekly* and the Bible.

The landscape, however, lent itself to escapist fantasies: nearby Burrow Mump rising from the Levels like a miniature Glastonbury Tor, with a shattered tower on its summit; Athelny, with its lingering fame as the hideout and stronghold of Alfred the Great; the rivers which joined nearby, and up which the occasional tidal wave came riding from the sea.

His imagination was also provoked, he claims, by the tedium of farming. Some people are born to the life, others are not, and Roger was one of them. To take his mind off mucking out, he would let his imagination go, building elaborate scenes that would later be acted out in complicated role-playing games revolving around Robin Hood.

The Garlands' ancestral home (still managed as a farm by an uncle) is an ancient structure, with walls as thick as a person that lean in places as a result of some misplaced bombs intended for Bristol. The dwelling was once a sixteenth-century longhouse, and there are photos of groceries being delivered to the place

△ **Fantasy Landscape**
Roger 1988
Oils. 12 x 18in (30 x 45cm)
Private commission, David and Lesley Stone.

Some visitors to the gallery wanted to buy *Horsegirl* (see page 8), but could not afford the asking price. So they commissioned a new painting and got this, which in Roger's opinion is far better, as well as having a pun on their surname worked into it.

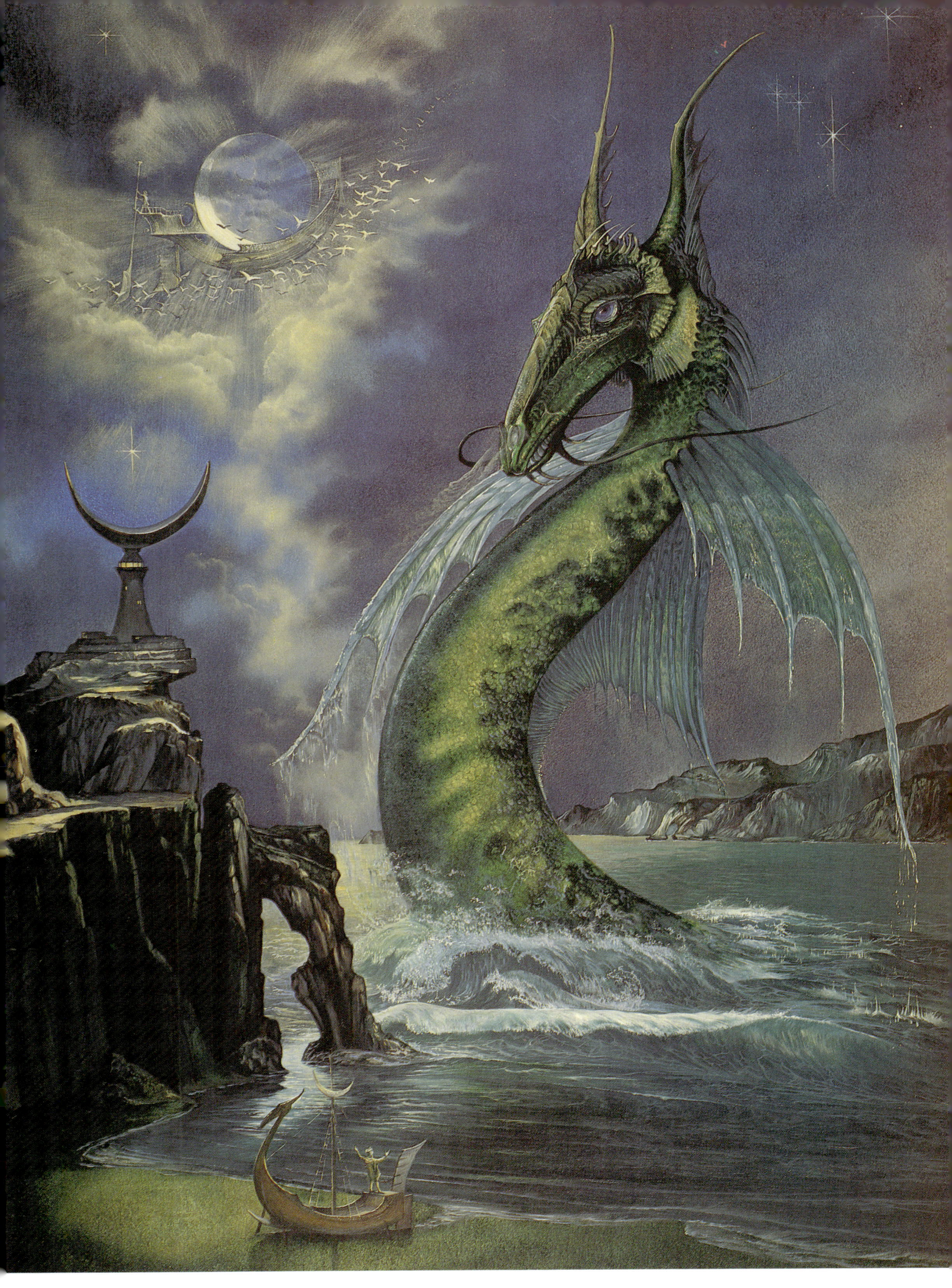

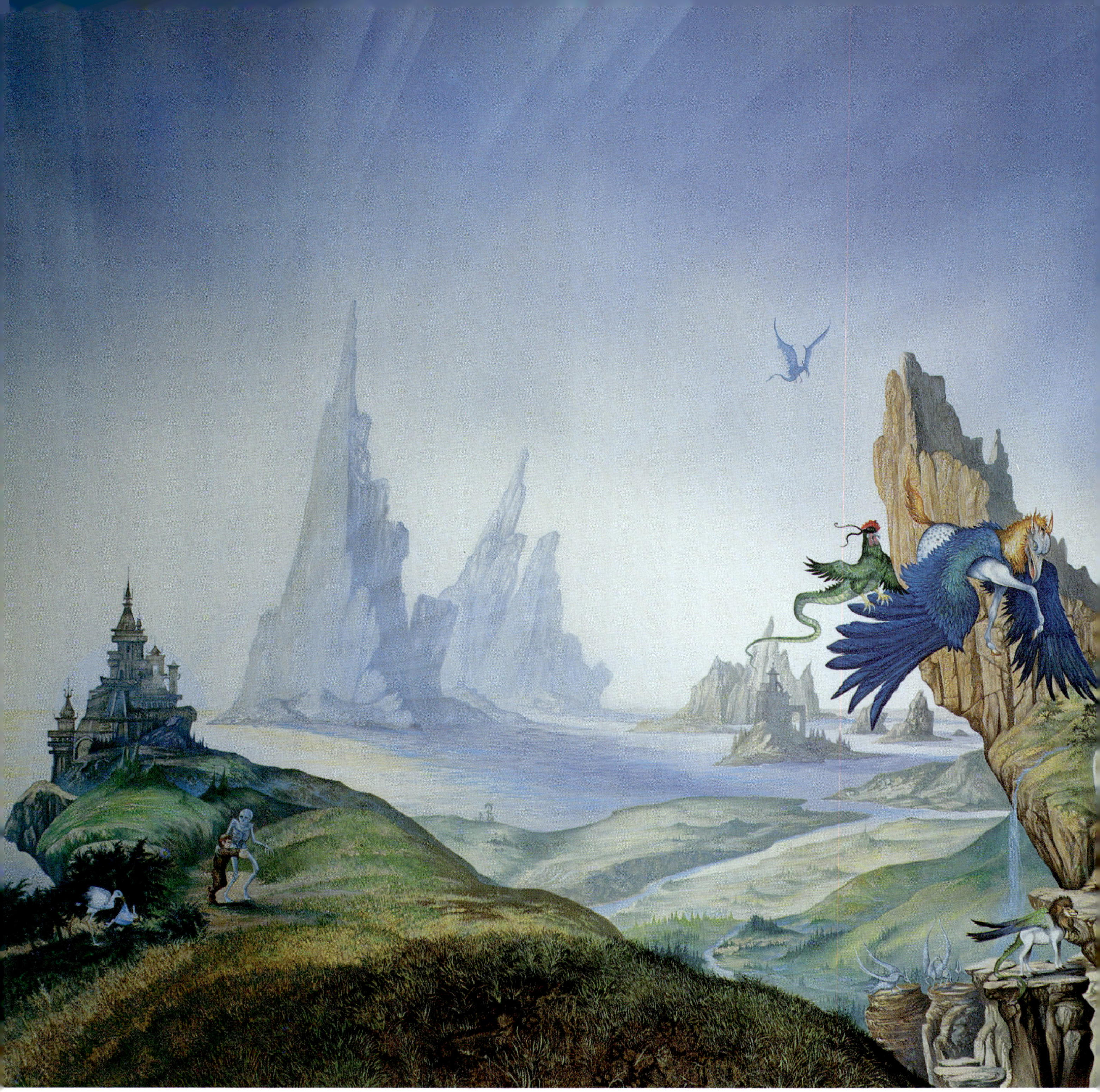

**(Previous page)**
**Cold-Drake**
Roger 1991
Oils. 9 x 12in (23 x 30cm)
Private work.

Inspired by Tolkien, but not illustrating any particular creature or incident in his writings, this picture sprang from a desire to paint a different kind of dragon. The arched cliff is a favourite, and recurring, motif.

by boat during some particularly severe flood. When Linda first visited, hitching down with Roger from Wolverhampton as a student, she says it felt just like walking into *Lark Rise to Candleford*. In Somerset she discovered that not only did such a life exist, but she was being invited to join it.

The family's intention was for Roger to go into agriculture, and there was disappointment at his lack of enthusiasm. Apart from definitely not wanting to be a farmer, Roger had no clear direction until the age of seventeen, when he was lucky enough to get an inspirational art teacher who demonstrated the wonder of capturing real things like fuchsias on paper with a pencil. Dropping all other

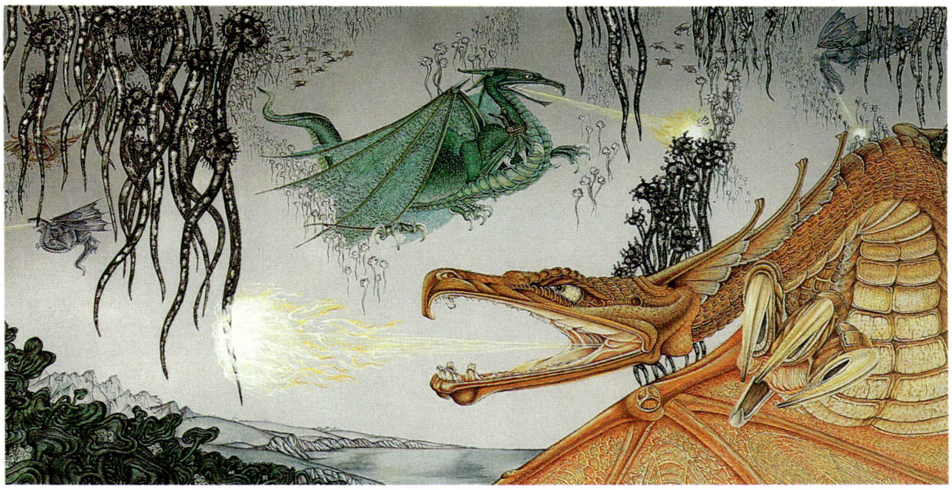

△ Dragonflight
Roger and Linda 1978
Oils and Acrylic. 11 x 17in
(28 x 43cm)
Illustration for *Alien Landscapes*, Pierrot.

The picture shows Pern, Anne McCaffrey's fantasy world, which is periodically assaulted by a virulent silver thread, which would destroy it if dragons did not consume it with fire.

The painting represents several firsts. It features Roger's first published dragons; and as Linda drew the characters and some of the landscape, it is their first joint picture. It also shows Roger's first use of marbling (in its widest sense). To give the thread an organic look, turpentine was dripped on to a plain grey paint surface.

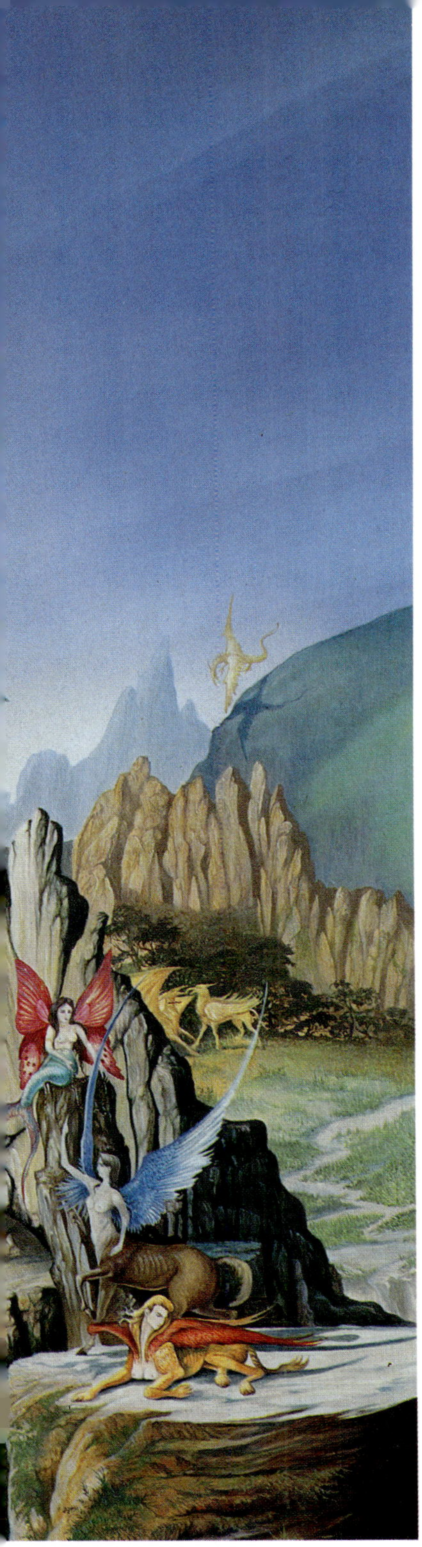

△ The Gathering at Dawn
Roger 1988
Oils and Acrylic. 14 x 19in
(36 x 48cm)
Cover for *Heaven Scent* by Piers Anthony, Hodder and Stoughton.

Roger got a bit carried away here, and a simplified version of the picture had to be produced for publication. The crowd is gathering for a wedding.

subjects, he took Art 'A' Level in half the usual time and went on to an excellent foundation course in Plymouth. Here, among other things, he learned etching, which became an abiding love, and for which he only wishes he had more time.

Art has been a passion ever since, and all of what may be termed Roger's hobbies have something to do with it. When he tires of painting, he turns to related crafts for refreshment – framing, etching, printing. 'I don't want anything else,' he says, 'which is really quite sad I suppose, but nothing else is as satisfying.'

While he had found a vocation at seventeen, it took much longer to find an individual style, initially his greatest hurdle. At college, all kinds of artists, like Norman Rockwell, were held up as exemplars of individual style; but when asked how one acquired it, all the tutors could say was: 'It just comes, or not. Just keep on drawing.'

One obvious approach was to imitate contemporary illustrators, but this seemed too easy, and pointless, if what you are looking for is individuality: 'It is possible, though, to borrow techniques without stealing style. I still avoided contemporaries, though. What I did was turn back to the old masters and see how they had worked. Brueghel particularly influenced my landscapes, as did Dürer, whose linear style I was naturally drawn to. What was most frustrating in the early days was having ideas but not being able to express them.'

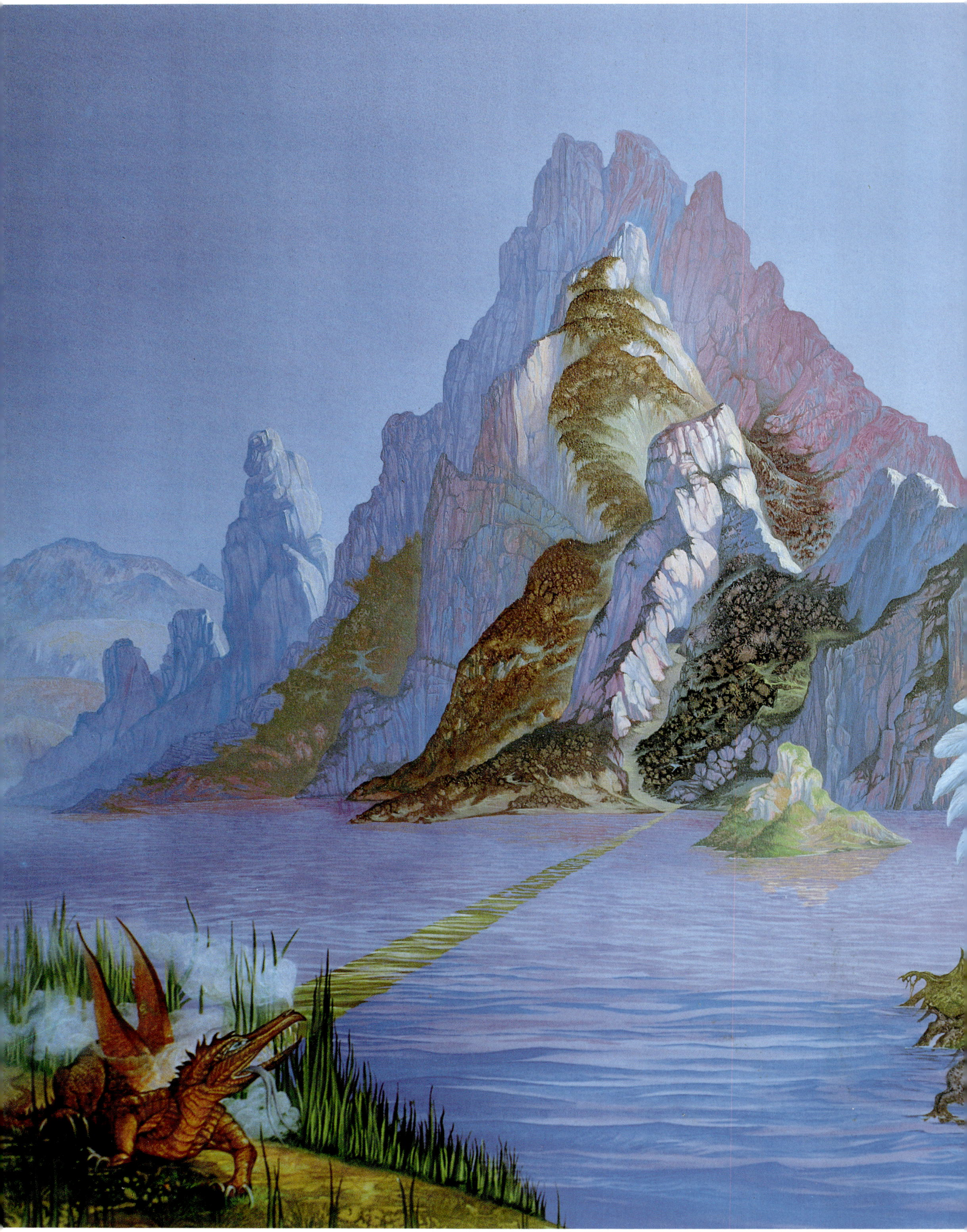

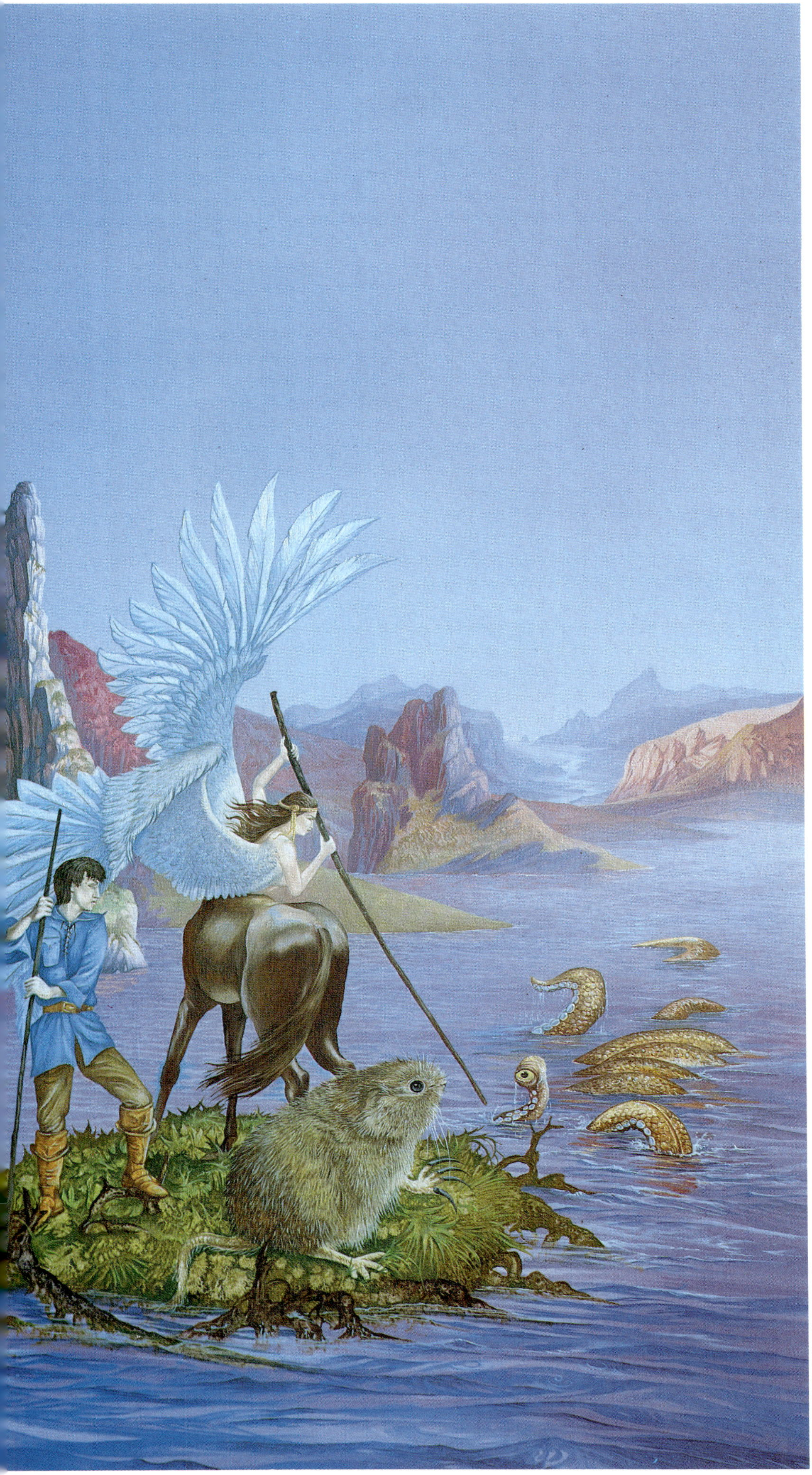

◁ Vale of the Vole
Roger 1988
Oils and Acrylic. 13 x 18in
(33 x 46cm)
Cover for a book by Piers Anthony, Hodder and Stoughton.

One of a series of very good books (in Roger's opinion), aimed at a young audience with a taste for role-playing games. Much of the action revolves around puns.

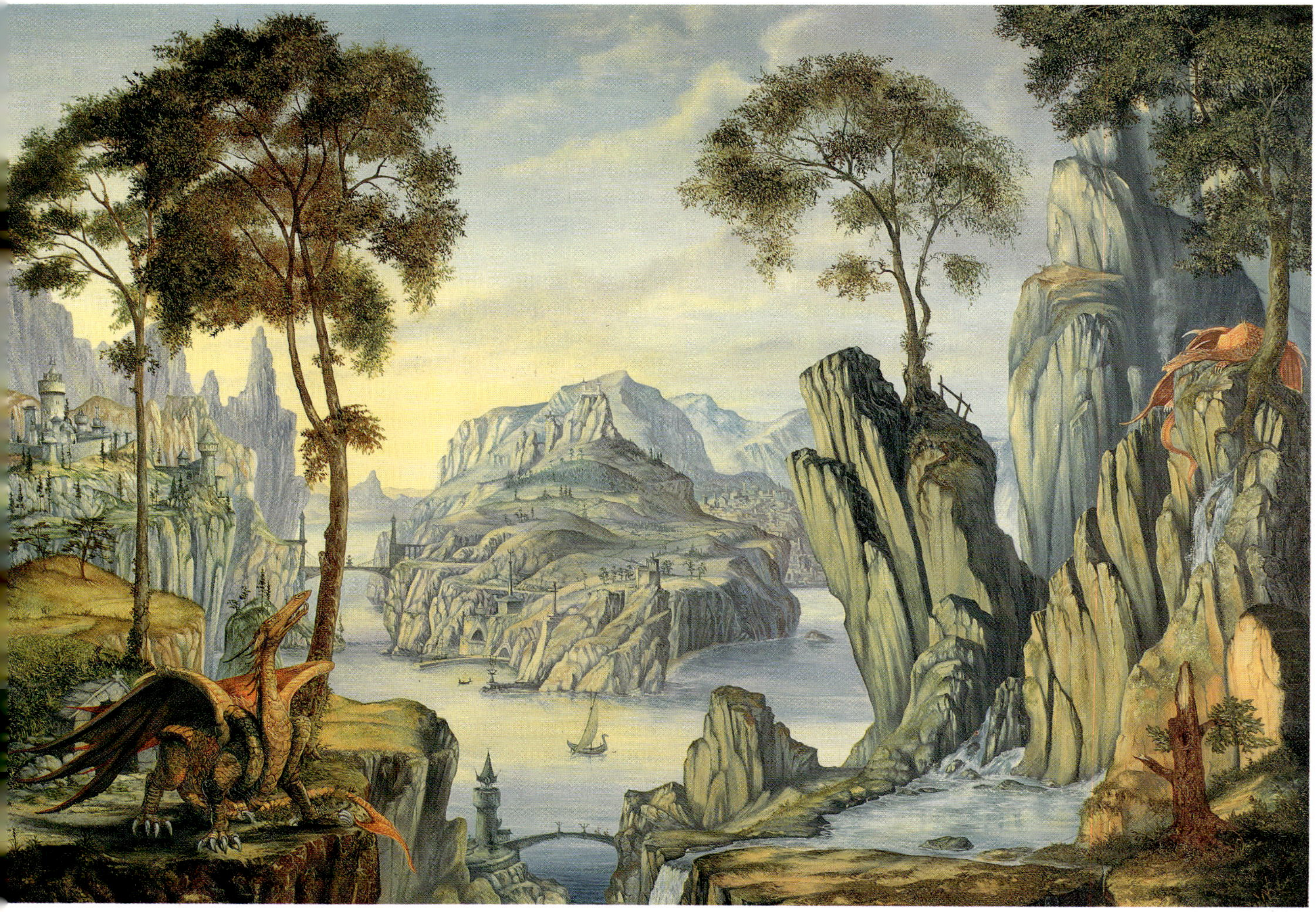

Somehow a style did emerge, though Roger can no more explain the process than his college tutors – you just keep working away and eventually it either emerges, or it doesn't.

Linda introduced Roger to the Pre-Raphaelites, who were to become a major influence in common. Preferences vary slightly – his favourite being Burne-Jones, while Linda's is Rossetti – but overall their admiration is about equal; as it is for the Symbolists they discovered later.

Like Linda, Roger has on occasion been asked what he takes to get some of his ideas, to which he replies that no stimulation is needed: 'It's strange sometimes realizing that not everyone has the same kind of imagination as you. I don't need to look for ideas, they are all around. I would have no problem conjuring up my next year's work by spending a day wandering round the woods in Lifton Gorge. It's almost like there is another world you can just sometimes catch out the corner of your eye. The spirits are there if only you can open your mind to see.'

'For example, I have a picture in mind of a mayfly-type dryad, who has just crawled out of a stream to dry herself on a rock in the sun. I can show you the place where it could, or should, have happened. It's what my mind's eye saw there.'

'My fantasy work comes almost wholly from the effect nature has on my imagination. Certain parts of the country have a special presence that affects

△ **Guardians of the Isles**
Roger 1992
Oils. 11 x 17in (28 x 43cm)
Private commission,
David and Wendy Spy.

Purely imaginary worlds are what Roger enjoys painting most. The chance presented itself here when a Scottish visitor to the gallery asked for something Tolkienesque. Thinking of Scotland suggested islands as a theme, the rest just followed naturally.

▷ **Fire-Drake**
Roger 1992
Oils. 9 x 12in (23 x 30cm)
Card design, Lakeside Gallery.

The model for this dragon was a gangling Irish Setter. Marbling was used to give the rocks an organic feel. For some reason cheap white spirit worked better for this than turpentine, and then only with certain colours.

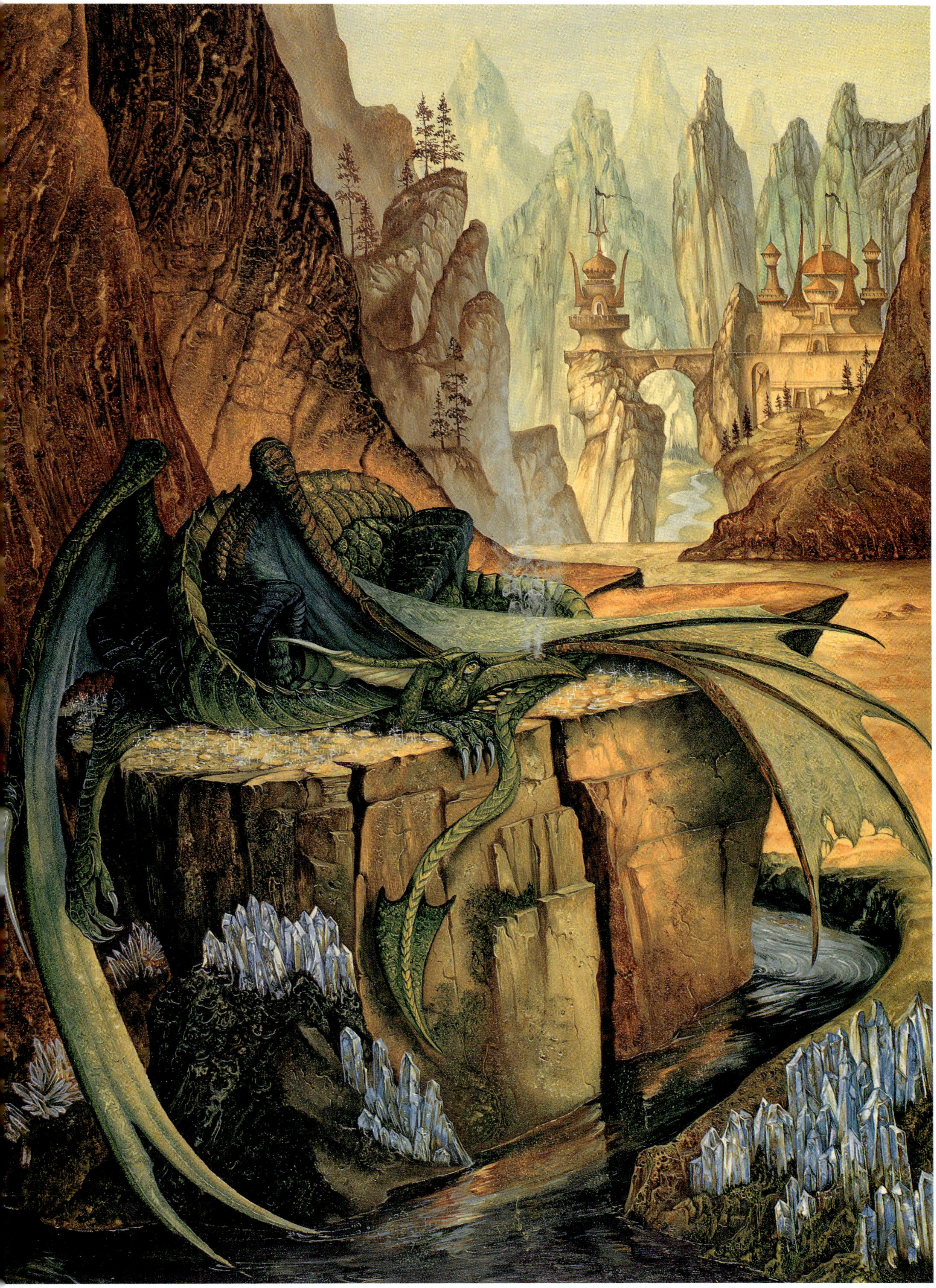

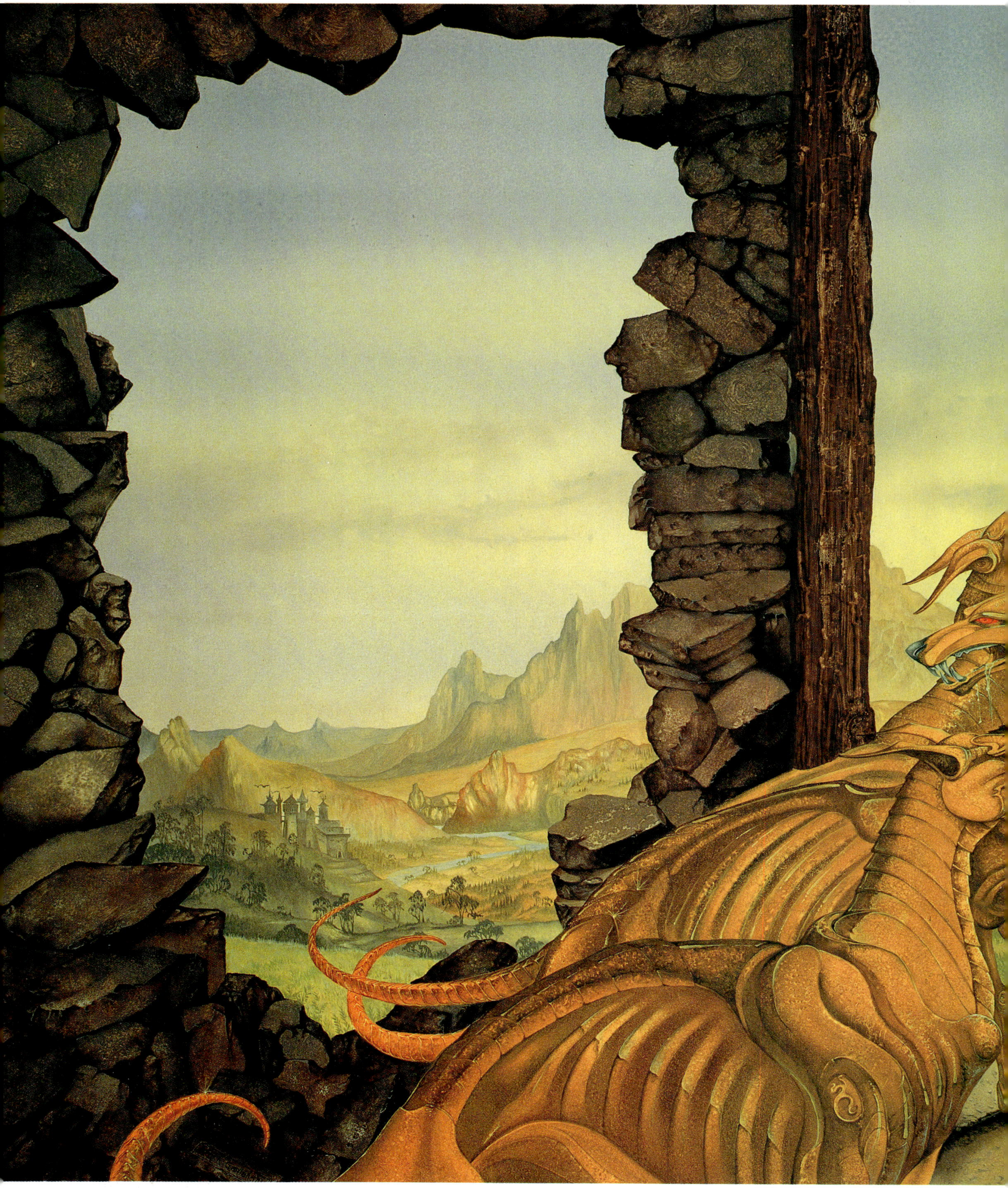

many people in the same way, that is why legends grow up around them. My own favourite places generally have running water, rocks and trees. I'm inspired by closed-in areas rather than moors, because it's so easy to see things coming out of the shadows. Cliff paths also appeal, and one of my few regrets about where we live now is being so far from the coast. Perhaps being Pisces draws me to water.'

From time to time, Roger has quite adventurous dreams. Although often creepy, he has yet to succeed in painting one successfully, however vividly he remembers them. At most, a few details have crept into other scenes.

In general, Roger tries to avoid crowding his pictures: 'Too much detail can exclude viewers and take away the mystery. To me what is not painted is almost more important than what is; it gives the viewer's imagination something to do. That is part of the attraction of Symbolist art for us – the mysteriousness that defies explanation, a strange waiting for something to happen. There is, in Symbolist paintings, a decadence and insecurity that speaks to me. Someone once compared them to Mahler – terribly imperfect in places, but with flashes of brilliance.'

Gustav Moreau is probably the main Symbolist influence on both Garlands; but there are others like Bocklin and Klimt who are almost equal favourites; and many individual paintings, like Jean Delville's *Satan's Treasures*, which have shaped their art as much as anything by Rossetti or Burne-Jones.

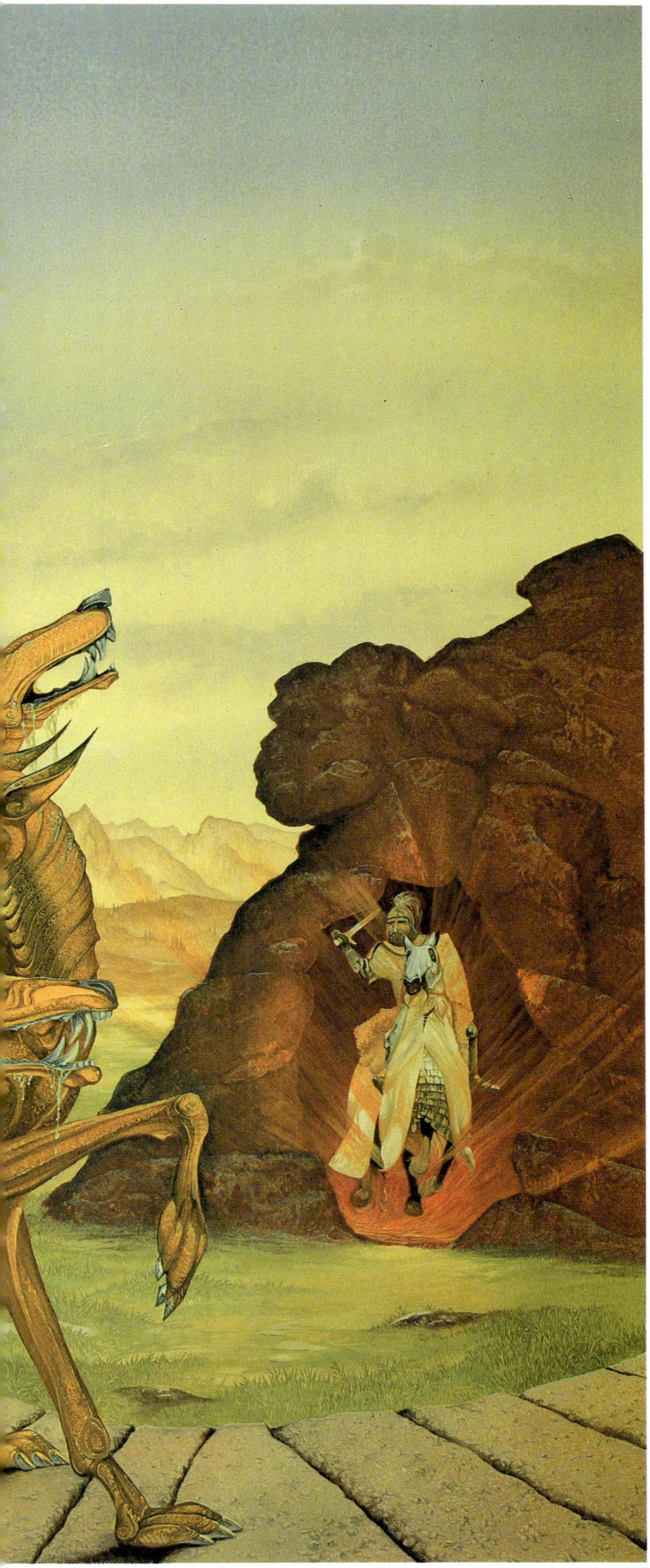

◁ **Goldendogs**
Roger 1978
Gouache. 17 x 21in
(43 x 53cm)
Cover for *Knights of Dark Renown* by David Gemmel, Century Hutchinson.

This story was based on a Celtic theme, in which the best smith in the land creates living metal dogs. Again, the model for them was an Irish Setter.

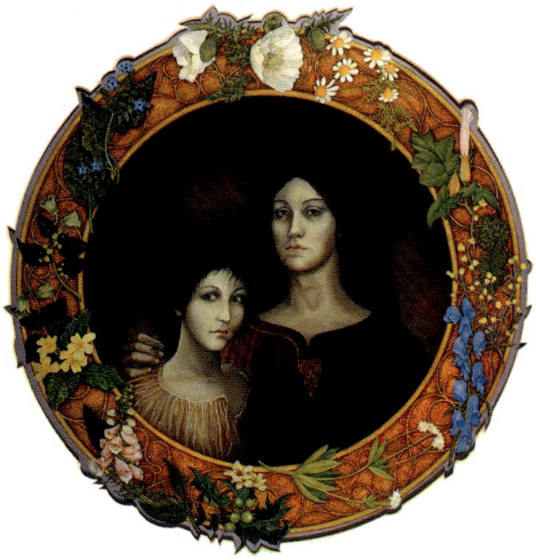

# GARLANDS OF FANTASY

*"The attraction of illustration is that it is one of the few outlets for figurative artists. A drawback is that often little or no recognition goes with the work."*

It was Tom Phillips, illustrator of Dante's *Inferno* and part-time tutor at Wolverhampton Art College, who introduced Linda to *The White Goddess* and themes which have preoccupied her ever since. She has never systematically read the book from start to finish, but prefers to plunder it more or less at random, like rooting through a treasure chest. 'It contains all the information about myth that you could ever want', she says, and although other volumes, like Frazer's *Golden Bough* sit beside it on the studio shelf, it remains her fount of inspiration.

The theme of Linda's diploma show at college was 'Nightmare' although, having to conform to prevailing norms, she explored it in very abstract terms – aiming for a stained glass effect, which resulted in something resembling a psychedelic Brigit Riley. 'Dreadful,' she says of it now, 'but it met the requirements.'

Leaving college meant freedom to work in a more natural medium, the results of which soon led to a demand for similar work for book jackets, which is about as near to heaven as any kind of artist can get – finding an appreciative audience without the strain of integrity.

The attraction of illustration is that it is one of the few outlets for figurative artists. A drawback is that often little or no recognition goes with the work, because publishers tend to be possessive about their artists, trying not to print their names in an attempt to prevent rivals poaching them. Often the Garlands have been told, on showing their portfolios, that if the client had known they had painted a particular piece, they would have been contacted long before.

One's work tends also to be seen as secondary to whatever is being illustrated; but occasionally the position is reversed, as when one publisher told Linda of 'some bloke in Gloucester who's buying our books as they come out, just for your covers.'

The art of book illustration is one the Garlands more or less taught themselves as they went along. The only useful contribution from their official college training, that they can both think of, is the lasting habit of self-evaluation.

△ **Wise Child**
Linda 1987
Oils. 14in diam. (36cm)
Cover for a book by Monica Furlong, Victor Gollancz.

Linda still laments the take-over of this publisher by a larger group, and the subsequent loss of their offices in Covent Garden, which had a wonderfully old-fashioned feel that was a cross between a labyrinth and a bordello. They also produced some lovely books, including this one by Monica Furlong about an ancient Celtic herbalist who takes on an apprentice. A faint model for the girl was a haunting photograph of Alice Liddel, Lewis Carrol's inspiratrix for the Alice stories. The border contains a muted Celtic pattern overlaid by a collage of herbs, including aconite and digitalis.

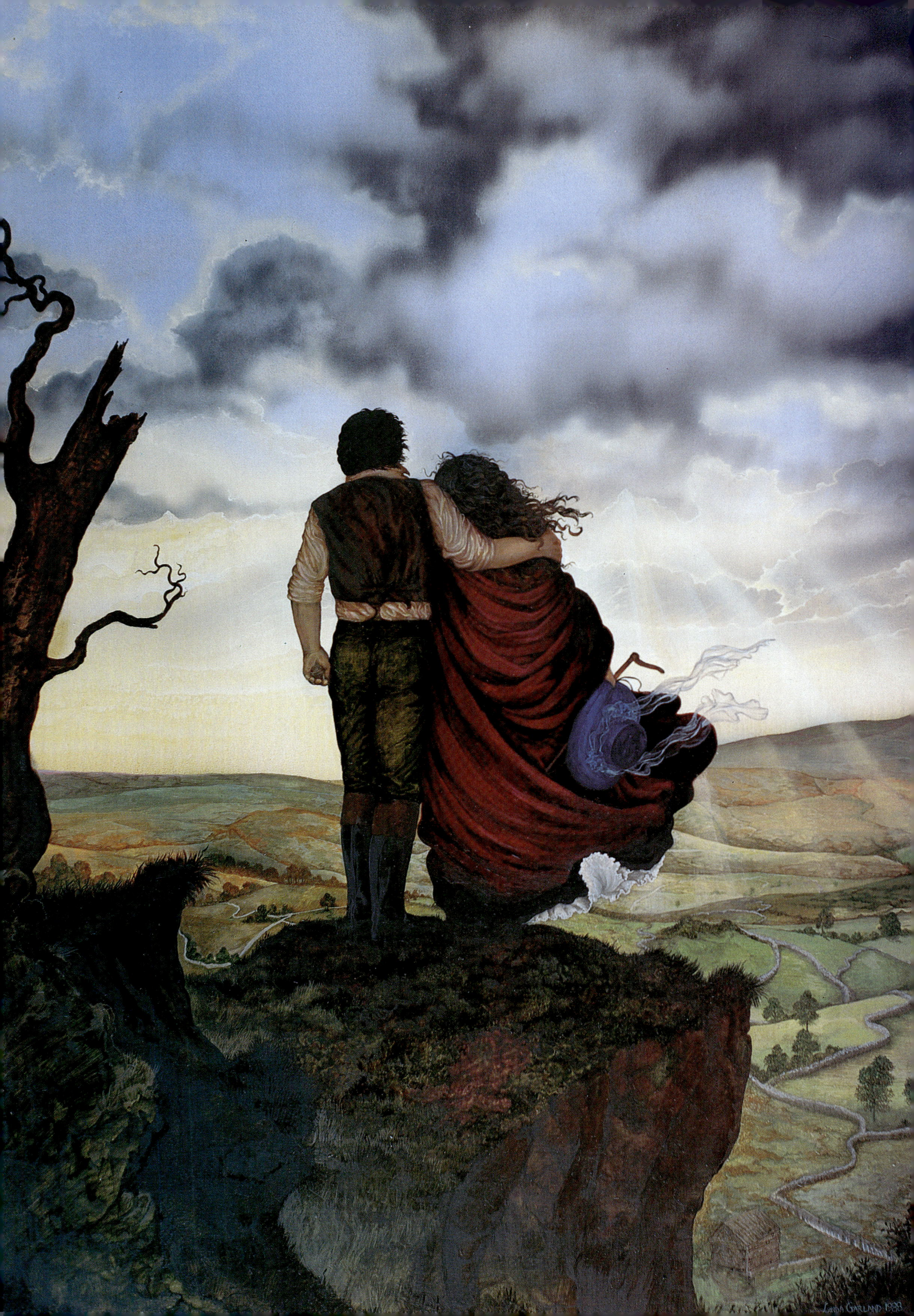
LINDA GARLAND 1988

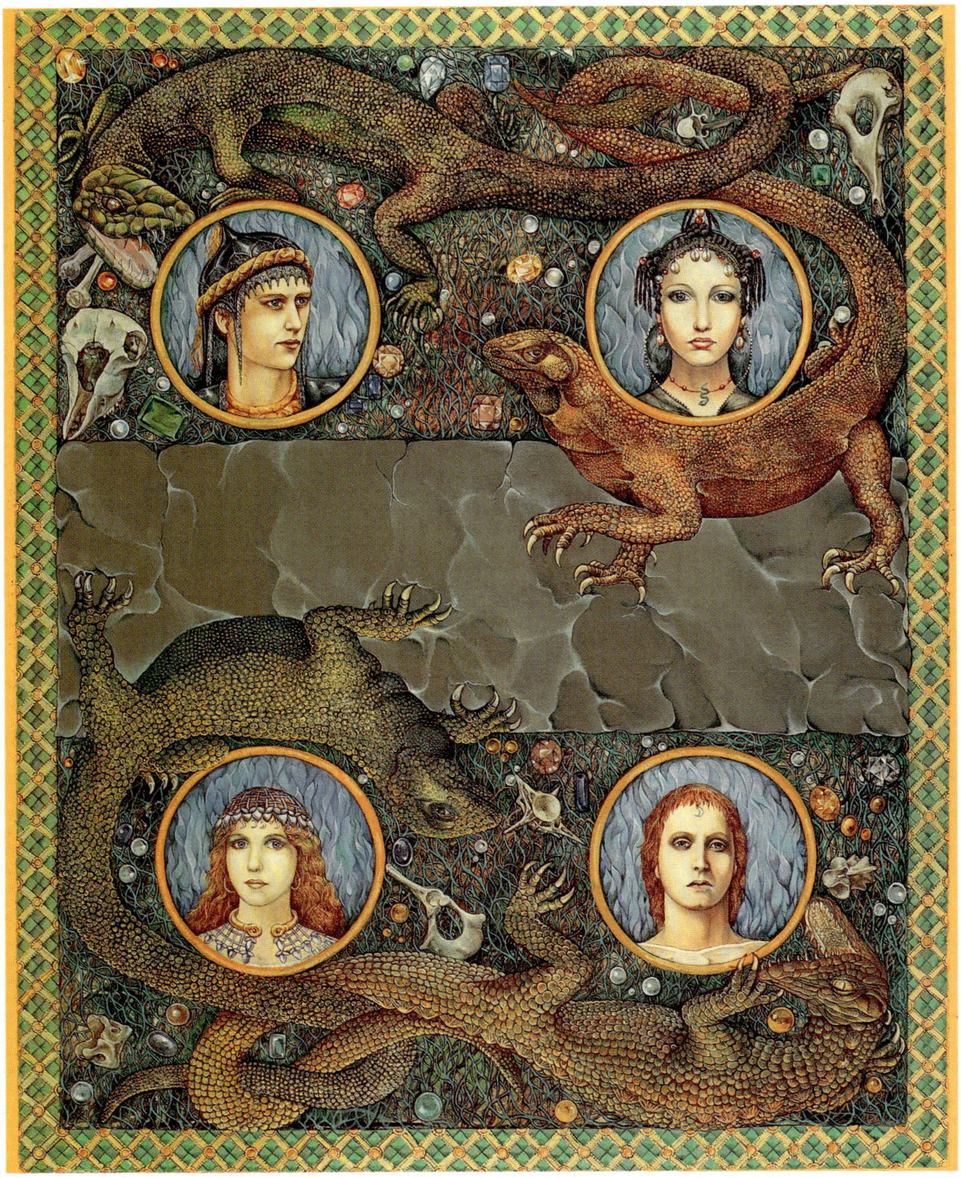

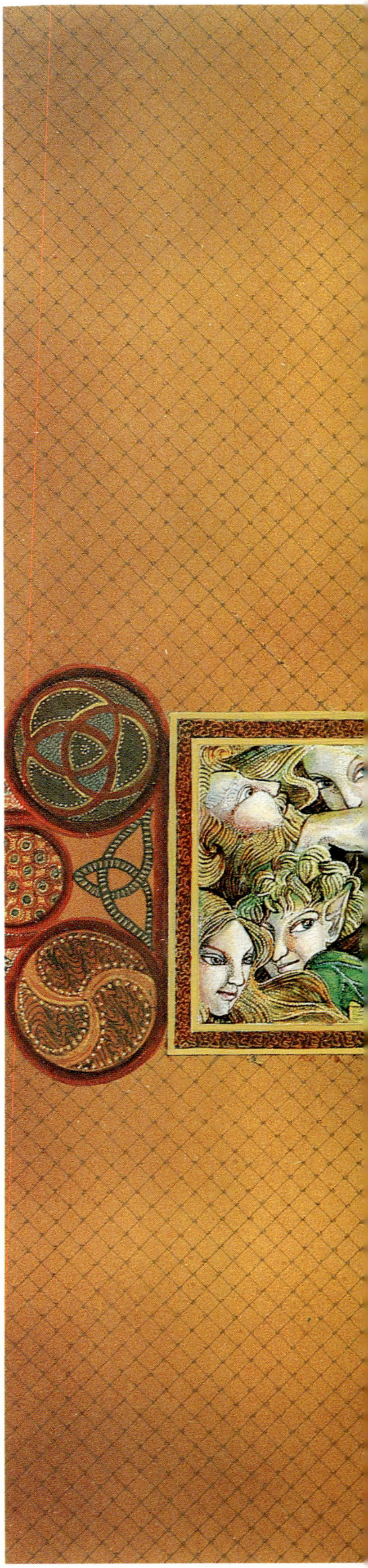

(Previous page)
**Wuthering Heights**
Linda 1988
Oils. 18 x 30in (45 x 76cm)
Promotional poster, Piancastelli Productions.
This picture, and its accompanying brochure, was used to attract finance for a stage musical of *Wuthering Heights*. A rear view of the figures was required so they would not clash with the actors in the production. The scene is the Yorkshire moors, where the story takes place. For a while, there was talk of Linda being commissioned for the stage sets, but this sadly did not come to fruition.

△ **Four Heads With Lizards**
Linda 1985
Oils. 9 x 11in (23 x 28cm)
Private work.

Shown as a sample to clients, this enigmatic painting has led to many similar commissions which mingle patterns and figures.

▷ **The Haunted Mountain**
Linda 1978
Oils. 11 x 13in (28 x 33cm)
Cover for *Lions* by Mollie Hunter.

This was one of Linda's first covers, and was commissioned for a story based on an old Scottish ballad about having to hold on to an enchanted lover as they move through a series of shape-shifts, from snake to fire and ice and more, or lose them forever. In this story, a boy's father is taken by the fairies, and when they finally meet again he must hold on to his father to get him back. The design was based on those in the *Book of Kells*.

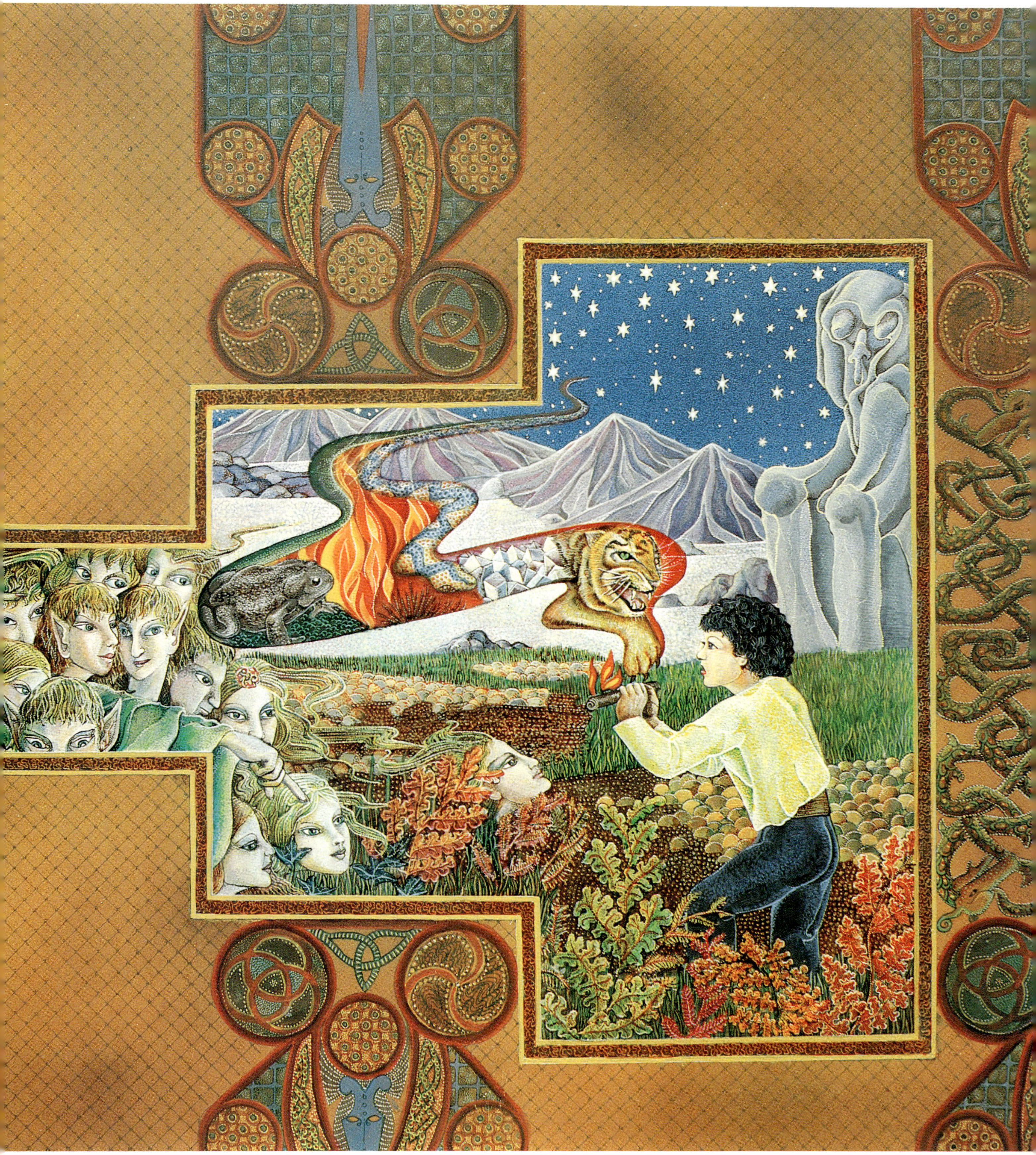

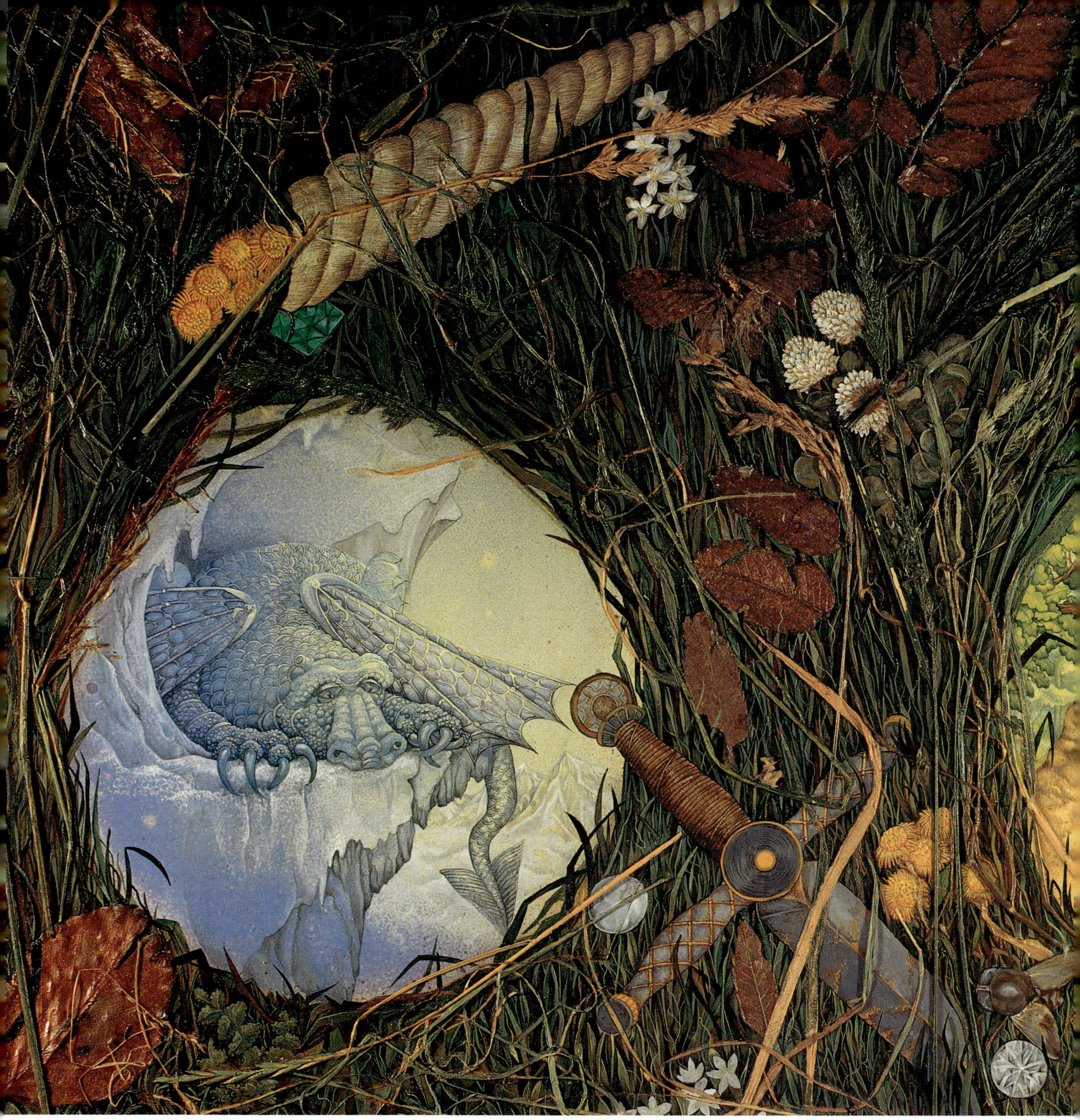

△ **The Unlikely Ones**
Linda 1986
Oils. 13 x 20in (33 x 51cm)
Cover for a book by Mary Brown, Century Hutchinson.

This cover was for a story, aimed at teenagers, about a hideous witch who steals the jewel hoard of the glum-looking dragon on the left. She embeds them in the bodies of the motley crew on the right, thereby deforming each of them in some way. They band together to try and return the gems, even the goldfish which has a tiny jewel in its throat. Much of the picture is a collage, mingled with paintings of the jewels and other items mentioned in the story.

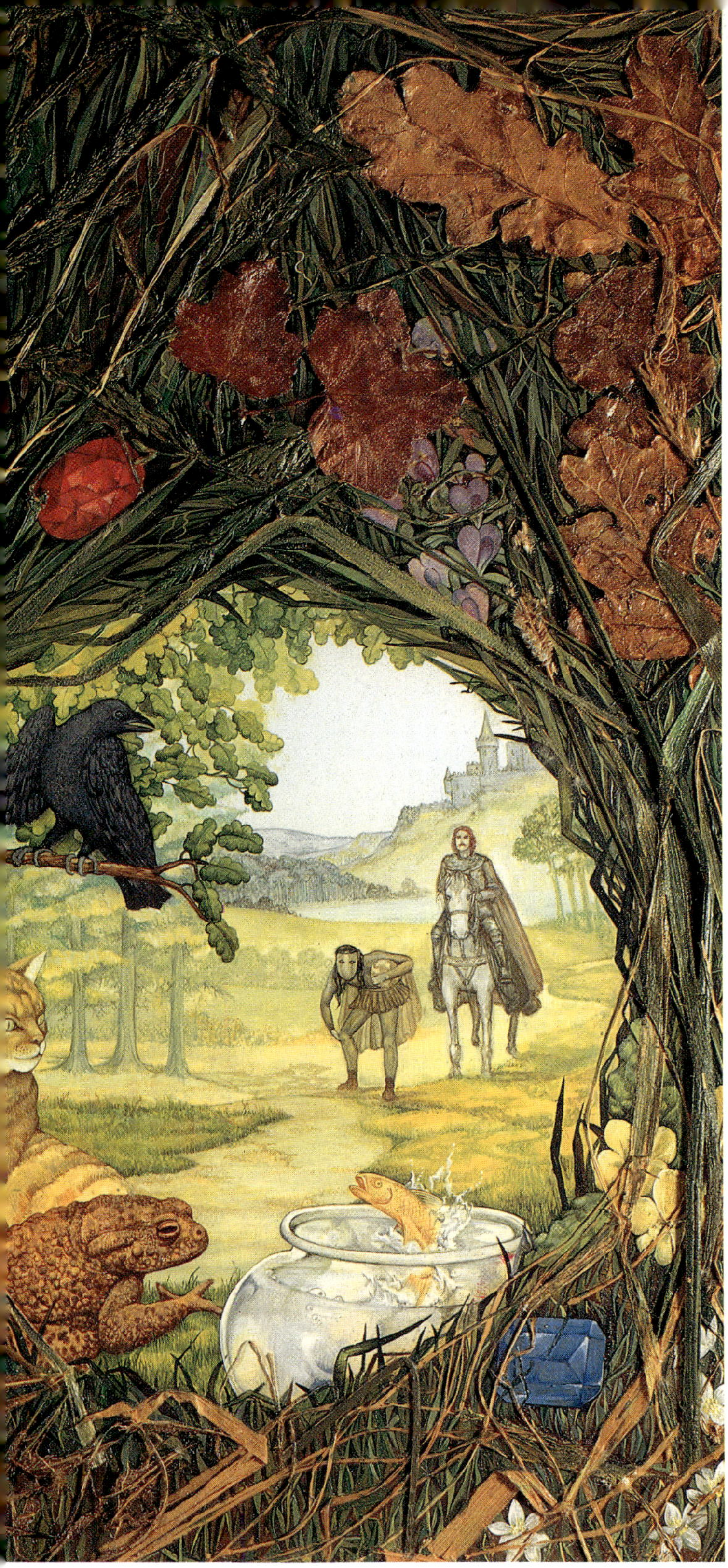

The effect is often subliminal, but still important. Roger: 'Without training it is easy to be satisfied with whatever you do. College teaches you to step back from your work and view it the way a tutor would. There is a danger of getting over critical though, which I think we have fallen into at times. I often admire the speed and recklessness with which some people paint, relying on talent and energy to get them through.'

Usually, with covers, they work to three times the printed size and do preparatory drawings on thin layout paper, which allows ideas to be developed quickly by being traced from one sheet to another. Roger's first drawings are thumbnail sketches, only two or three inches square, on which he works out the overall composition before scaling it up to working size.

The airbrush is an instrument the Garlands have never been happy with, and have now more or less abandoned it, except for mists. It used to be indispensable for skies and backgrounds, but for these they have found other means, particularly sponges, which Roger discovered and which they now collect wherever they go. Roger: 'It was quite thrilling really, finding how much can be done with different sponges, experimenting with surfaces and getting away from traditional methods. Sponging gives a nice textured surface for painting over, and because you can use oils the result is purer than painting over the acrylics which the airbrush uses.'

The dislike is a matter of personal temperament, for they admire several airbrush artists. The tool is just too mechanical for their taste, and although it is probably their fault for not changing the needle often enough, they have too many memories of it splattering in the wrong place at the last moment. Also, there is the tedium of masking the picture, and the hard edges this leaves.

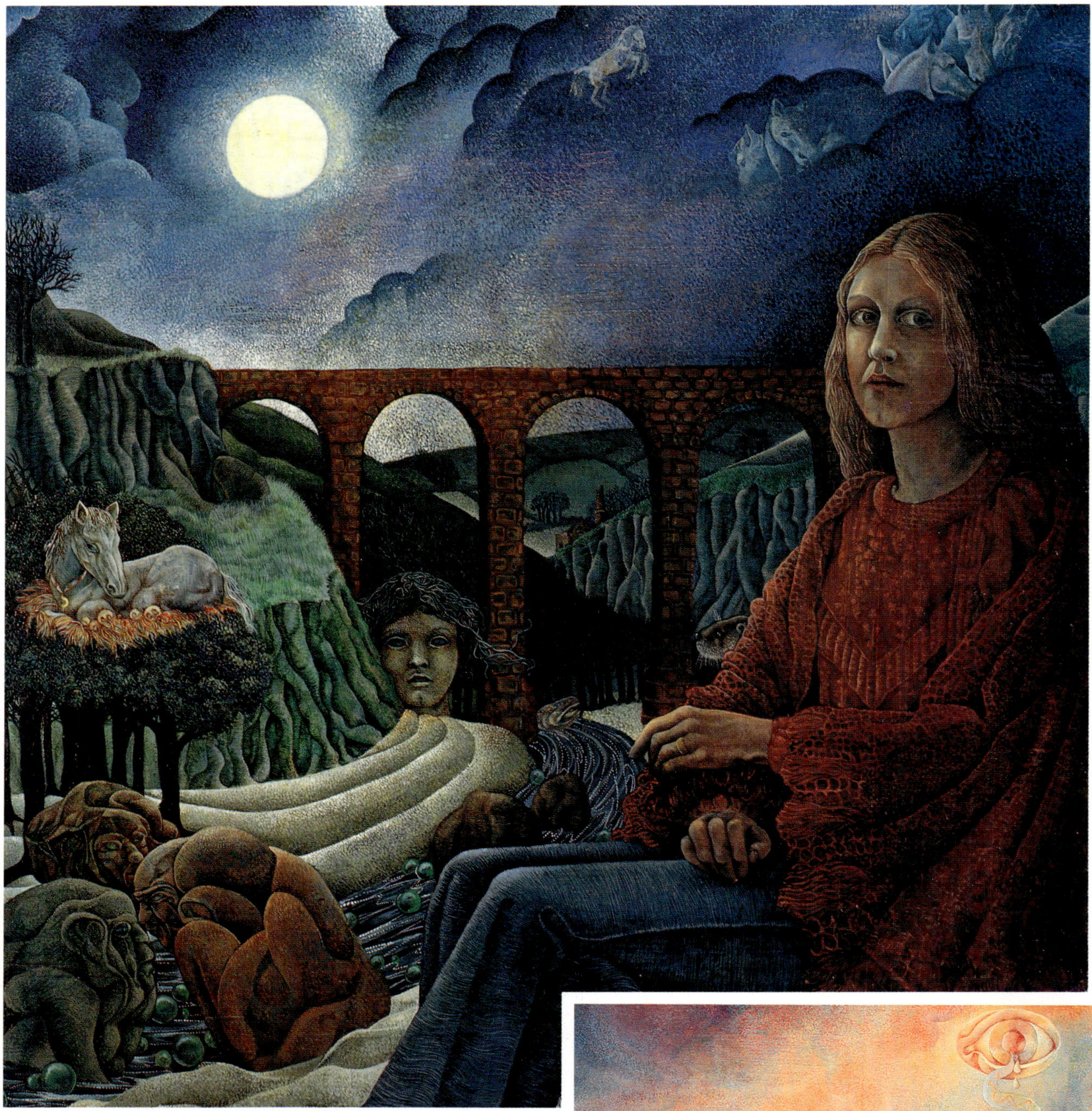

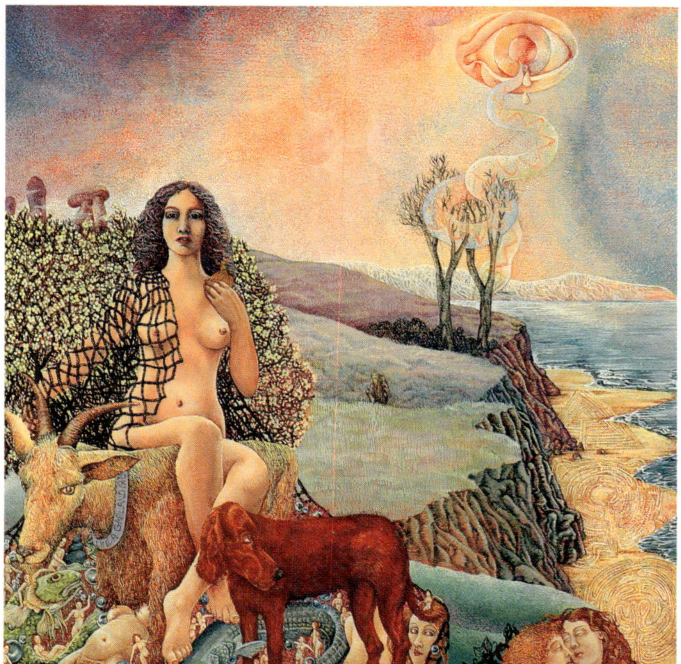

△ **Winter**
Linda 1976
Oils. 9 x 9in (23 x 23cm)
Private work.

The scene is Luxulyan Valley in Cornwall, which is full of wonderful rocks that look like hunched-up people. The rail bridge ingeniously doubles as an aqueduct that used to take water to the tin mines. The white horse in the tree is the original night-mare, surrounded by the skulls of her victims.

▷ **Spring**
Linda 1976
Oils. 9 x 9in (23 x 23cm)
Private work.

The masonically-posed lady represents May, particularly May Eve, when the normal rules of propriety were traditionally suspended, and the hedgerows were full of otherwise illicit lovemaking.

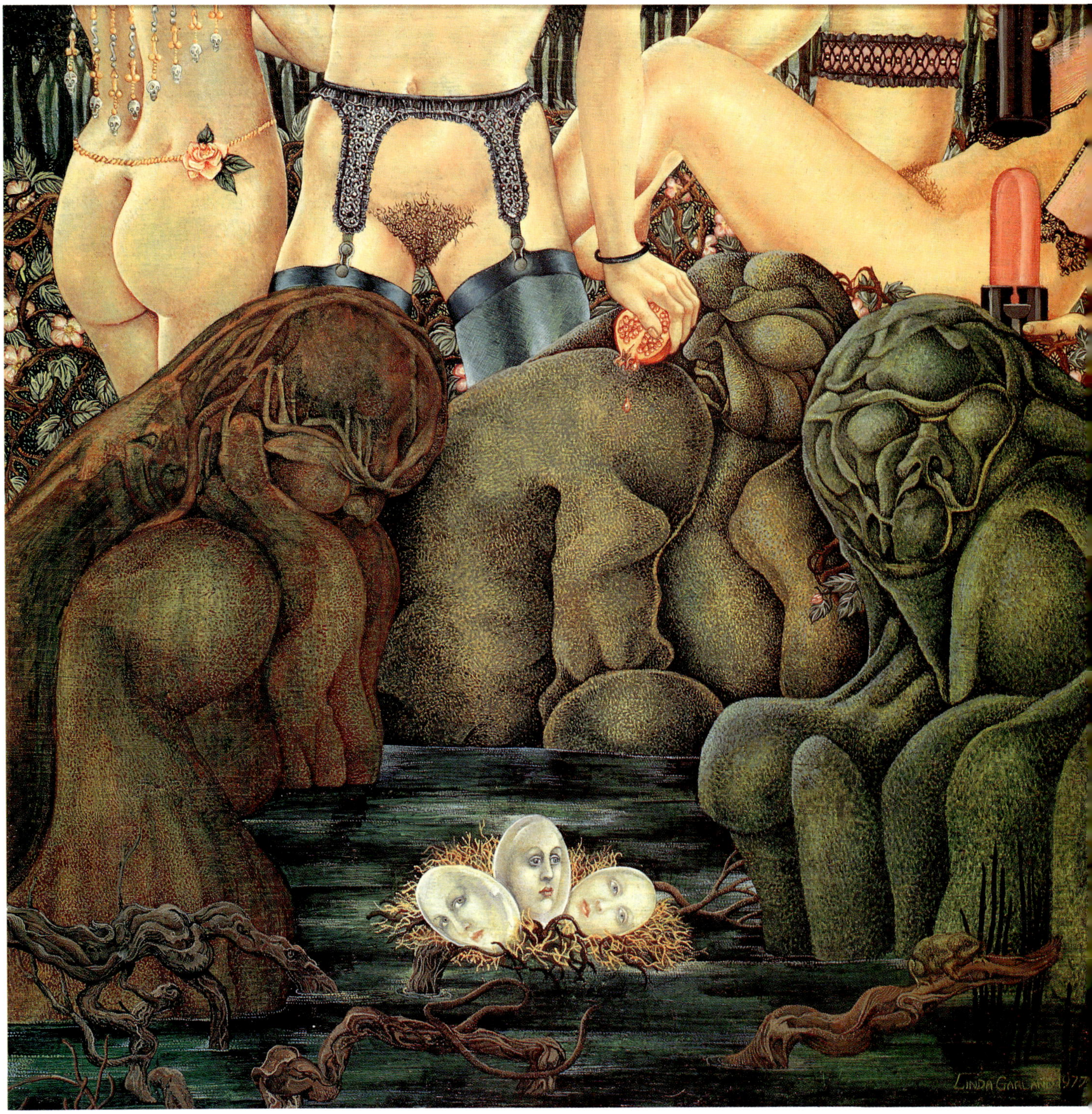

△ **Summer**
Linda 1977
Oils. 9 x 9in (23 x 23cm)
Private work.

This picture depicts the three stages of woman.

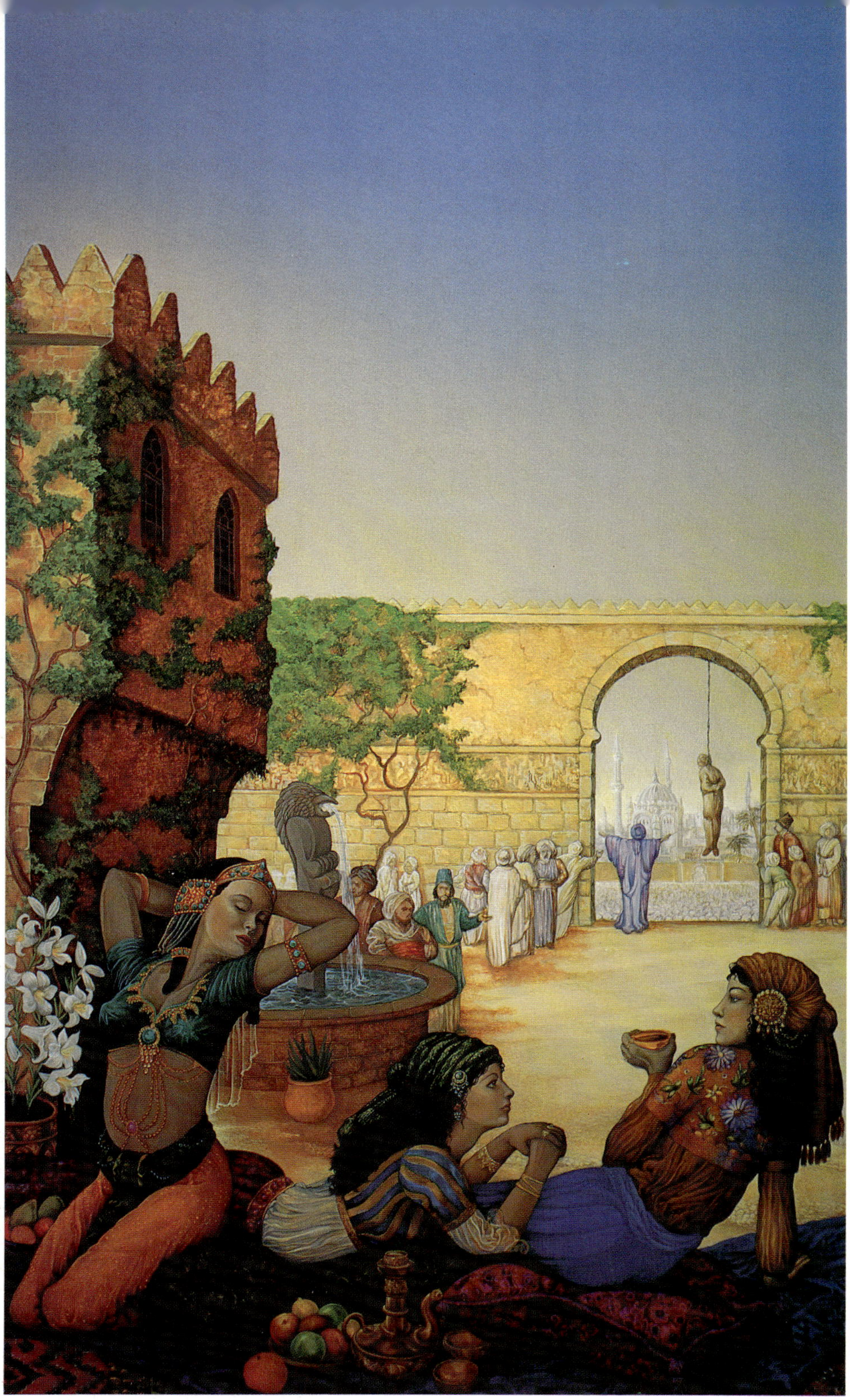

▷ **Caravan of Dreams**
Linda 1977
Oils. 8 x 13in (20 x 34cm)
Cover for a book of Sufi stories by Idries Shah, Quartet.

The motifs and clouds in this very early book cover by Linda were taken from Persian carpets and paintings.

◁ **Bagdad**
Linda 1987
Oils. 11 x 18in (28 x 46cm)
Cover for a book by Ian Dennis, Unwin Hyman.

This strange, erotic, Scheherazade-type book passed rapidly round the Garlands' circle of friends before disappearing at some point. The painting was sold at a local Phillips auction, fetching the highest price of the day, which led to a TV appearance for Linda and a rapid upward revision of prices back at the gallery.

Oil paint is the Garlands' favourite medium, because it is extremely versatile. It can be pushed around the surface, slipped or washed with sponges, or simply wiped off if necessary to start again. Linda particularly likes oils for skin tones because, unlike acrylics, they do not dry to a different shade. They are also slightly transparent, allowing the ground to shine through. Usually this is white, producing a stained glass effect; but occasionally the surface is underpainted for particular effects, such as underpainting blue with purple. The only problem with oils, they have found, is that they tend to wear out sable brushes, at the rate of about two per painting.

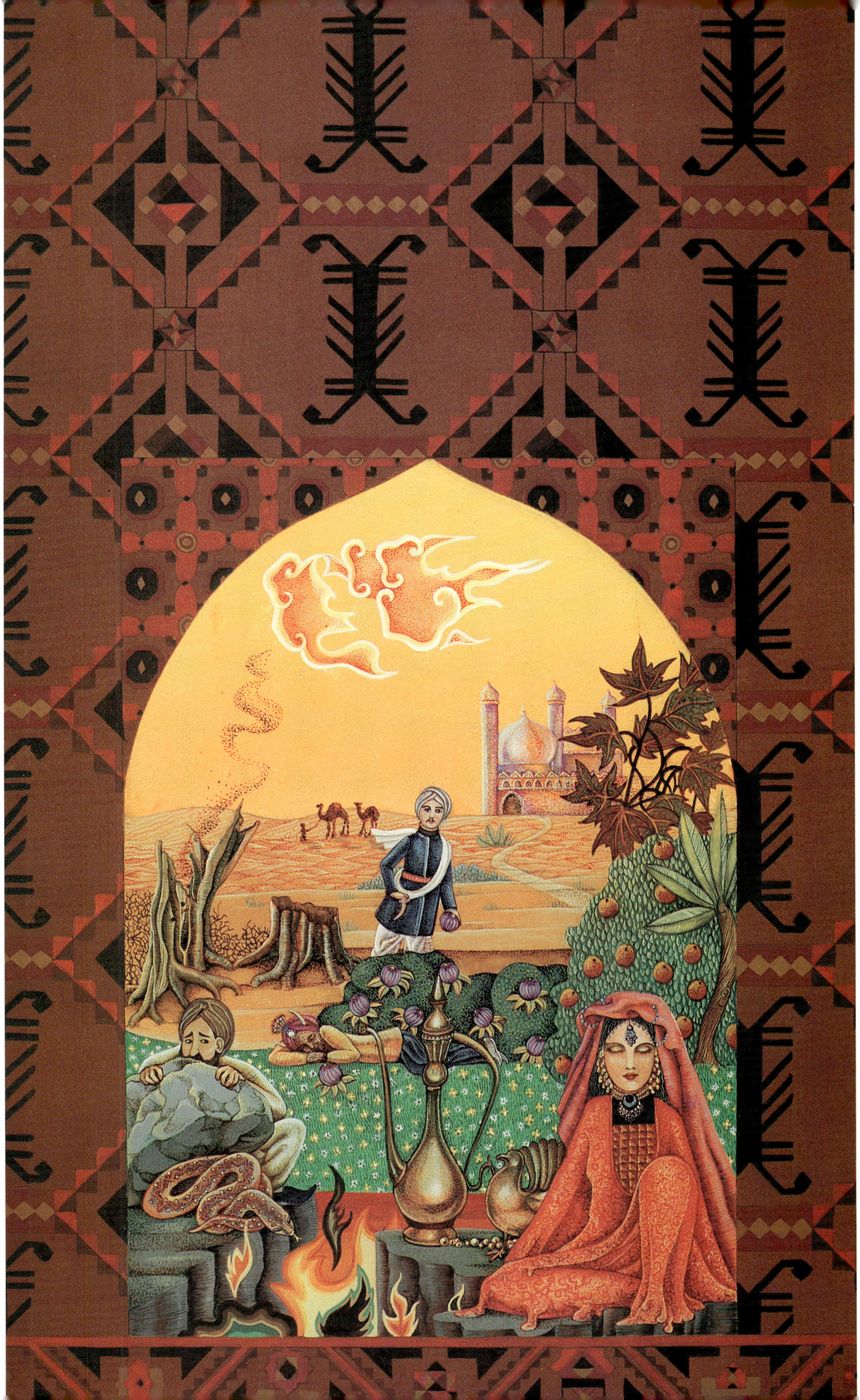

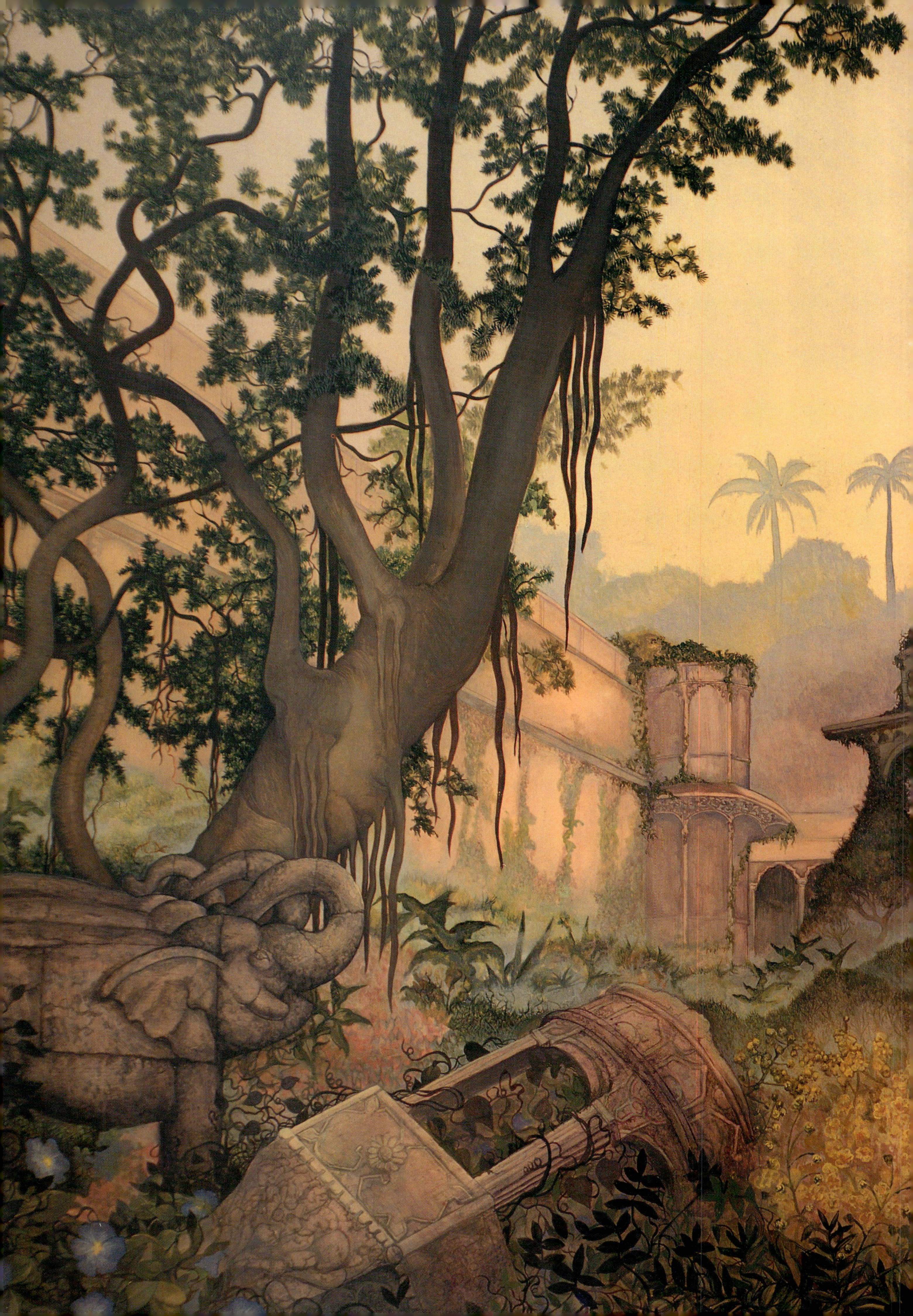

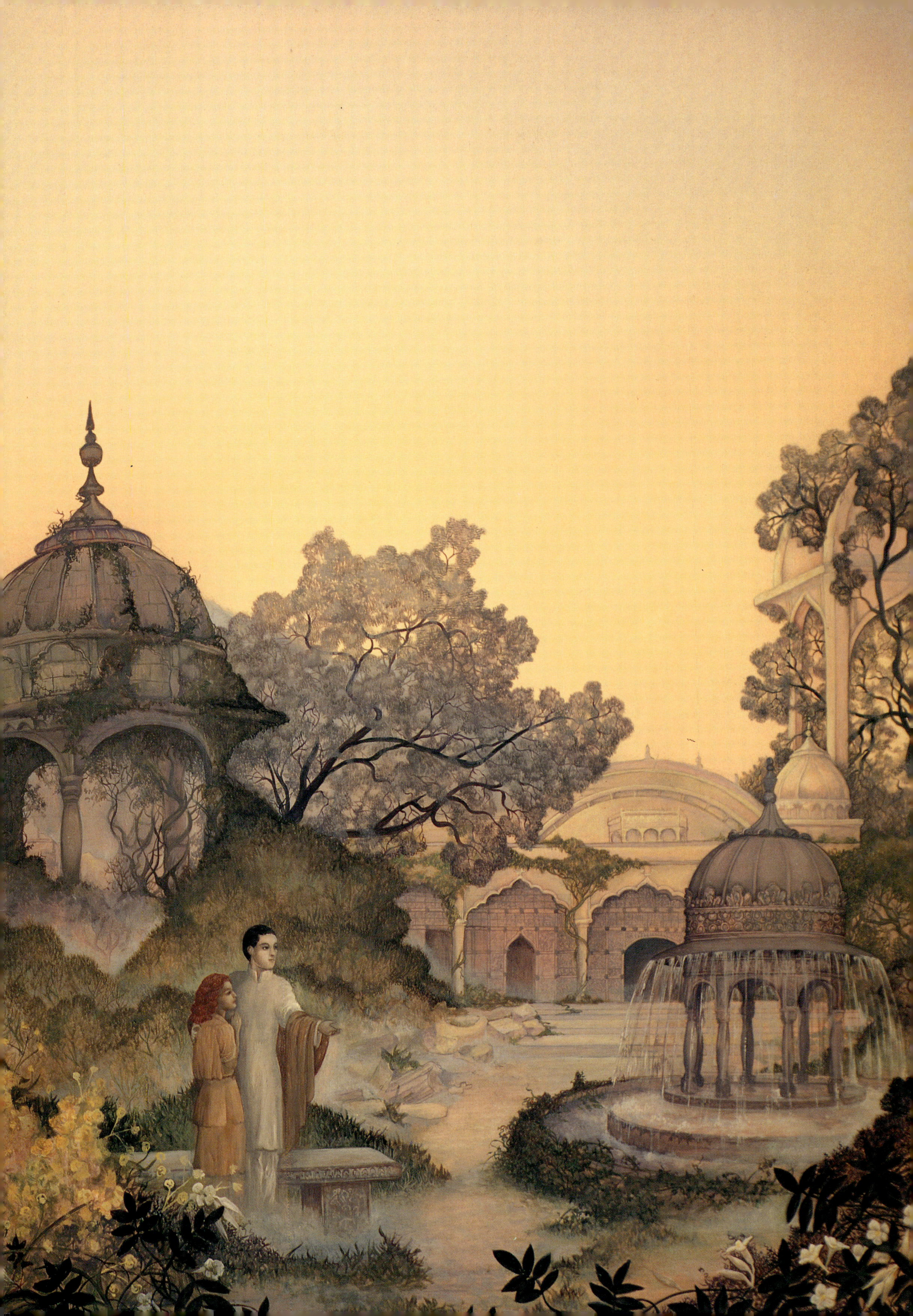

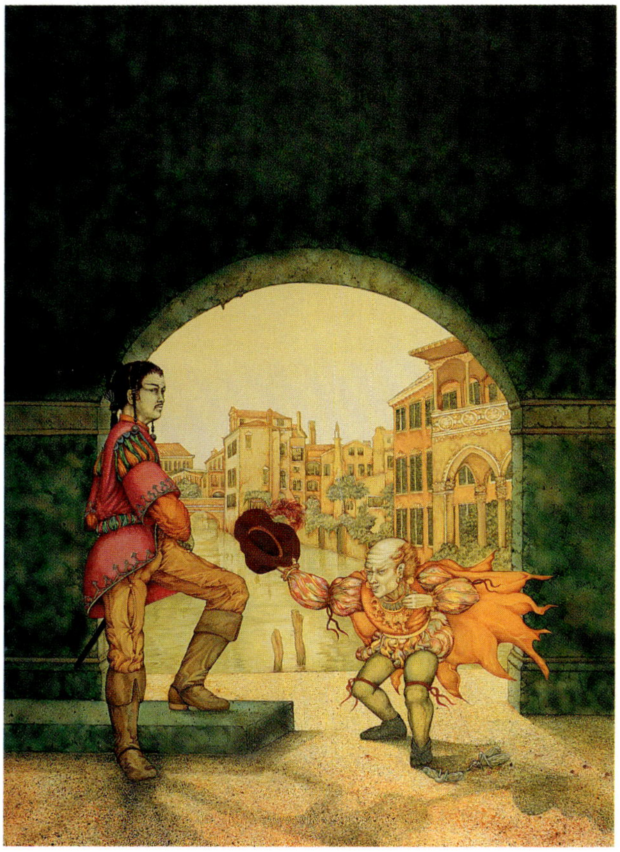

(Previous page)
**Ruined Temple**
Linda 1987
Oils. 13 x 19in (33 x 48cm)
Cover for *Spring Imperial* by Evelyn Hart, Century Hutchinson.

One of a pair of covers which represent Linda's first, and so far only, venture into romantic fiction. The story is set on the eve of the Second World War, and tells of the troubled love between a young lady of the British Raj and an Indian prince. Photographic reference for the palace and vegetation was provided by the author, who grew up in India.

△ Viriconium Nights
Linda 1987
Oils. 11 x 16in (28 x 41cm)
Cover for a book by John M. Harrison, Unicorn.

The Art Director's opinion of this picture was, 'It's the best book cover I've seen in years.' Linda's comment is, 'You raise your game when you get a good book like this. The story had a Venetian feel, so as a reference I used our own photos from a trip to Venice.'

Nylon brushes are cheaper and sturdier, but coarse, so it has to be nothing but the best. The drying time used to be a problem: oils can take up to three weeks, which is far too long for book jackets. For speed, they used gouache for early covers, until the invention of drying resins removed the problem.

Most of their paintings are done on prepared wooden board, which they adopted after some early paintings were severely mauled by printers trying to remove the top layer for scanning. Notes were attached to the first wooden paintings saying: 'Try stripping this!'

Transparencies of finished paintings are taken by Roger using an old Kodak 5 x 4 camera mounted on a sliding frame, which he picked up for a hundred pounds, and which has saved them a fortune since, quite apart from the convenience of not having to cart paintings off to a photographer. An initial handicap was having to rely on sunlight for taking pictures, which often meant waiting for the clouds to lift before a piece of work could be sent off; but this was overcome by splashing out on a couple of spotlights.

Choosing a cover image is usually a matter of instinct. If no guideline has been given, the book is simply read through, and notes taken about the characters and passages which particularly conjure up the overall mood of the story. Usually, there are one or two decisive sentences which flash up and suggest the cover.

Both Garlands like to send fairly detailed drawings to the publisher for approval, as this saves a lot of argument later and means that the painting is mainly a matter of getting the colours right.

Have they had many flops? Roger: 'My only real flop was a cover for *Here be Dragons*. To give me an idea of what they wanted, the publishers sent a Noel Paton picture, a beautiful painting of a knight killing a dragon, and asked me to do something similar. I froze and came up with an awful image.

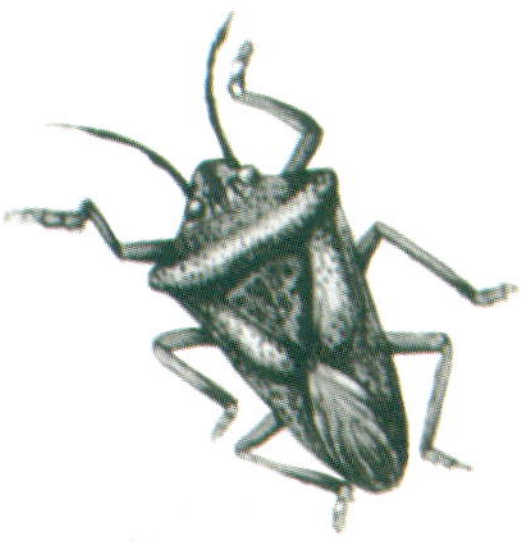

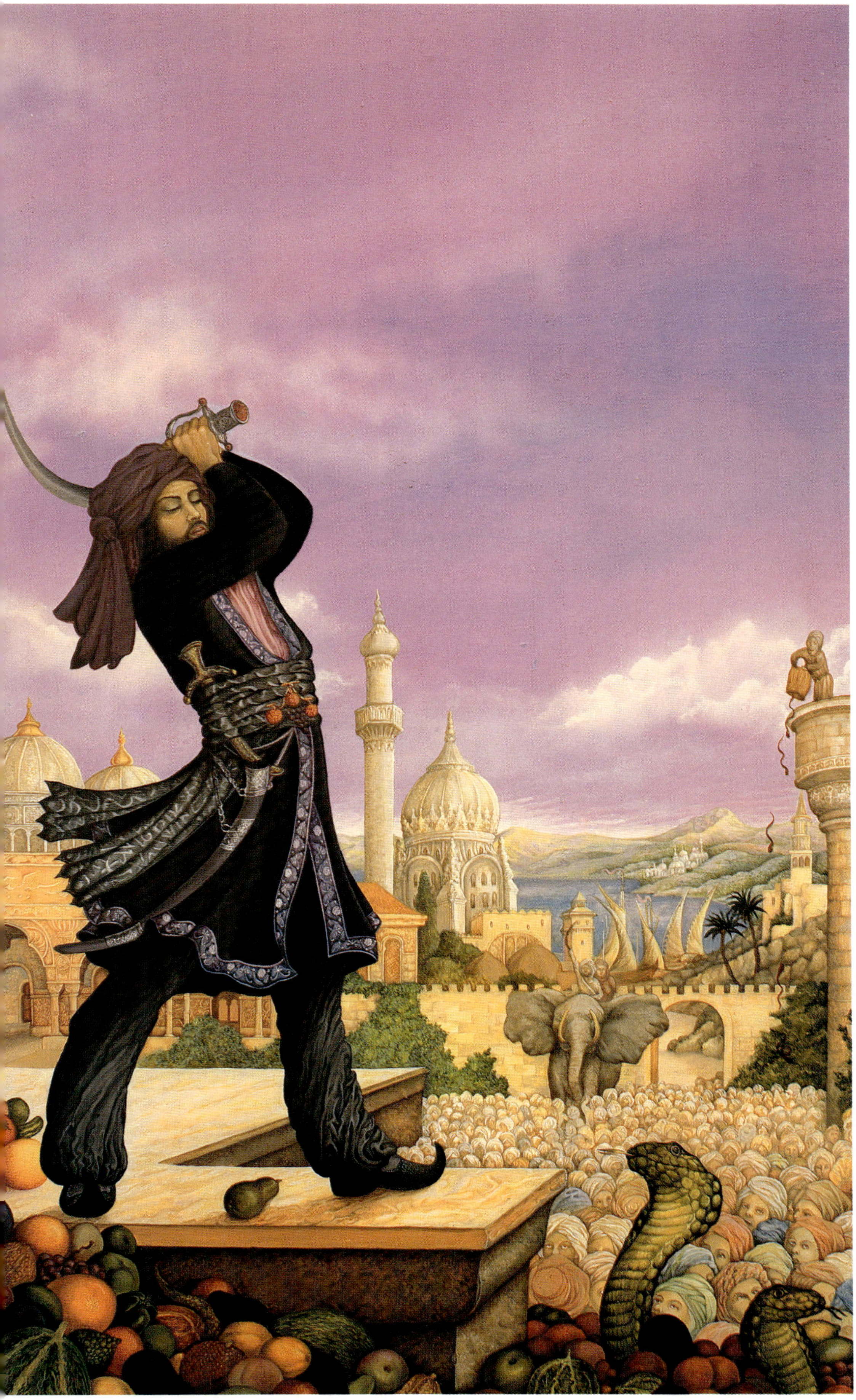

◁ Prince of Stars
Linda 1987
Oils. 11 x 18in (28 x 46cm)
Cover for a book by Ian
Dennis, Unwin Hyman.

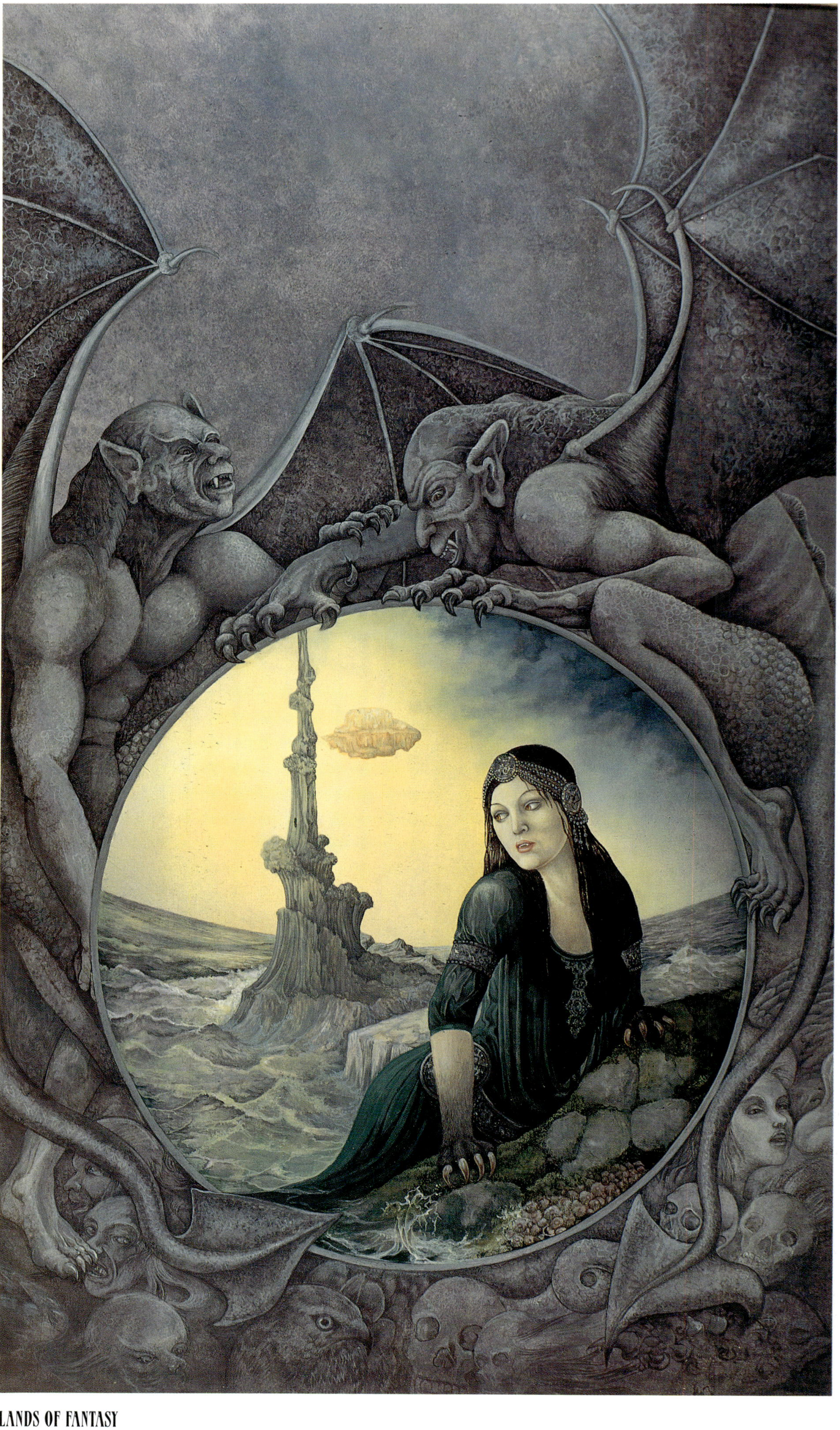

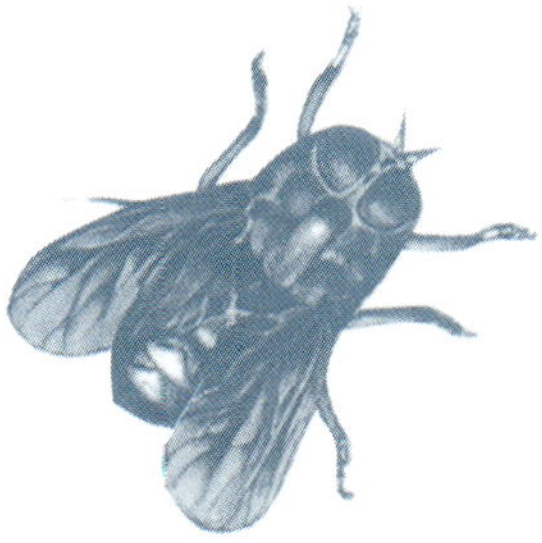

◁Gothic Siren
Linda 1987
Oils. 13 x 20in (33 x 51cm)
Cover for *Burning Realm* by
Michael Reeves, Orbit.

This painting was one of a pair of covers for some stories by Reeves set in a strange disintegrating world held together by a necromancer. The female is in the process of shape-shifting into a wolf.

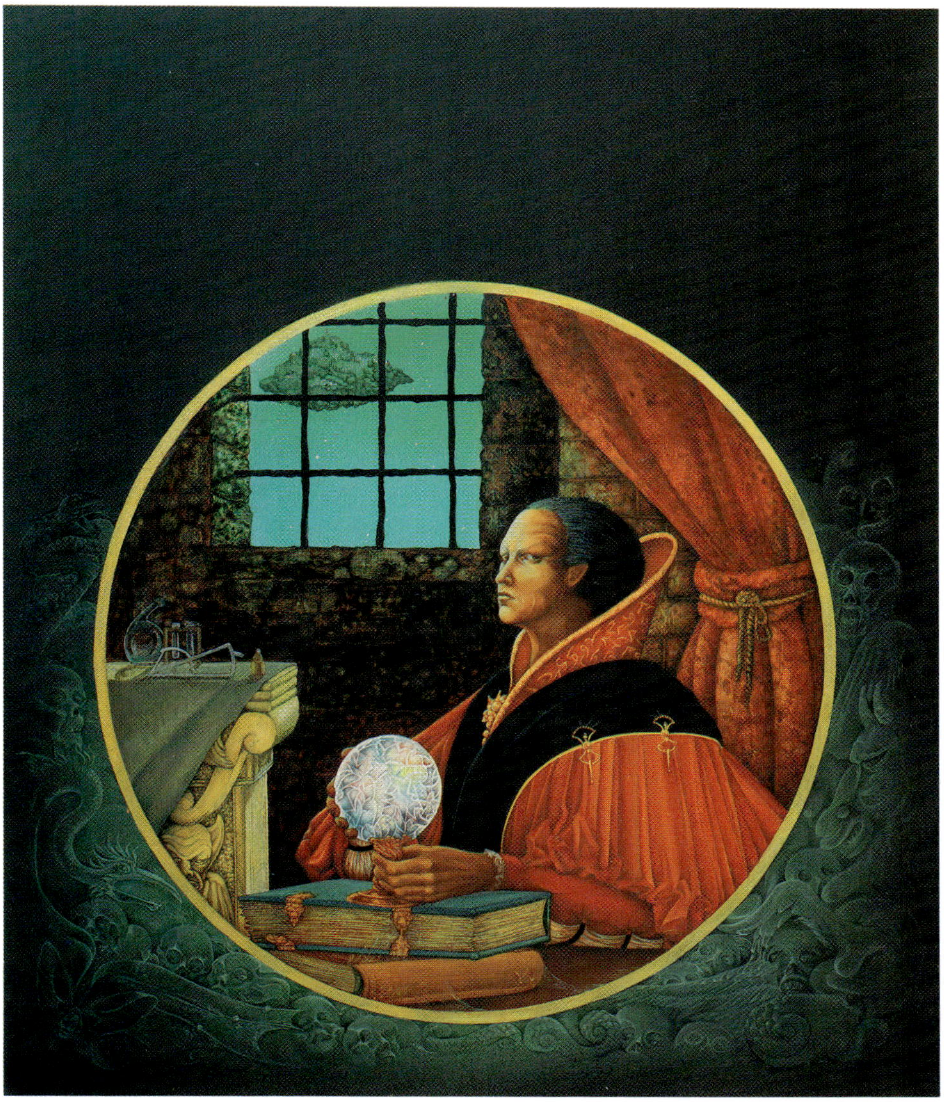

▷ The Necromancer
Linda 1985
Oils. 13 x 20in (33 x 51cm)
Cover for *Shattered World* by
Michael Reeves, Orbit.

If I hadn't been sent anything at all, it would probably have been all right, but I love Joseph Noel Paton's work too much to want to compete with it. I couldn't get over the feeling they should have just used the picture they sent.'

Linda: 'My only one was with *Scallagrig* by William Horwood, the *Duncton Wood* author. It's a terribly poignant story about a child who is highly intelligent, but has almost no bodily control. I cried all night when I read it, and it was the only time I couldn't come up with an image to fit the story. How can you illustrate a state of mind? And to go for a portrait of the child from outside seemed all wrong. I felt very humbled by the experience, but it had been sent to four other artists before me and none had been able to do anything with it. An incredible book.'

Book jackets were the Garlands' liberation as artists, but the time came to move on. Linda: 'Cover illustration is a young person's profession. It is not something you can do forever without getting stale and beginning to repeat yourself. There comes a point where you have to draw the line. Also, we are slow painters, so there was a quite modest limit to the number we could do in a year. Life began to feel too predictable.'

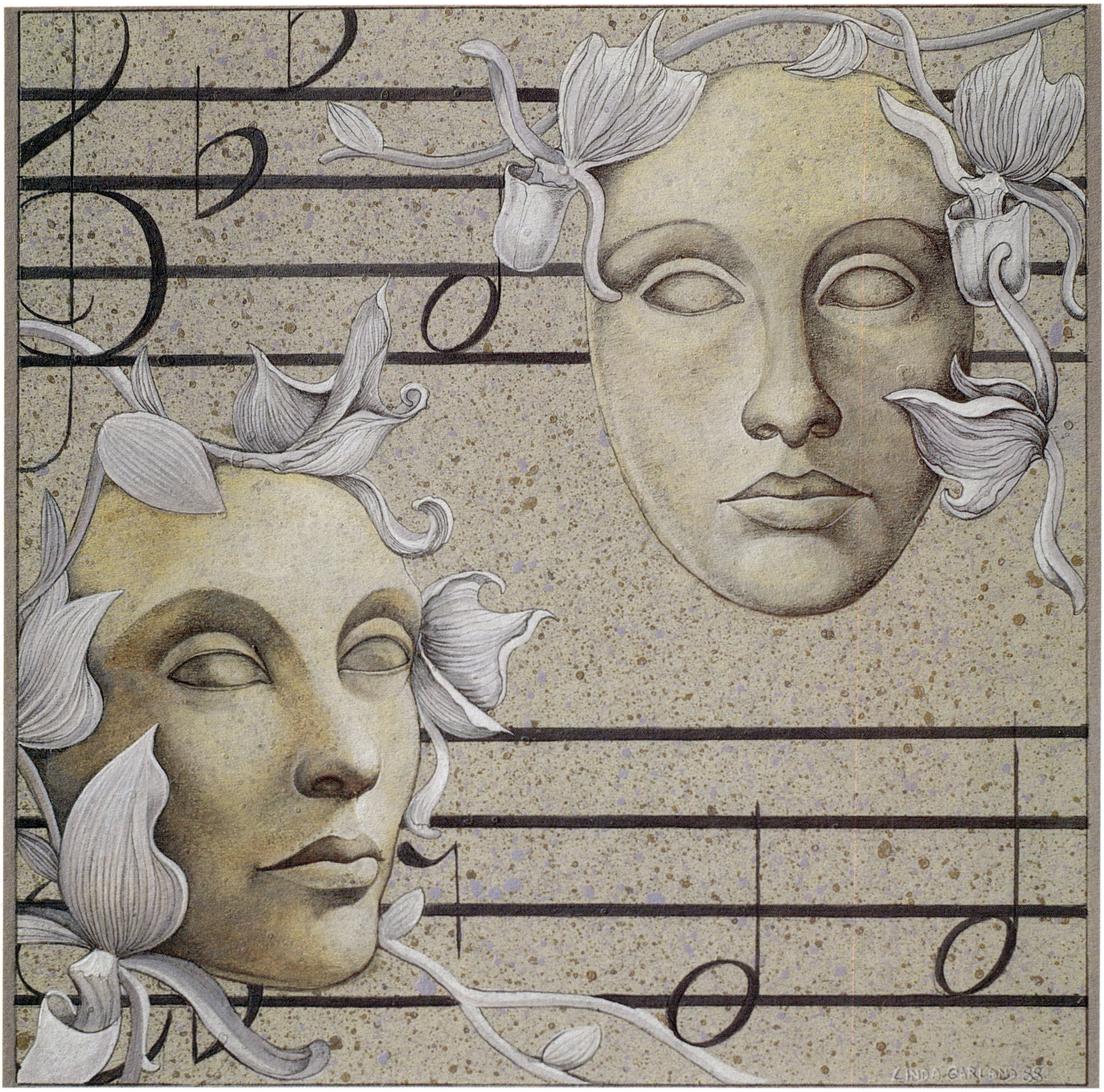


△ **Sentics**
Linda 1988
Oils. 9 x 9in (23 x 23cm)
Book cover, Prism Press.

The work was for a book on music therapy – the theory that certain musical notes are inherently calming.

This did not mean completely giving it up. Both have done covers since, but only ones of particular interest. They stopped actively seeking such work, and in the nature of things it tailed off quite rapidly. Roger: 'Unless you or an agent are up in London actively pushing publishers you soon get forgotten.' Which sounds a bit harsh, but made it easy to change direction.

In their painting, the Garlands have worked the hard way, sticking to the principle that they should be able to draw everything that goes into their pictures, instead of tracing some elements directly from photographs, a common illustrator's ploy.

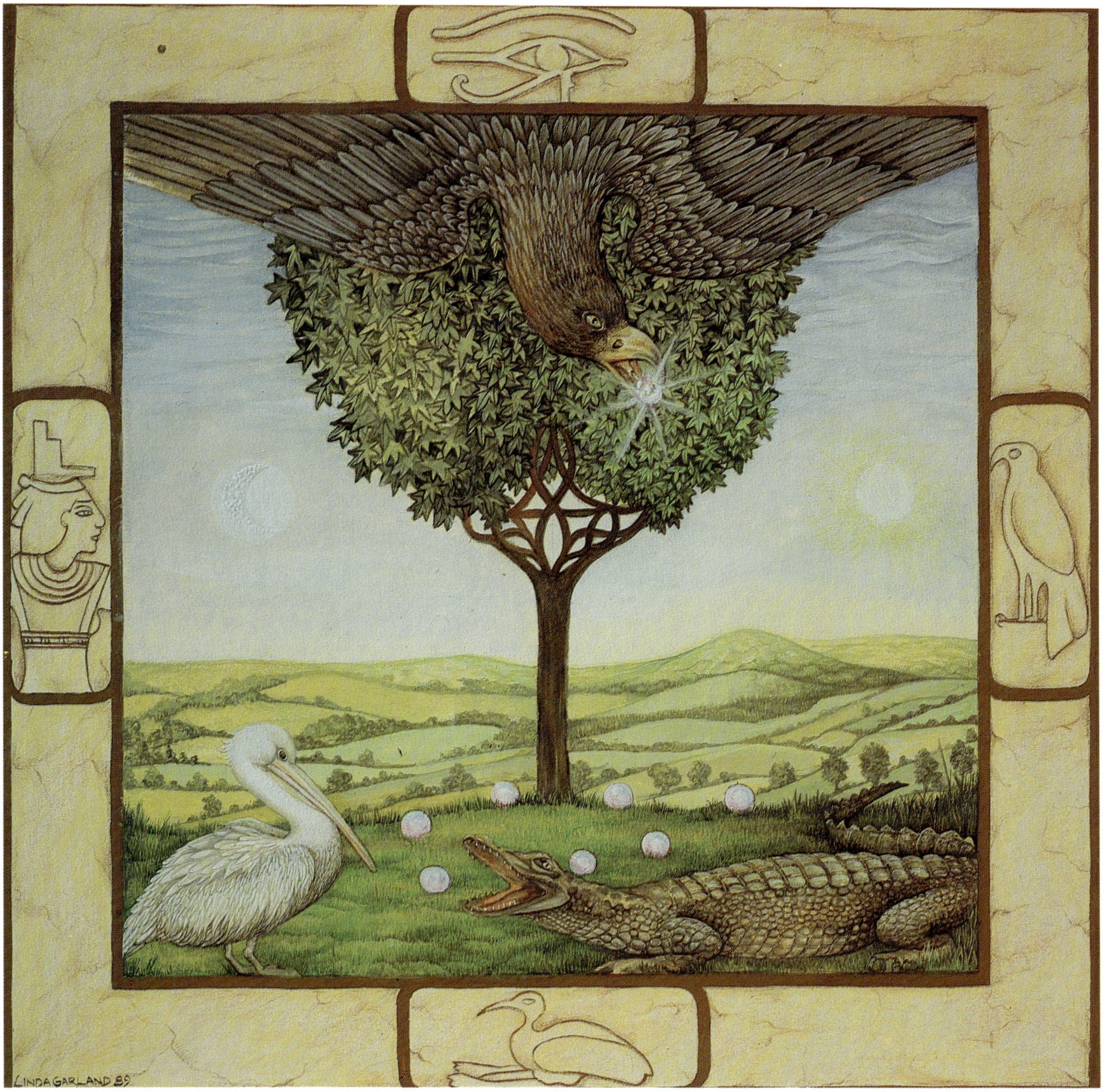


There have been a few extreme deadlines when all principle flew out the window, but they have been rare, and in the long term the thoroughness of their approach has proved itself.

In dire emergencies they use a photocopier for scaling drawings up or down; but they have resisted getting a light projector, which does this more effectively, on the grounds that scaling by hand and eye allows an extra opportunity for refining and strengthening a composition.

△ **Vision Quest**
Linda 1989
Oils. 9 x 9in (23 x 23cm)
Cover for a book by Neville Drury, Prism Press.

This work was commissioned for another Drury book, describing a series of visions, elements from which are included in the painting.

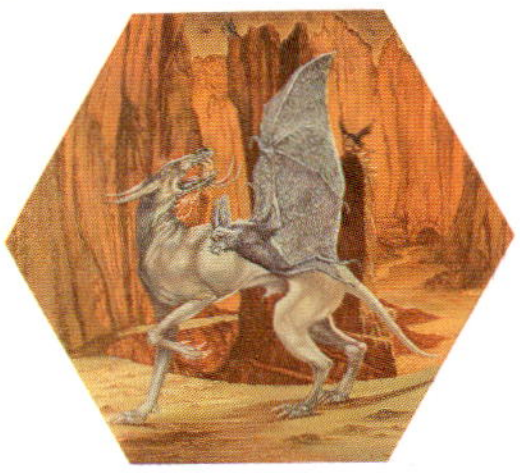

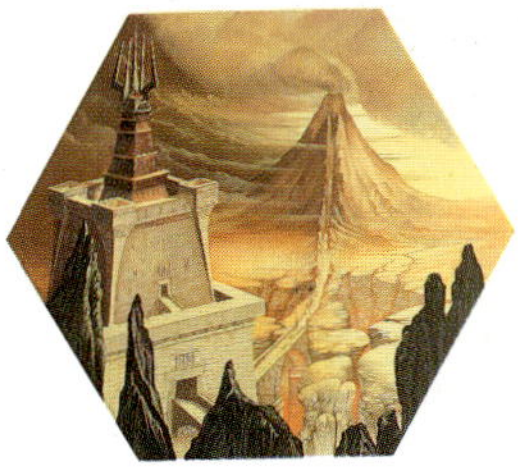

# MIDDLE-EARTH

*"Being asked to illustrate Tolkien by his publishers is something for which most fantasy artists would gladly sacrifice a spare limb or two...Roger remembers the excitement as if it were yesterday."*

Being asked to illustrate Tolkien by his publishers is something for which most fantasy artists would gladly sacrifice a spare limb or two. After Pauline Baynes, and Tolkien himself, Roger Garland was the first to whom it happened. How did it come about?

Not as the result of any determined effort. In 1981, he was contacted out of the blue by Eddie Poulton, the Art Director at Unwin Hyman. He had seen, and liked, Roger's work in the Young Artists catalogue, and would he be interested in painting a dragon for the cover of *Unfinished Tales*, the first of many volumes of Tolkien's posthumous writings edited by his son Christopher?

Roger remembers the excitement as if it were yesterday, having been as big a Tolkien fan as anyone at college. Exactly why he was chosen above the competition was never explained, so Roger can only assume it was *Serpentine* (see page 17) which caught the publisher's eye.

The commission felt like a privilege, even without knowing it would lead to a mountain of extra work. Roger pulled out all the stops to rise to the occasion, and the result was a portrayal of Glaurung, known as the First of the Dragons of Morgoth and the Great Worm. In the text he is described as being so heavy he can hardly lift his own weight, and so has to crawl and squirm along, scorching everything in his path.

The picture has been compared with Fafner, the worm in Arthur Rackham's *Ring Cycle* illustrations – a similarity which surprised Roger, but which is coincidental, as he only came across the Rackham pictures later.

The first picture met with Christopher Tolkien's approval and led to others, building up to the 1984 calendar which comprised Roger's book covers so far, plus several new paintings from the more familiar stories. The roughs for these were vetted by Christopher Tolkien before painting went ahead.

△ **Luthien and Beren**
Roger 1988
Oils. 8in diam. (20cm)
Audio cassette cover, Collins.

△ **Barad-Dur**
Roger 1987
Oils. 8in diam. (20cm)
Audio cassette cover, Collins.

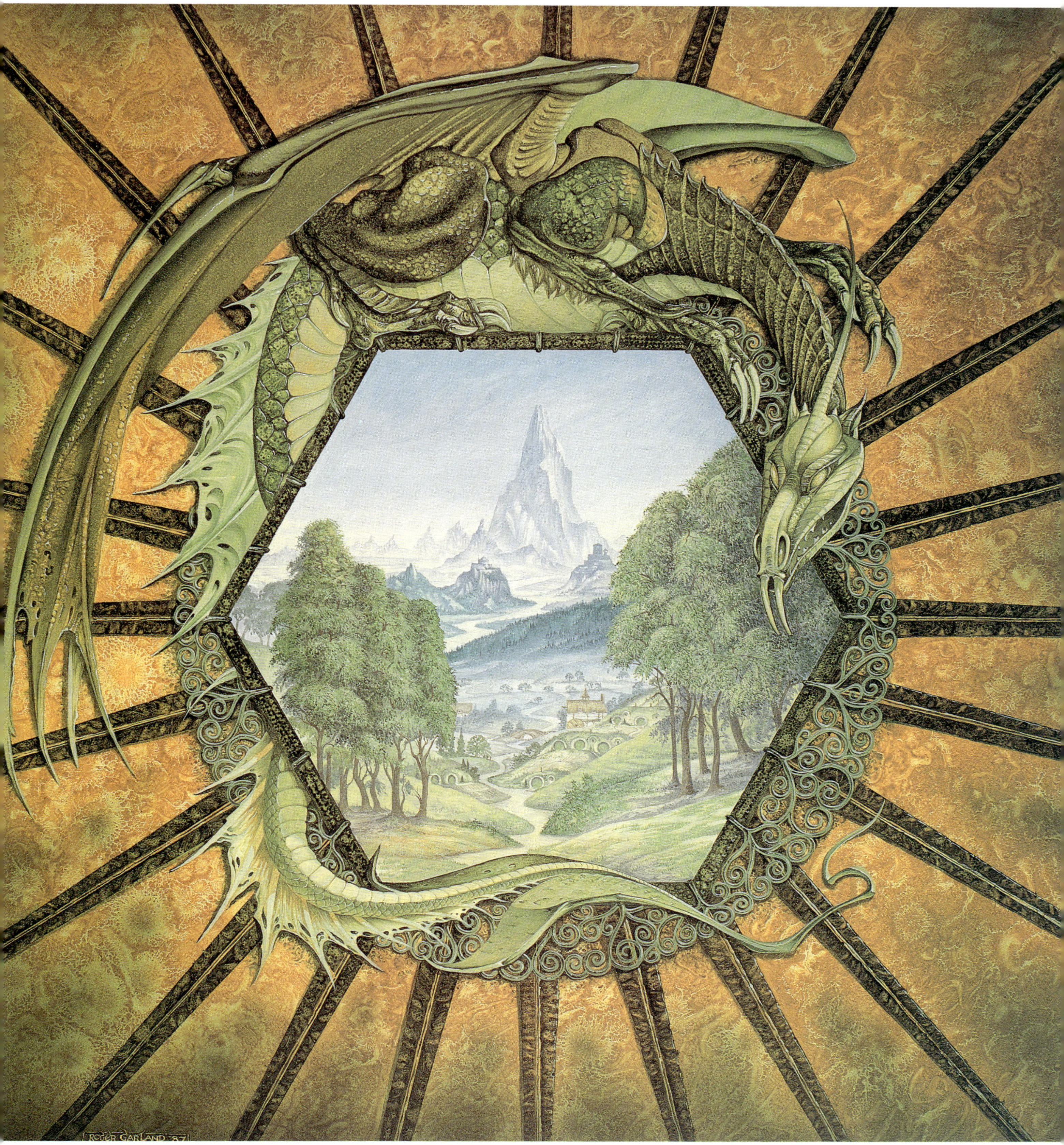
ROGER GARLAND '87

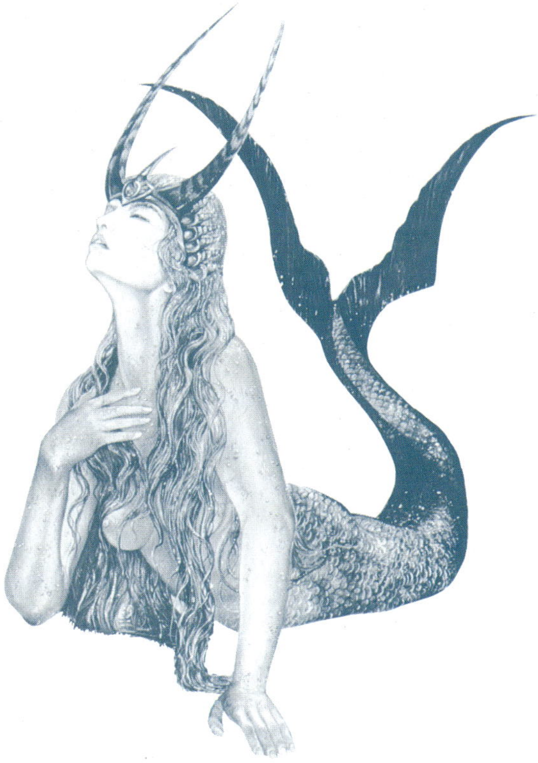

▷ **Glaudrung**
Roger 1981
Oils and Acrylic. 8 x 13in
(20 x 33cm)
Cover for *Unfinished Tales Book 1*, Unwin Hyman.

This was Roger's first Middle-Earth book jacket, whose approval by Christopher Tolkien led, as far as he knows, to the rest of the series. Glaudrung is described in the text as a 'worm', a cave-dwelling dragon, so he has no wings.

As a general guideline, it was suggested Roger try to avoid close-ups of the main characters, as readers tended to have very fixed ideas about them, and usually certain chapters, or sections, were pointed out for illustration. Otherwise, Roger was left to his own imagination.

It helped that his favourite Tolkien book is *The Silmarillion*, as about half the pictures he had been asked for concerned events in it. The imagery is more to his taste than *Lord of the Rings* and it is, he feels, a far more visual book than most people imagine, though there is, perhaps, only one good picture for every two pages, rather than every other paragraph, as in Tolkien's other works. However, it contains wonderful visions, like that of the Galleon of the Sun dripping light as it passes through the Gates of Night.

In following years Unwin Hyman commissioned calendars by other artists like Alan Lee and Ted Nasmith, but Roger's turn came around again in 1989, for which he produced three new paintings to top up his recent book covers. The launch of this calendar happened to coincide with the opening of the Garlands' gallery, and a consequent TV news item helped make it the best-selling publication in the South West for a while – far outstripping its sales elsewhere, and prompting puzzled queries from the publisher as to what exactly they were up to down there.

Curiously, the success of his Tolkien covers and calendars did not lead to a rush of demand for Roger's talent from other quarters. It may even, he believes, have backfired by making him seem either too exclusive, or too associated with one theme, for other clients to consider. But he has no regrets.

**(Previous page)**
**Middle-Earth**
Roger 1987
Oils and Acrylic. 14 x 14in
(36 x 36cm)
Audio cassette cover, Collins.

This work represents one of a series of covers for tapes of readings by Tolkien himself, and renditions of his songs by Donald Swann (of Flanders and Swann fame). The hexagon's surround, holding it like a jewel, is based on the sunray pattern of a door from Selfridge's, now in the Victoria & Albert Museum, London. The design was repeated on all the covers with different inserts.

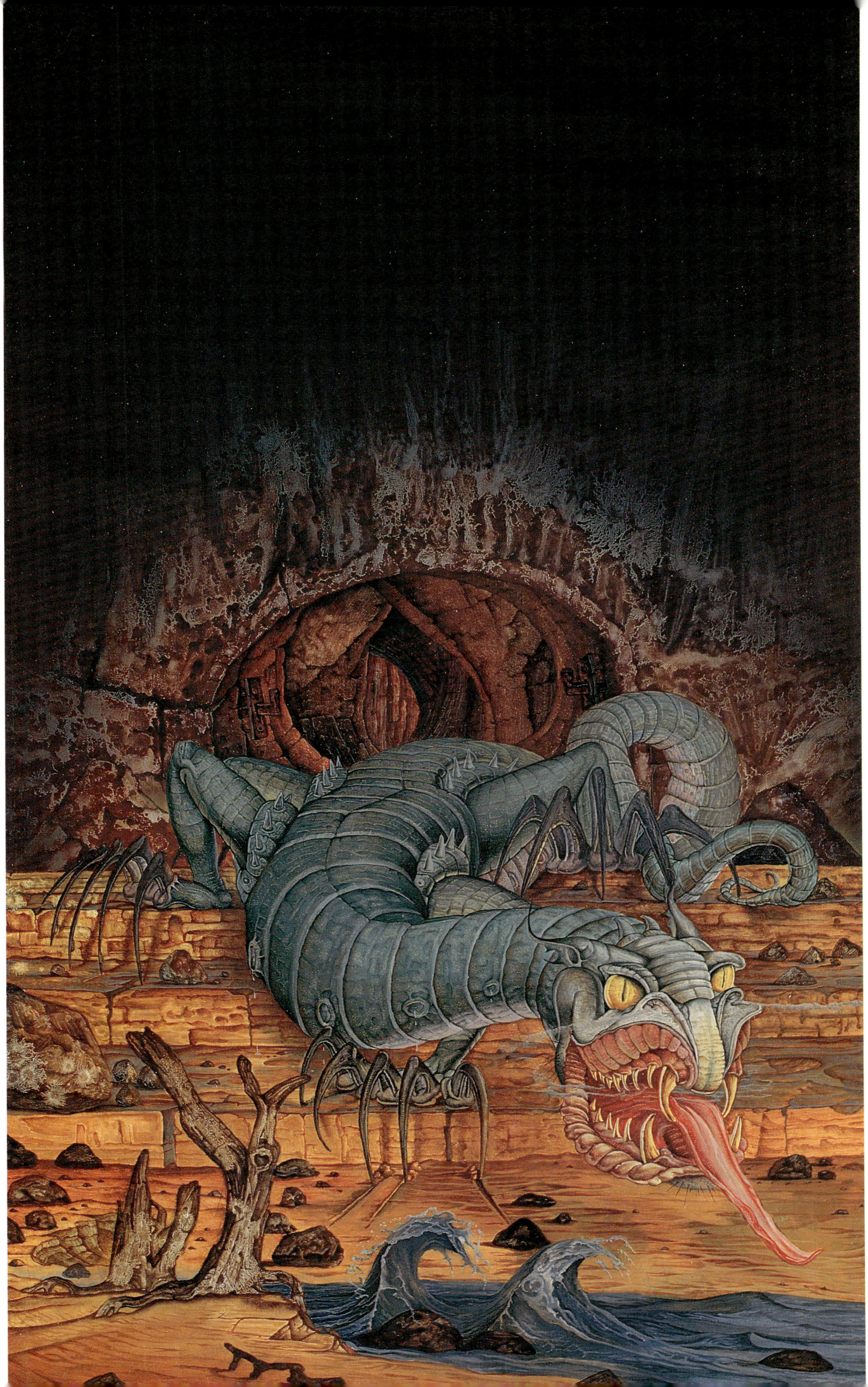

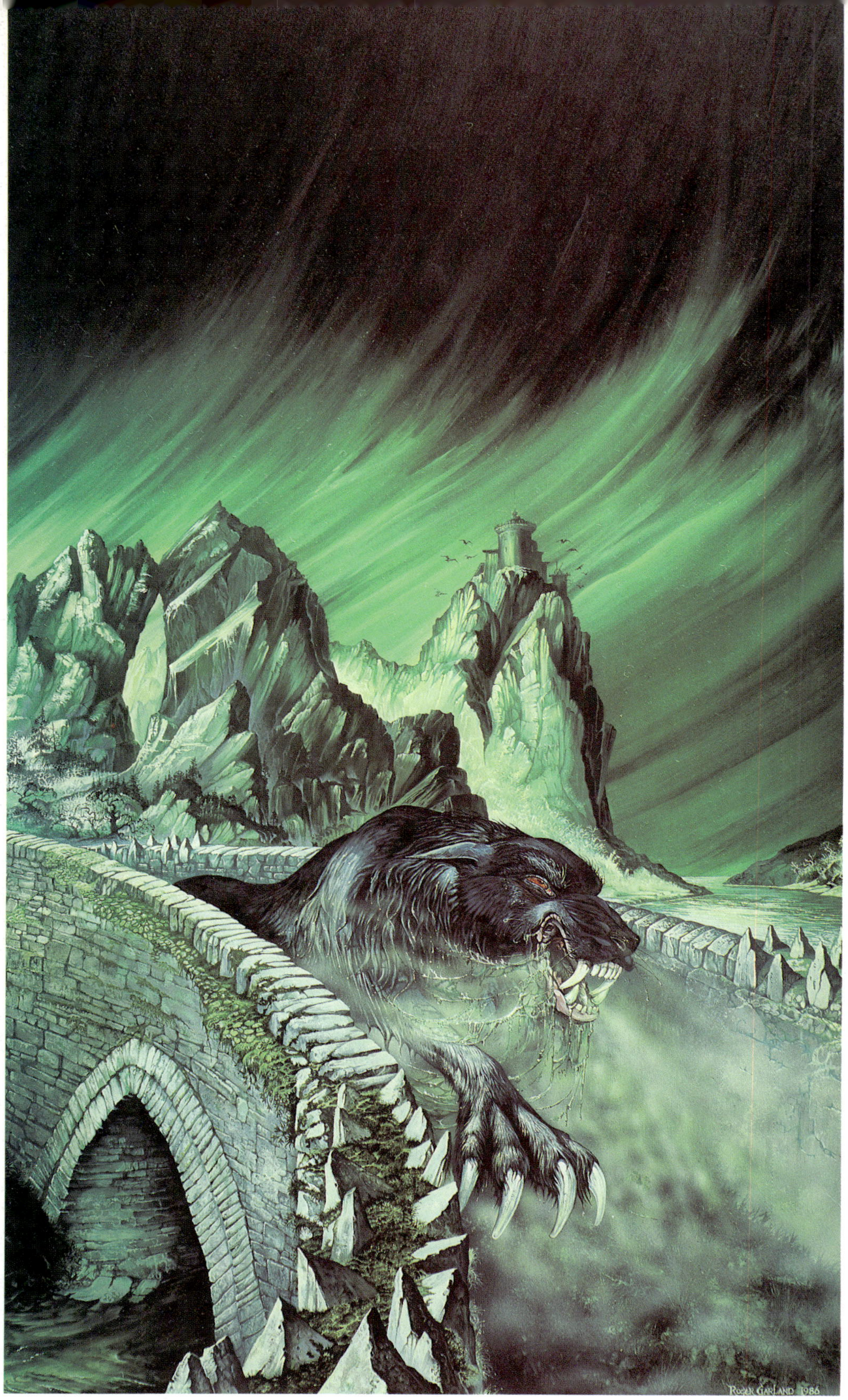


△ Thu, as Wolf More Great
Roger 1986
Oils. 12 x 19in (30 x 48cm)
Cover for *The Lays of Beleriand*, Unwin Hyman.

The bridge featured in this painting is a typical Cornish one, whose parapet stones at either end neatly echo the monster's claws and fangs. In the background is Sauron's stronghold, Angband.

▷ The Haven of Morionde
Roger 1989
Oils and Acrylic.
11 x 18in (28 x 45cm)
Cover for *The Lost Road*, Unwin Hyman.
Cover for *The Tolkien Calendar 1989*, Unwin Hyman.

Here we see Sauron in one of his incarnations, having just raised a tidal wave, casting sea-going ships far inland, to demonstrate his power.

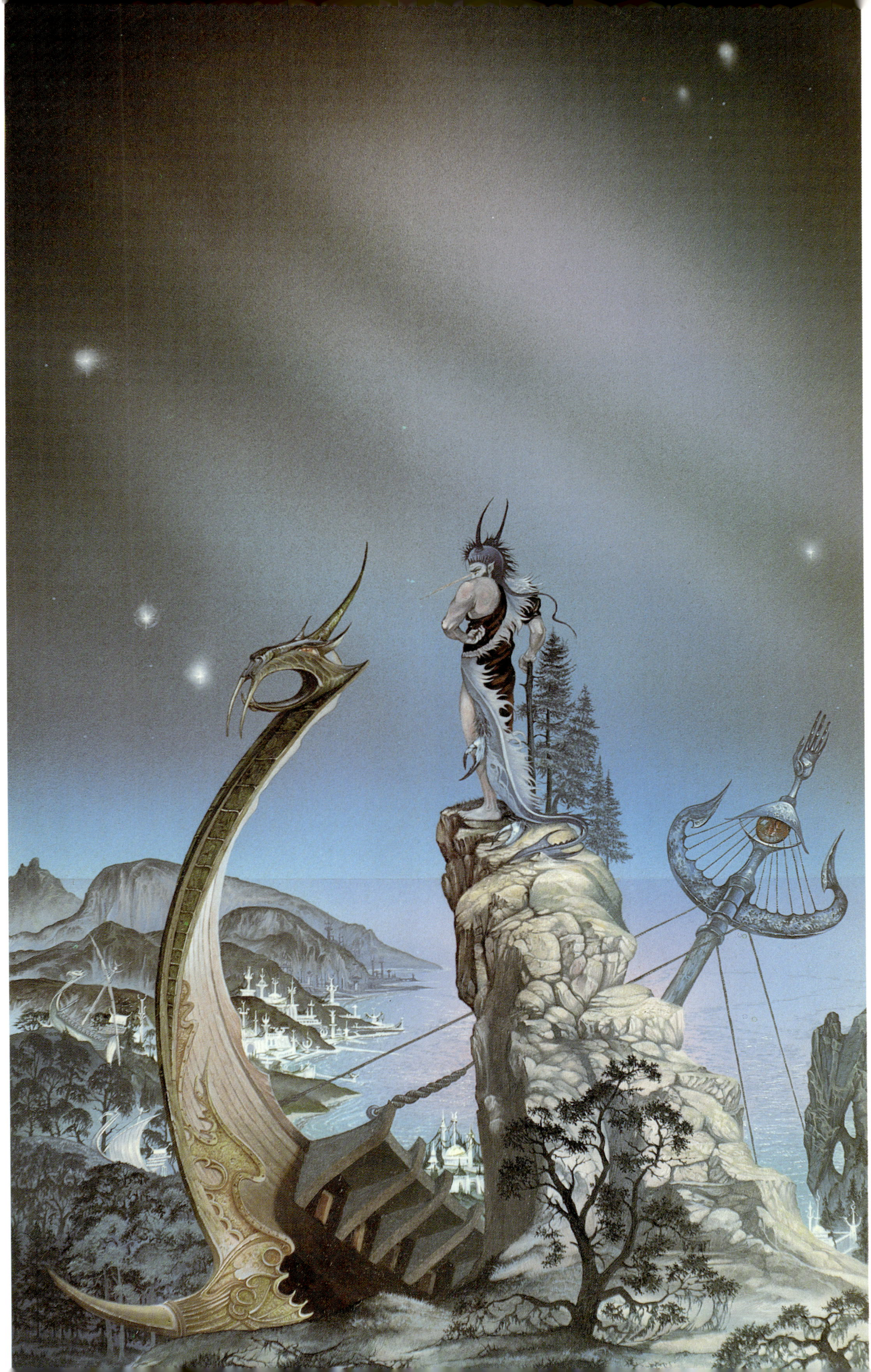

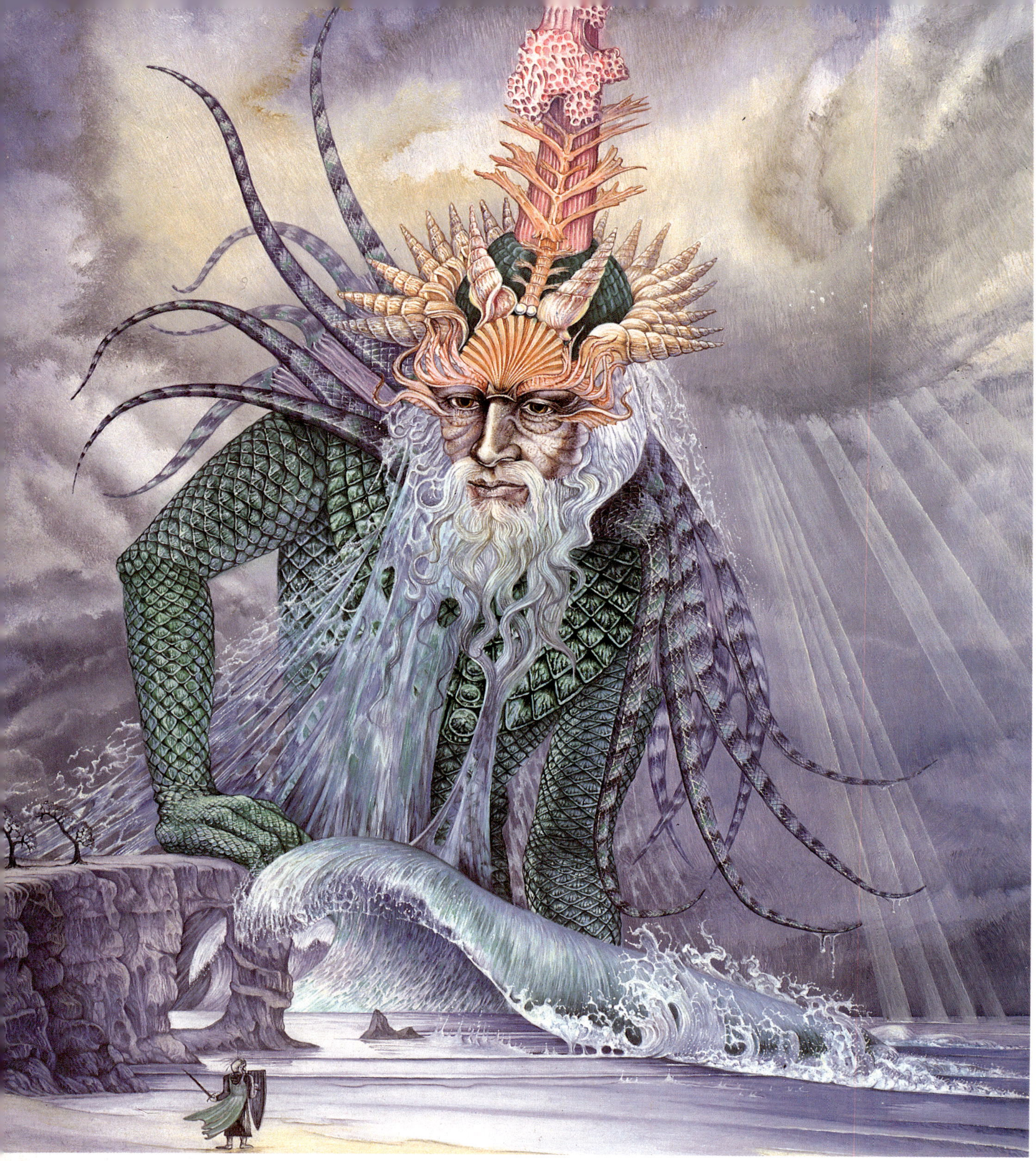

△ **Ulmo, Lord of the Waters**
Roger 1983
Oils and Acrylic. 9 x 11in
(23 x 28cm)
1984 calendar illustration,
Unwin Hyman.

In the mythology of *The Silmarillion*, and associated writings, Ulmo was one of the Valar, the supernatural Powers, who remained friendly to Elves and Men, even when they were shunned by the other Valar. Only rarely did he manifest himself like this. Usually, he moved invisibly through all the waters of Middle-Earth and spoke to its dwellers only through the music of spring, stream, river and sea. And because these reach almost everywhere, all news normally came to him first.

▷ **Earendil and Elwing**
Roger 1987
Oils. 11 x 17in (28 x 43cm)
Illustration for *The Tolkien Calendar 1989*, Unwin Hyman.

This picture depicts the scene at sunset when Earendil, the Silmaril on his brow, returns from the oceans of heaven in his ship, Vingilot, seen from a distance as a bright star, to be greeted by Elwing, who appears as a white bird (*The Silmarillion*, chapter 24).

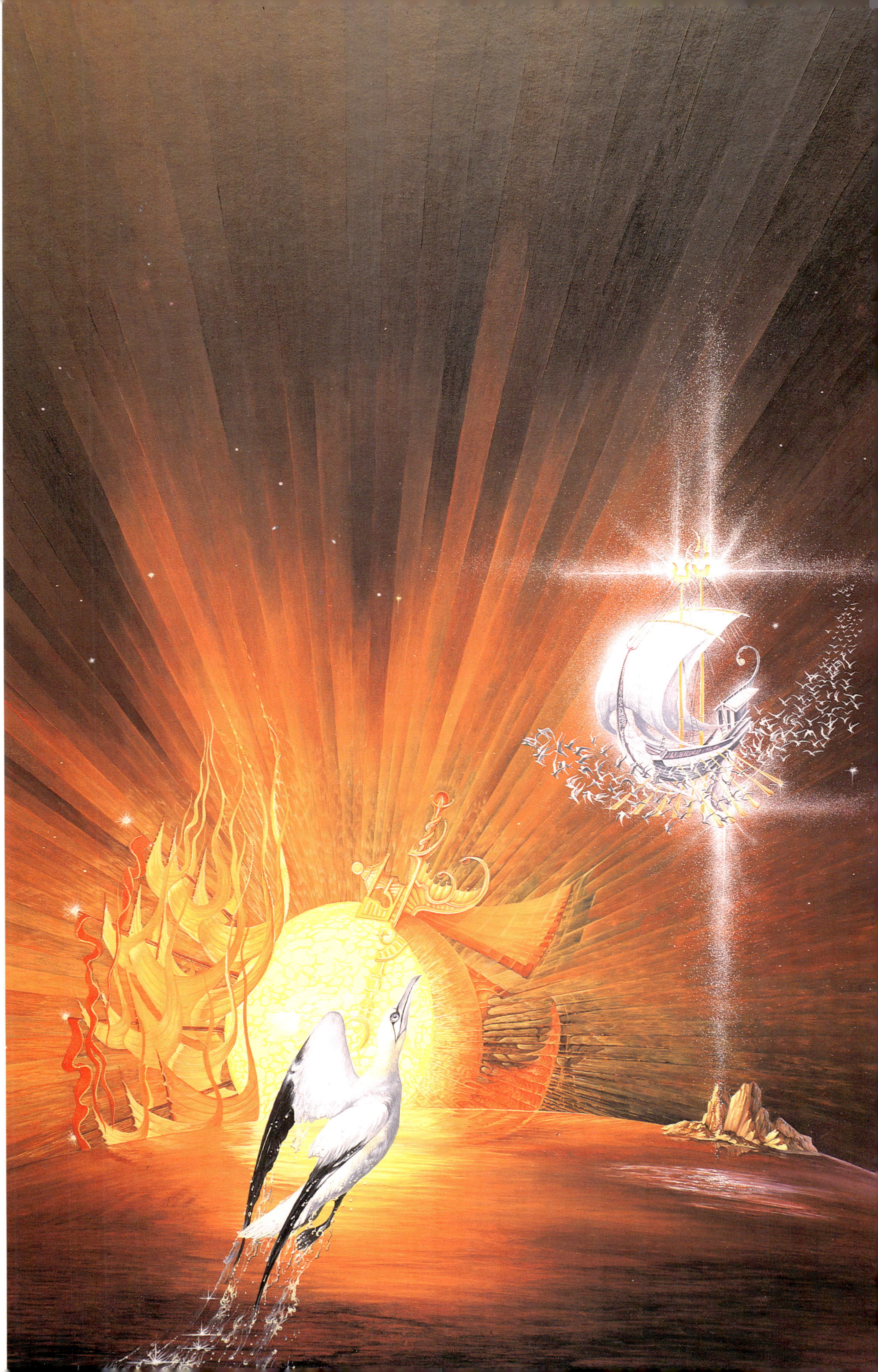

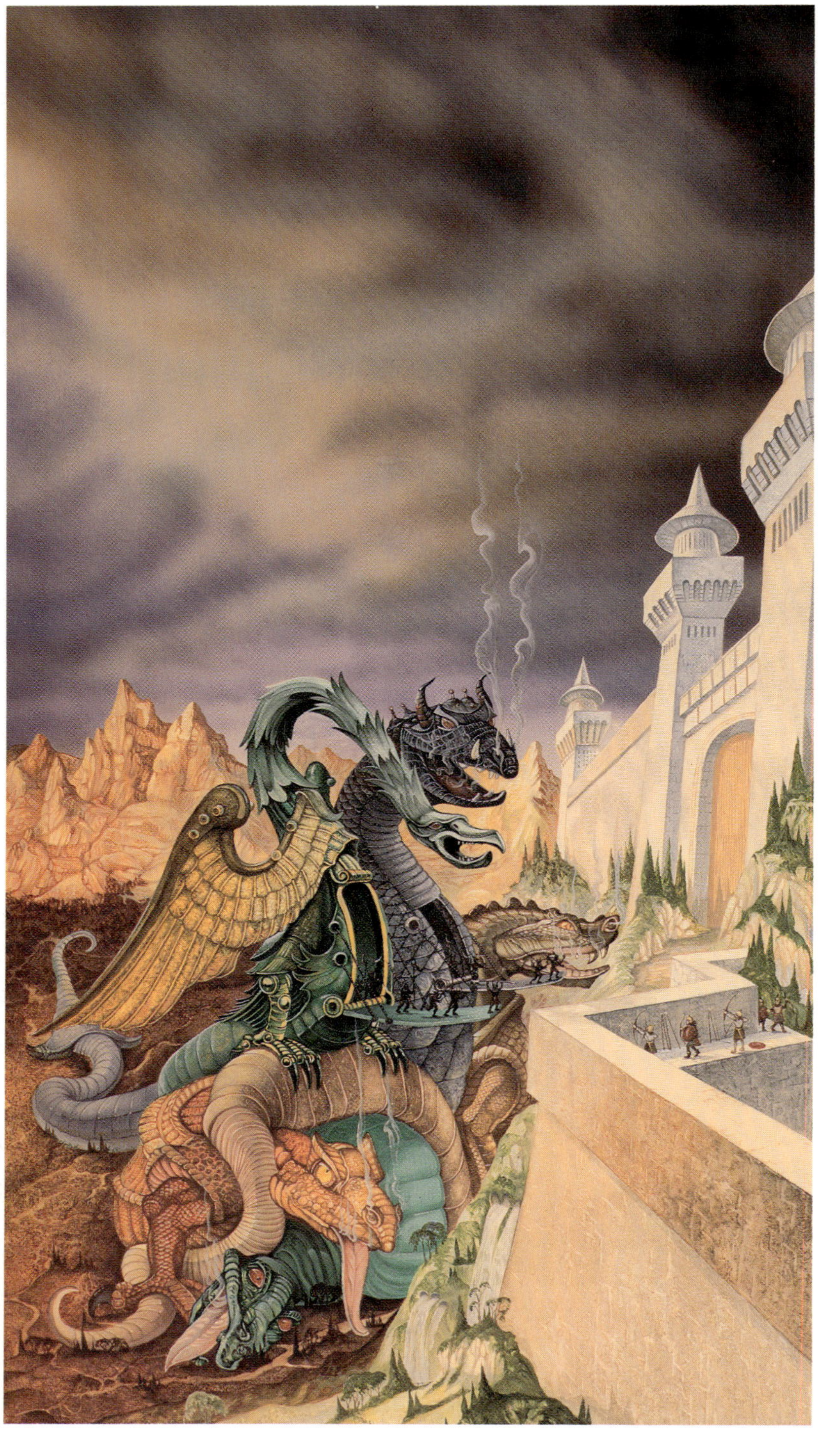

△ **The Fall of Gondolin**
Roger 1987
Oils and Acrylic. 9 x 17in
(23 x 43cm)
Cover for *The Book of Lost Tales: Part 2*, Unwin Hyman.

Real and mechanical dragons aid the orcs in their overthrow of the city. The green one is based quite closely on the figure of a dragon holding a lamp in Venice.

▷ **Gollum**
Roger 1983
Oils and Acrylic. 10 x 14in
(25 x 36cm)
1984 calendar illustration, Unwin Hyman.

On the advice of Art Director, Eddie Poulton, Roger kept the figure of Gollum small and concentrated on the landscape.

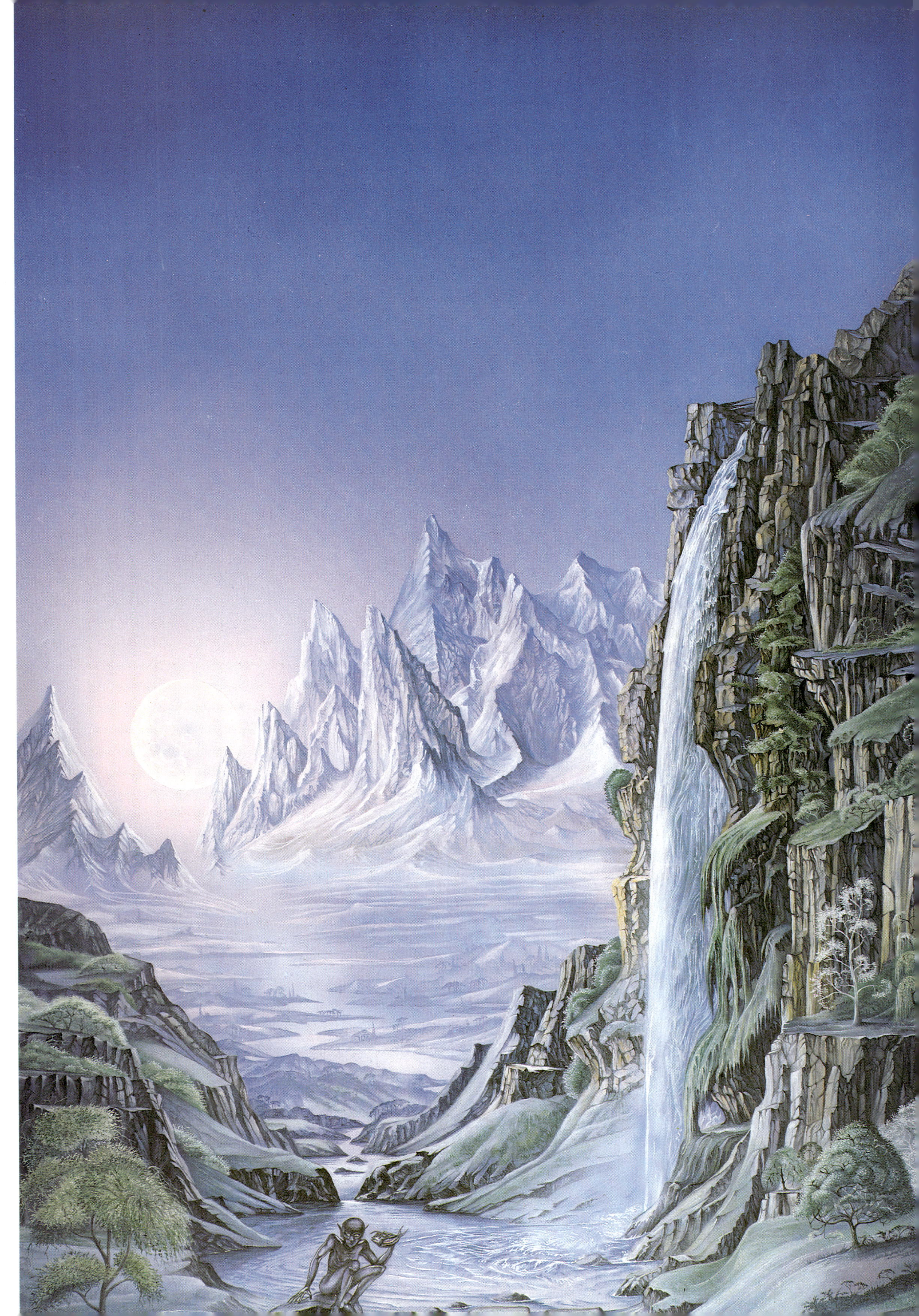

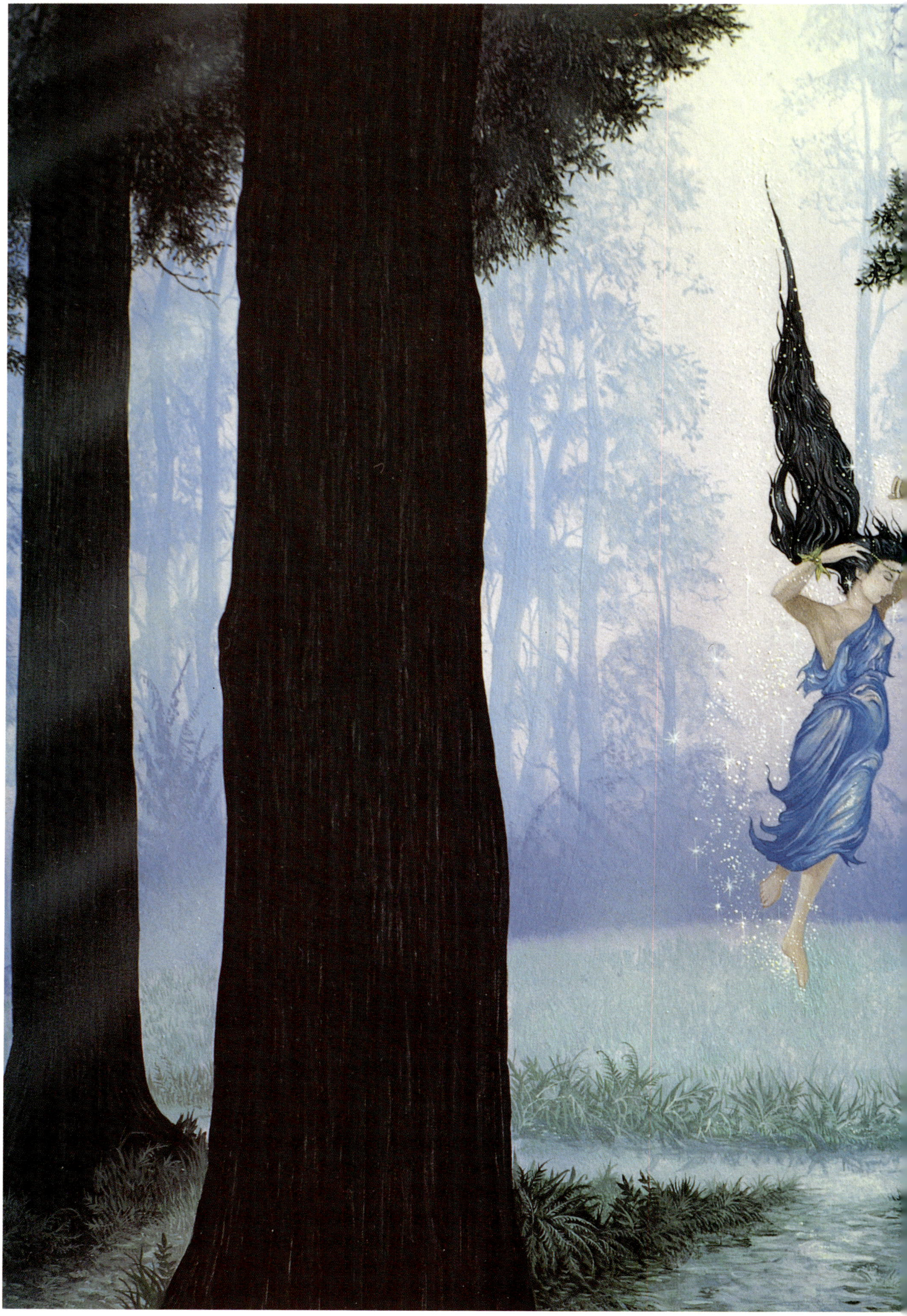

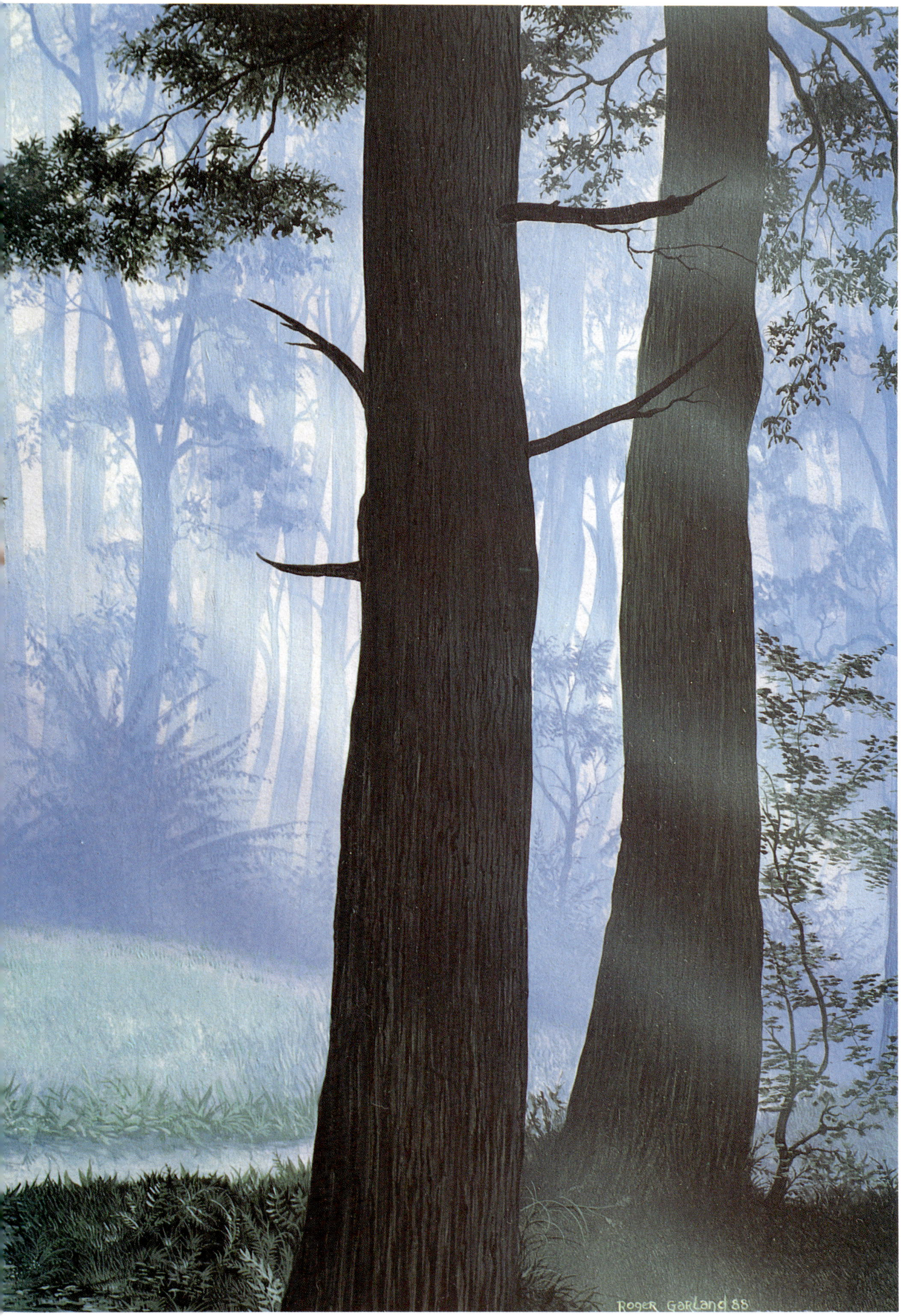
ROGER GARLAND 88

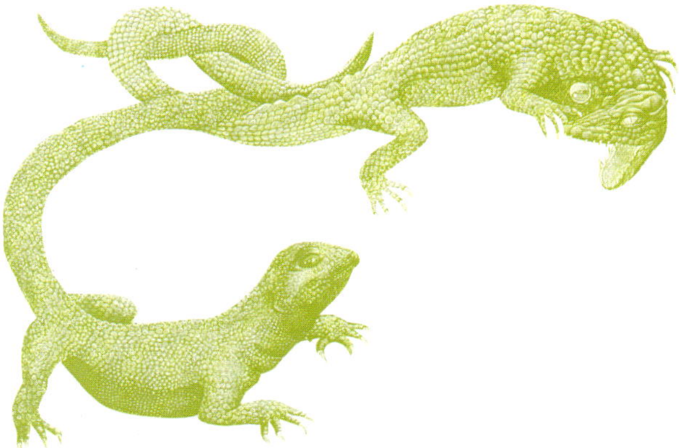

▷ **Gandalf**
Roger 1983
Oils and acrylic. 10 x 12in (25 x 30cm)
1984 calendar illustration, Unwin Hyman.

Anyone who illustrates Gandalf runs the risk of clashing with other enthusiasts' perceptions of the wizard. Roger is on firmer ground than most, since this picture was based on a postcard which Tolkien, himself, had said reminded him of Gandalf. Roger's mother posed for the first version, which came back from Christopher Tolkien with the comment that he loved the composition, but the wizard looked like someone's aunt, so the features were sharpened up.

None of these Middle-Earth pictures are for sale. Instead, they have been left in trust to the Garland children, an echo of Tolkien's own careful arrangements which Roger applauds.

Whether one can really shield offspring from the pits of insecurity in you own life is, he agrees, debatable. Particularly with a teenage son resisting pressure to study something sensible, like physics, in favour of becoming an artist too. Which is a compliment to the parents, but also puts them in an awkward position. It is one thing not to regret any crises safely in the past, another to imagine having to face them again.

Do the Garlands have any regrets about their career? Roger: 'Only when the money dries up and I think of the steady job I threw in. I think it's a male thing – feeling I'm the one who has to earn the money. Linda and I are equal partners, but when we hit hard times I'm the one who seems to feel most guilty about it.'

'Other than that, I suppose I occasionally feel guilty about being an artist instead of an ambulanceman, or something practical like that. But if you sit around justifying it too much, it's like going back to college where everyone spends so much time talking about art very little gets done.'

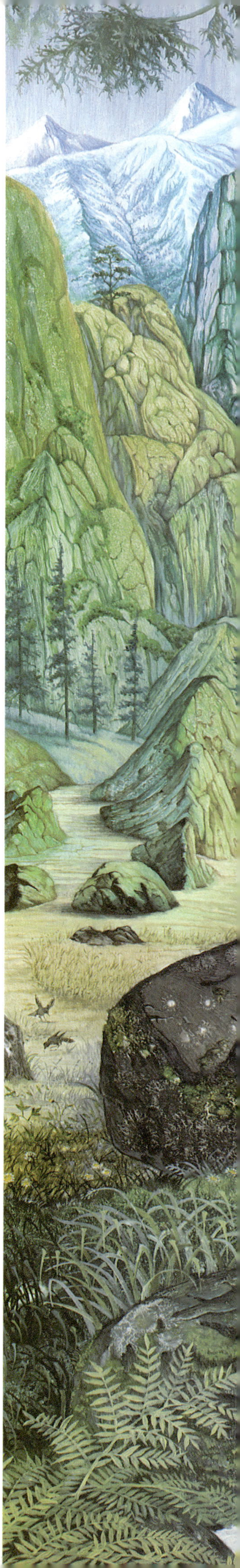

**(Previous page)**
**Luthien in the Woods**
Roger 1988
Oils and Acrylic. 9 x 13in (23 x 33cm)
Illustration for *The Tolkien Calendar 1989*, Unwin Hyman.

Luthien was one of the Maia, a princess who fell in love with the mortal Beren, and after the latter's death, chose to share his fate.

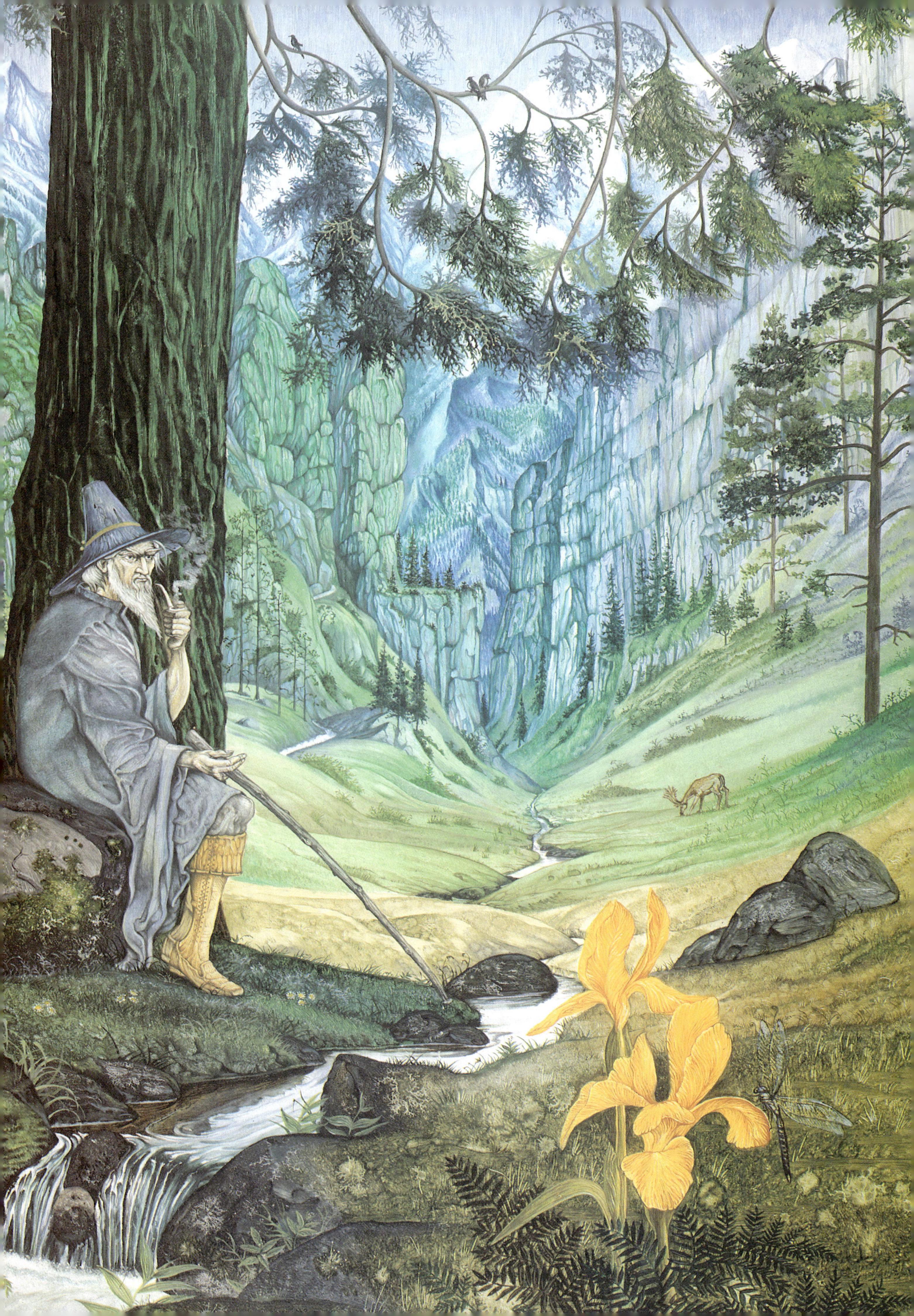

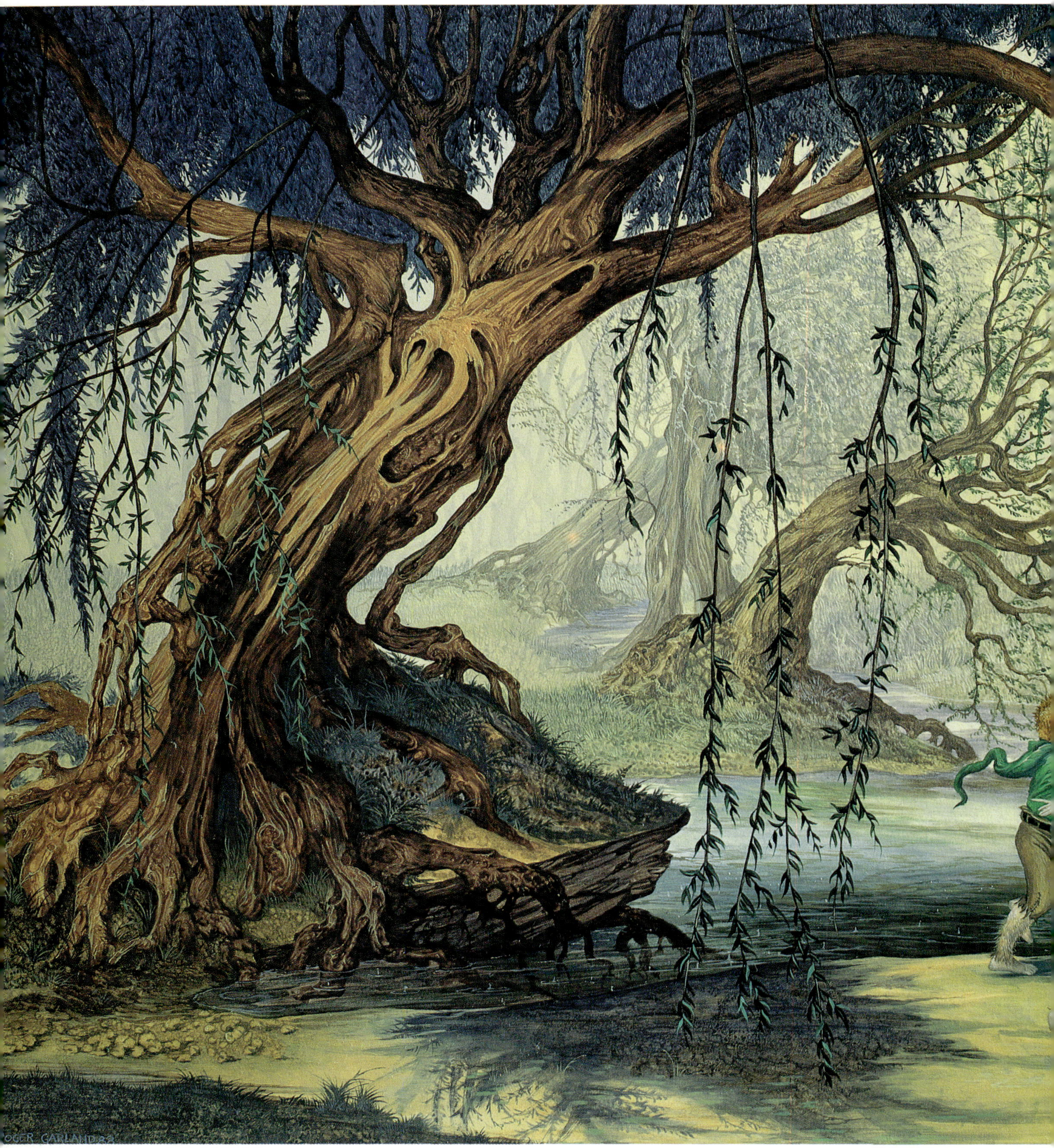

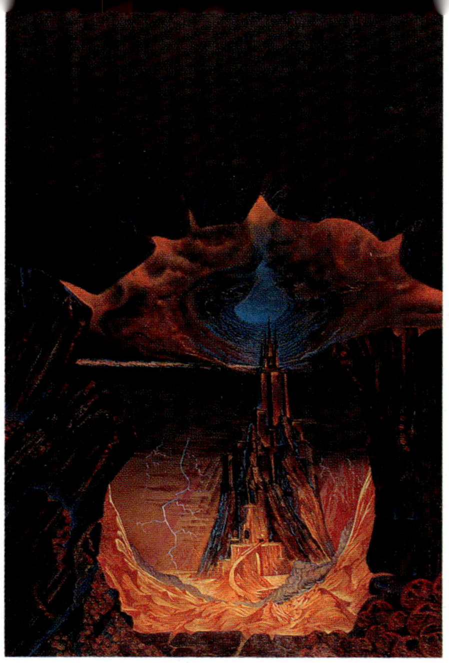

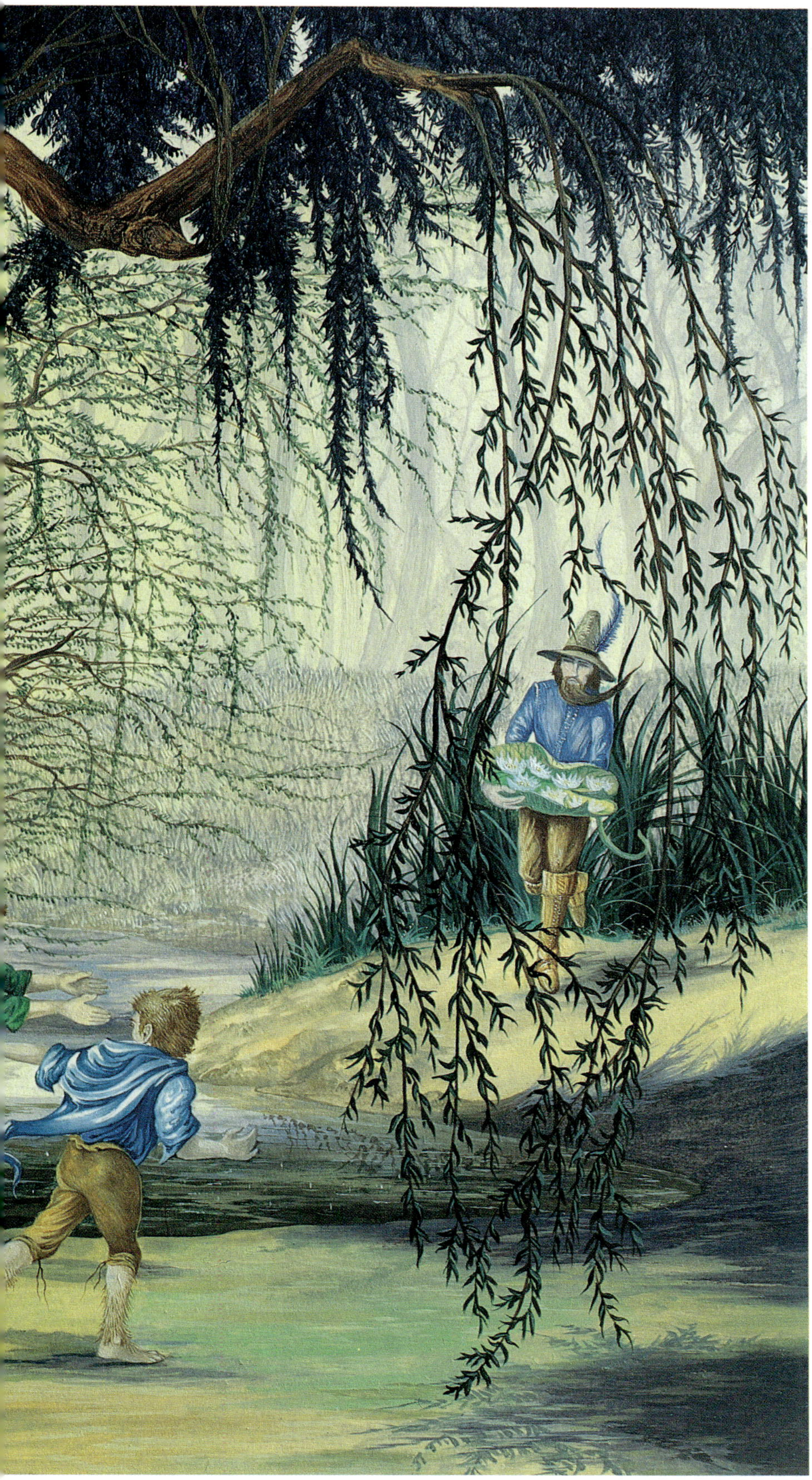

△ **Lord of the Rings**
Roger 1982
Oils and Acrylic. 12 x 17in
(30 x 43cm)
Trilogy cover, Unwin Hyman.

A view of Barad-Dur from within Mount Doom. Sauron's eye can be seen beaming out from the top of the tower.

◁ **Old Man Willow**
Roger 1988
Oils and Acrylic. 9 x 13in
(23 x 33cm)
Illustration for *The Tolkien Calendar 1989*,
Unwin Hyman.

Drawn from childhood memories of the Somerset Levels, this scene shows Tom Bombadil arriving just in time to rescue Merry and Pippin, who have been swallowed by the tree. Frodo is the hobbit on the right. The depth of the scene was achieved by building it up in layers, starting from the far distance and working towards the foreground, as if it were a stage set.

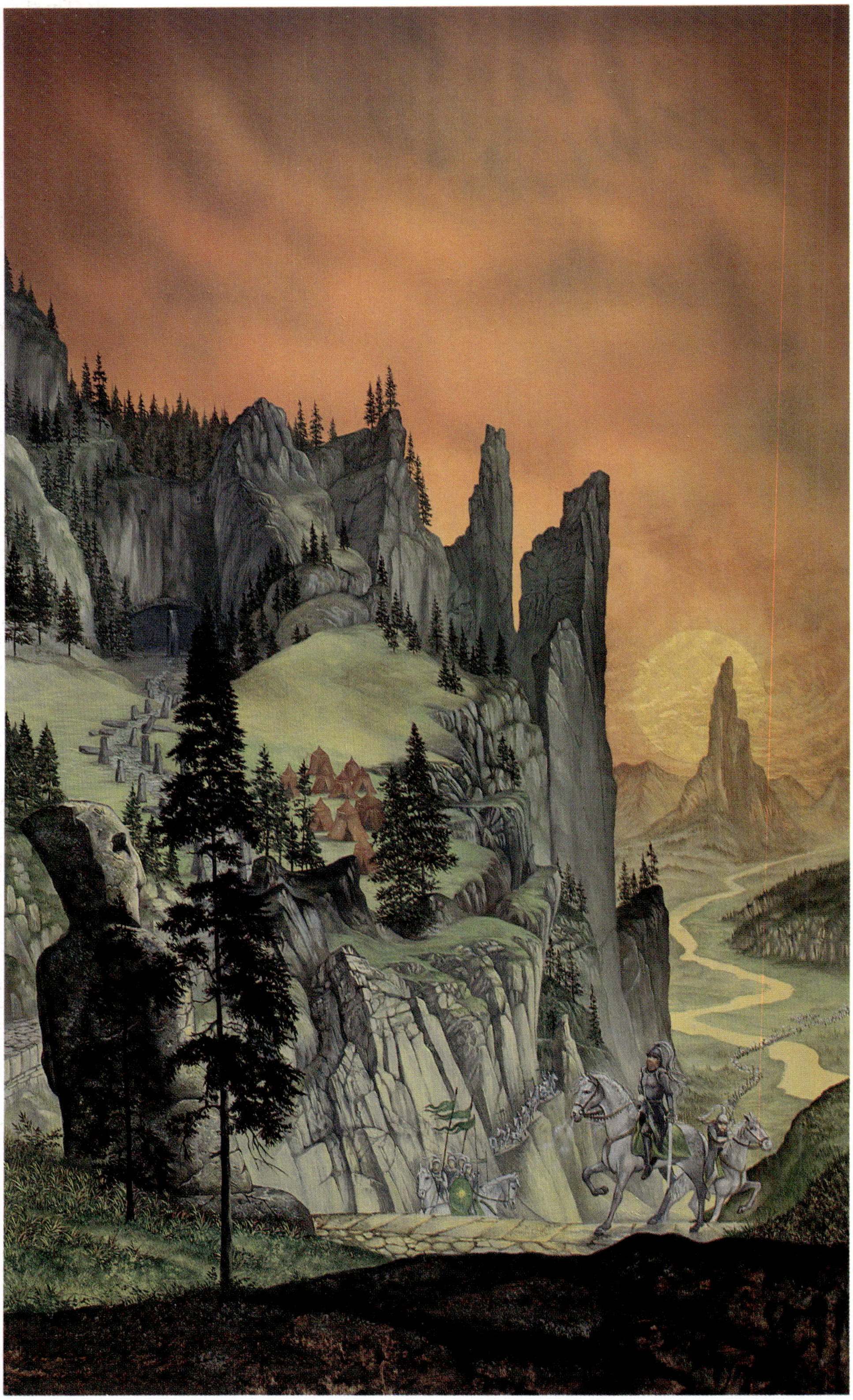

△ **The War of the Ring**
Roger 1991
Oils and Acrylic. 10 x 15in (25 x 38cm)
Book cover, Unwin Hyman (HarperCollins).

Commissioned for the book of the same title, edited by Christopher Tolkien, the scene shows the Riders of Rohan approaching Dunharrow. The colour range used was tricky to work with, but Roger feels it was successful in the end.

▷ **Boromir**
Roger 1991
Oils and Acrylic. 12 x 19in (30 x 43cm)
Cover for *The Treason of Isengard*, Unwin Hyman (HarperCollins).

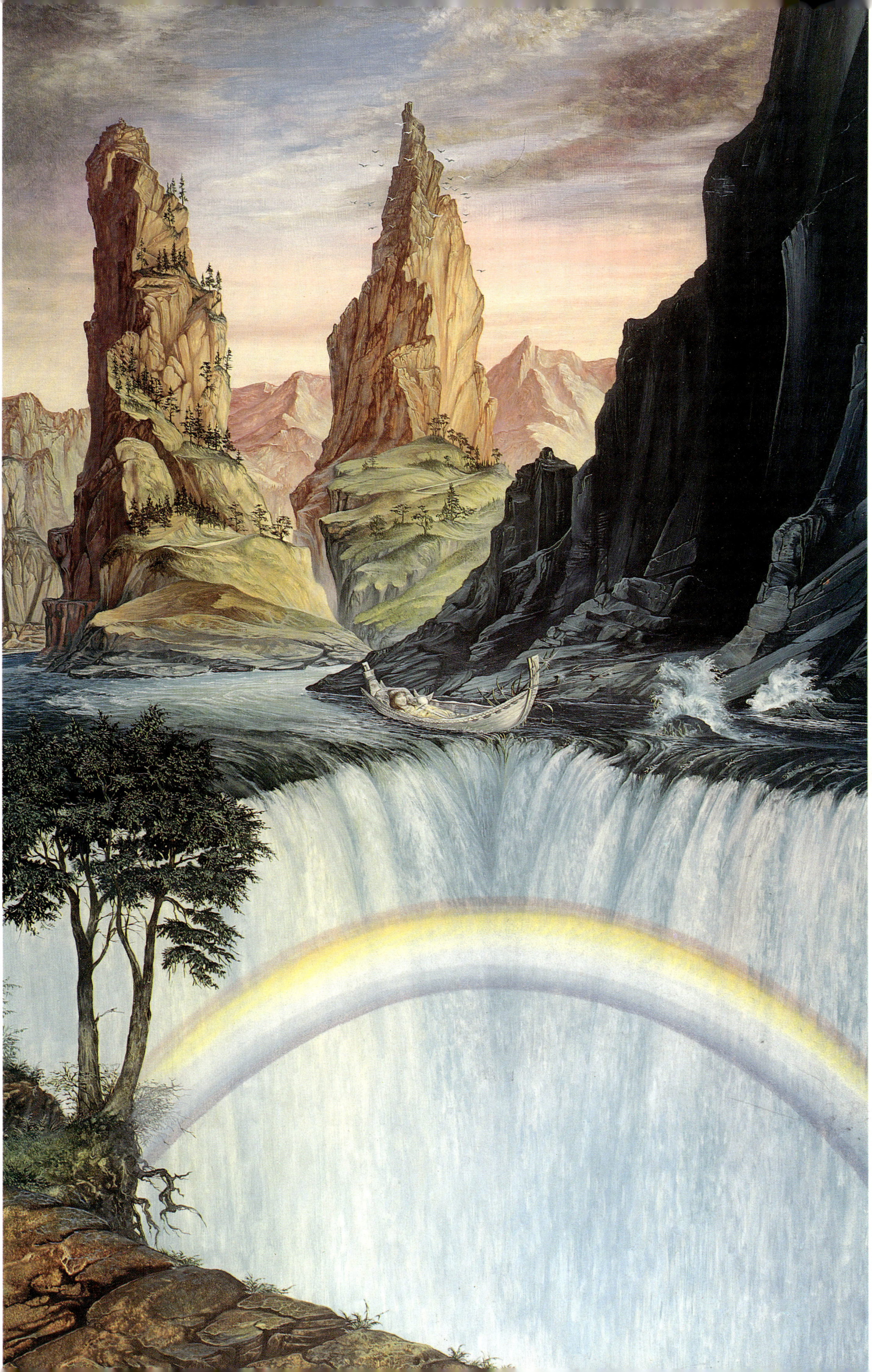

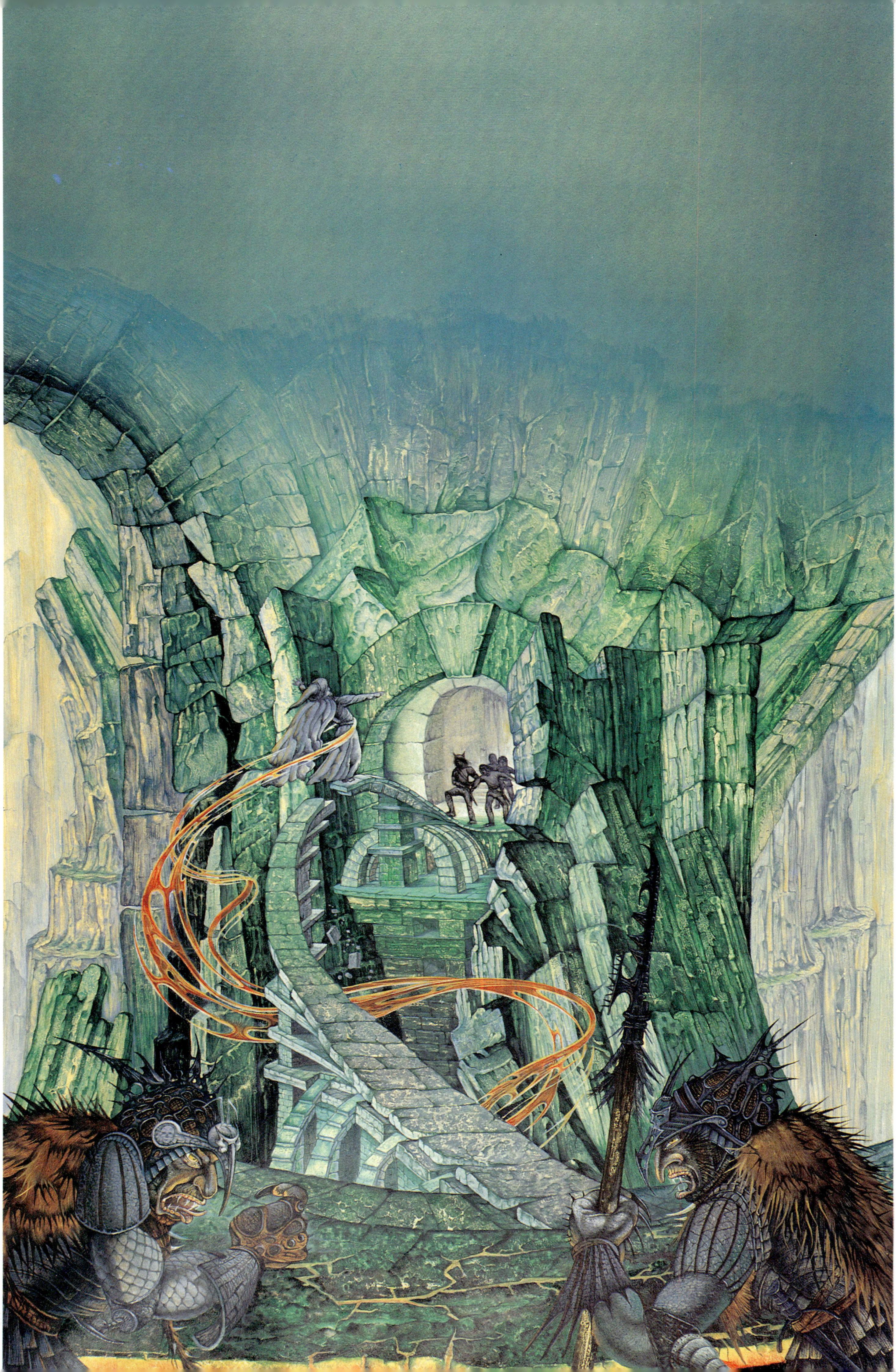

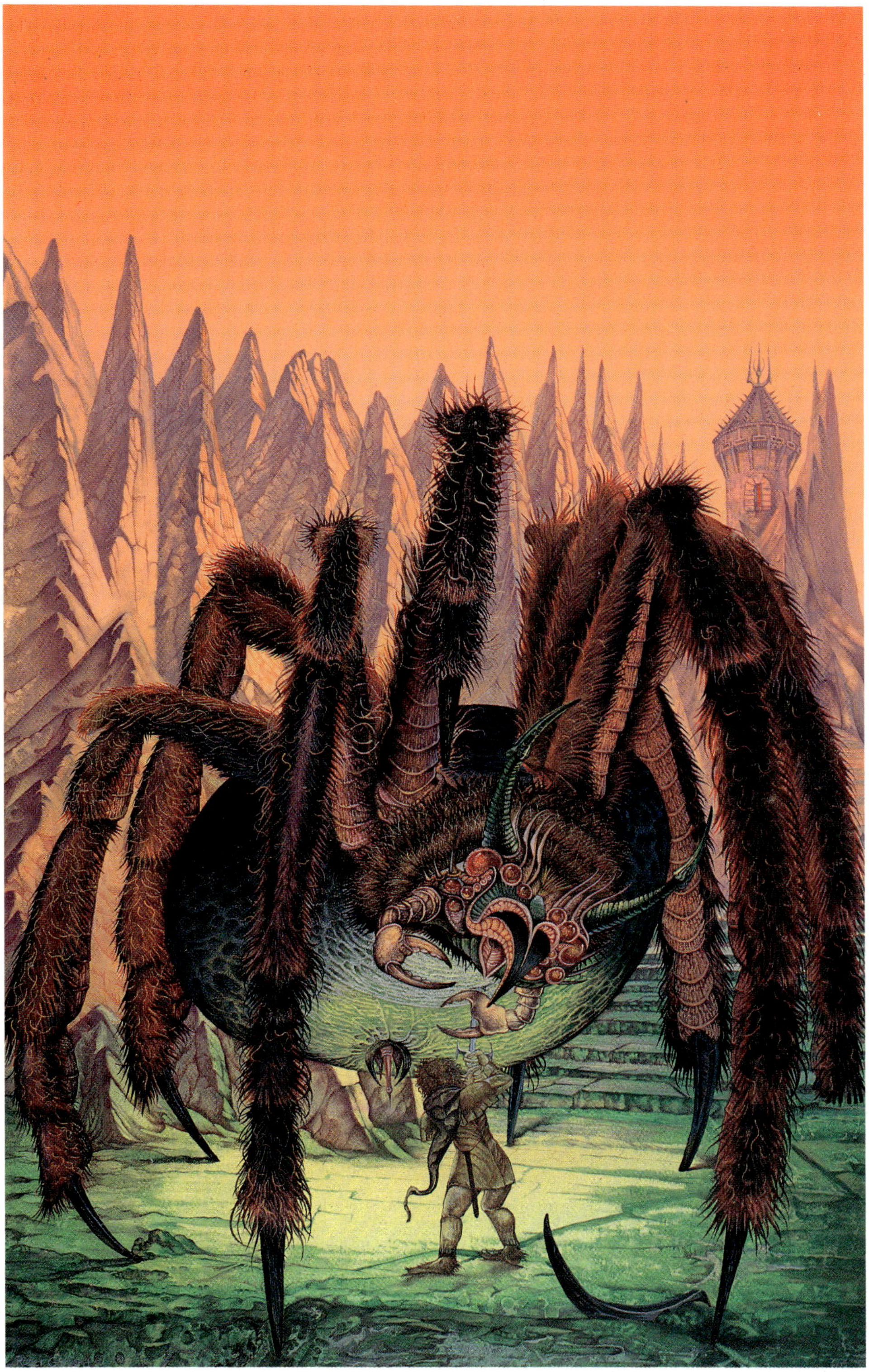

◁ **The Bridge of Khazad Dum**
Roger 1983
Oils and Acrylic. 11 x 17in
(28 x 43cm)
1984 calendar illustration,
Unwin Hyman.

This is the scene from *The Fellowship of the Ring*, in which the dreadful Balrog is cast into the pit, but in a final act of spite, lashes out with his whip and drags Gandalf in with it.

▷ **Shelob**
Roger 1983
Oils and Acrylic. 11 x 17in
(28 x 43cm)
1984 calendar illustration,
Unwin Hyman.

This scene shows Sam entering, for him, the most desperate stage of the great adventure, Frodo having been bound and poisoned by the monstrous Shelob.

The self-discipline required of a freelance artist did not come hard to Roger: 'Though when I left teaching I wondered at first how I would cope without the framework of a timetable. A friend warned me that self-employment could be a worse tyrant, and I soon learned what he was getting at. As a freelancer you soon have to fight the compulsion to say "yes" to every offer that comes along, and deadlines soon force a discipline on you.'

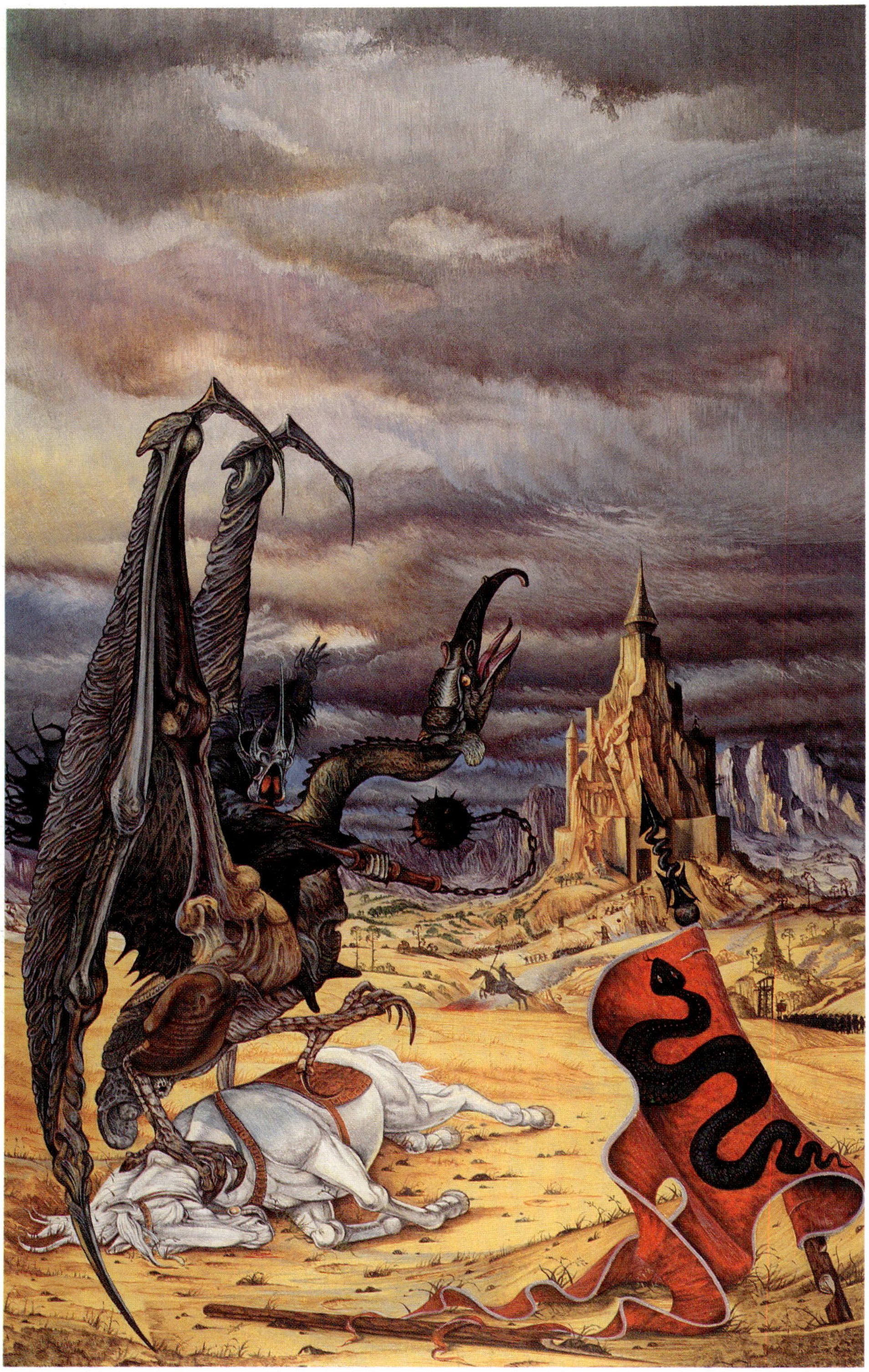

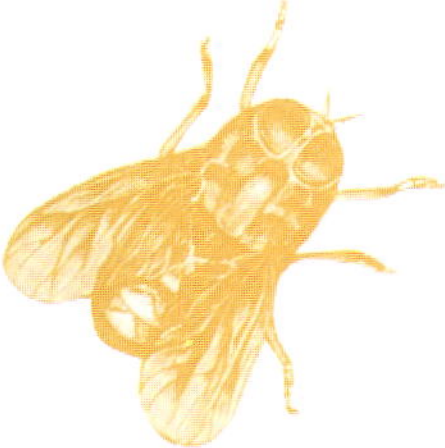

△ **The Lord of the Nazgul**
Roger 1983
Oils and Acrylic. 10 x 14in
(25 x 36cm)
1984 calendar illustration,
Unwin Hyman.

The dramatic scene in the Battle of the Pelennor Fields, when Theoden of the Mark, in his moment of triumph, falls victim to the Nazgul-riding Ringwraith.

▷ **Sauron Defeated**
Roger 1992
Oils and Acrylic. 12 x 19in
(30 x 48cm)
Previously unpublished.

One idea for the cover of the book of the same name, edited by Christopher Tolkien, turned down in favour of another view of Barad-Dur.

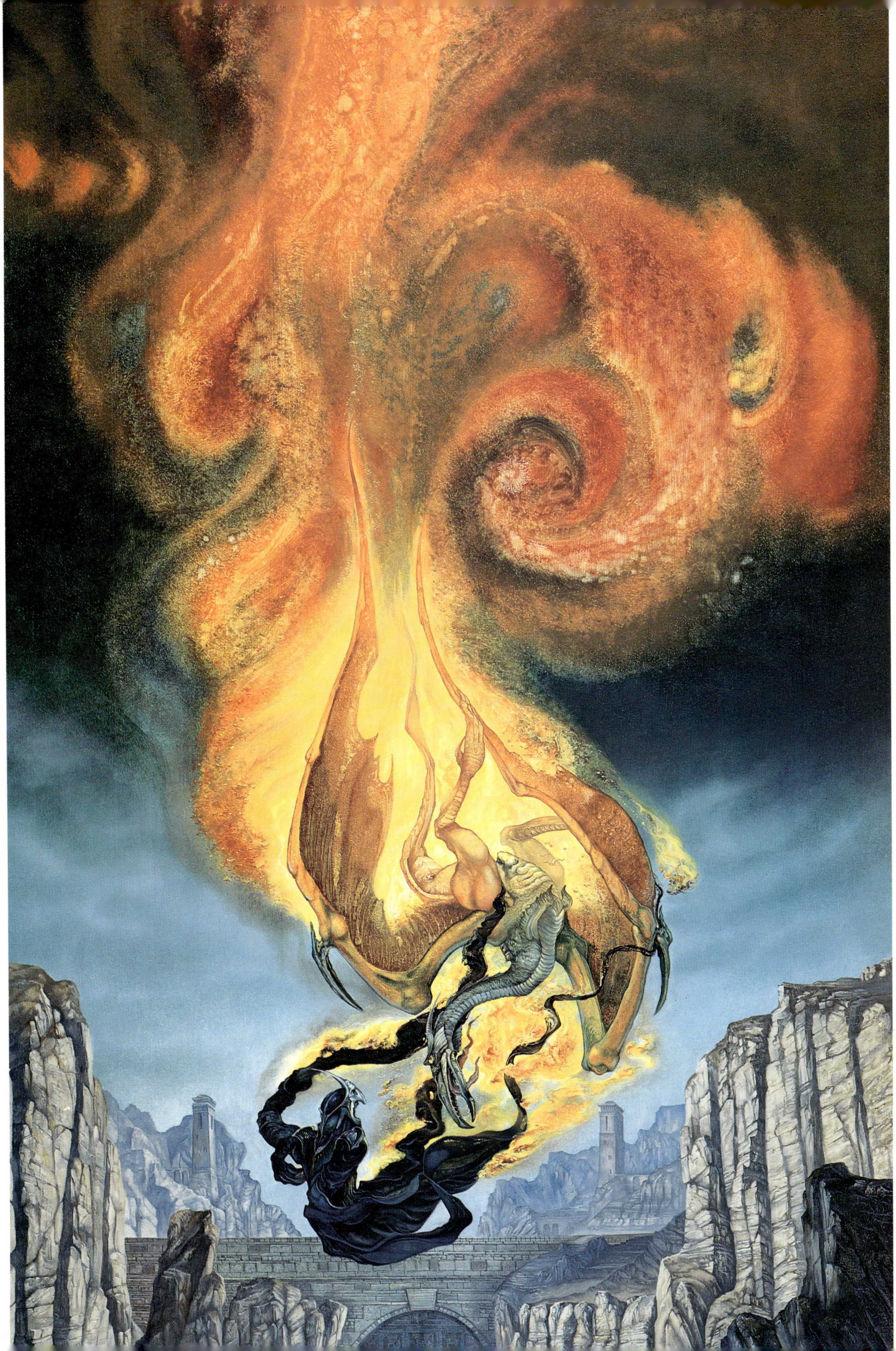

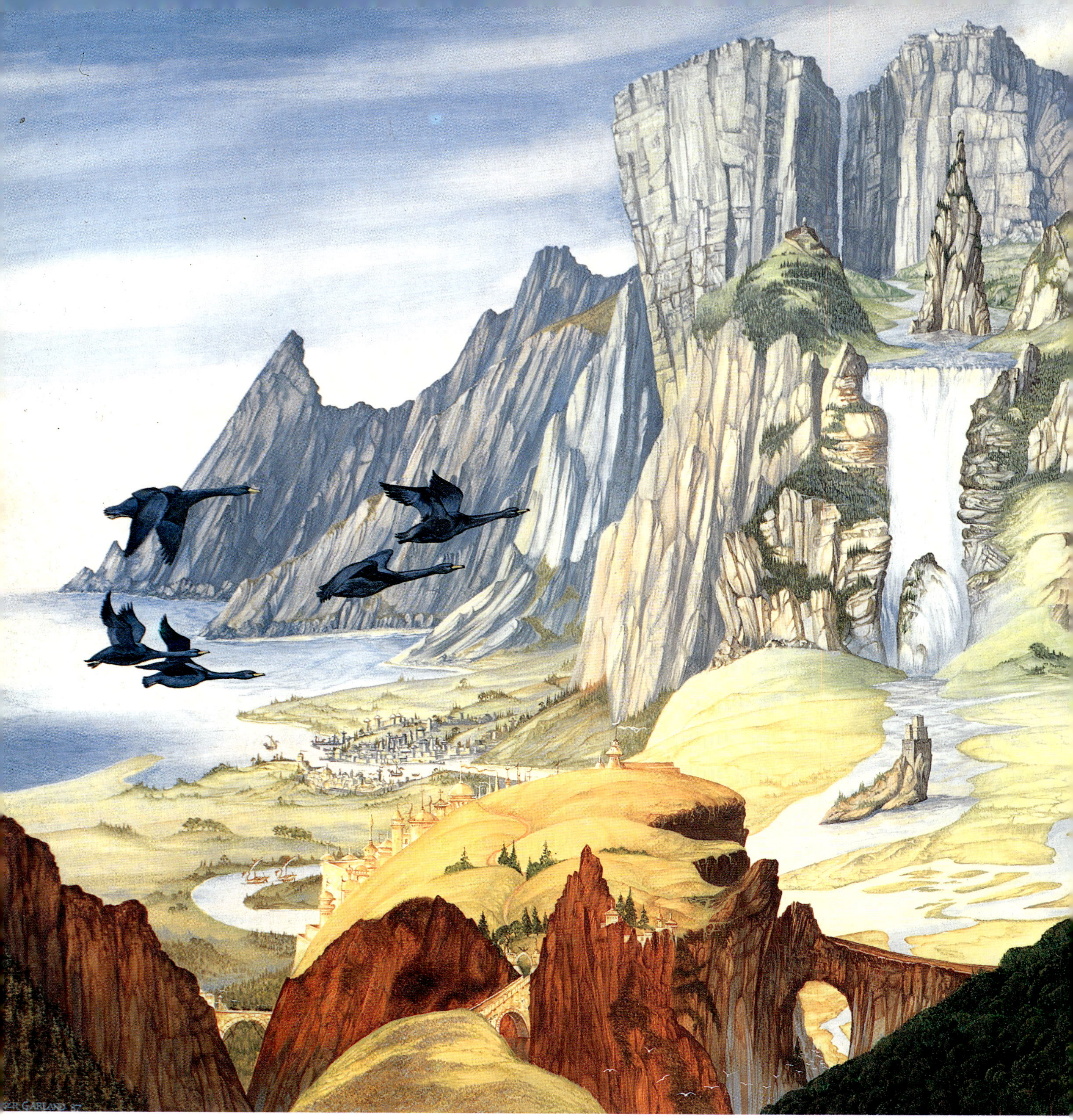

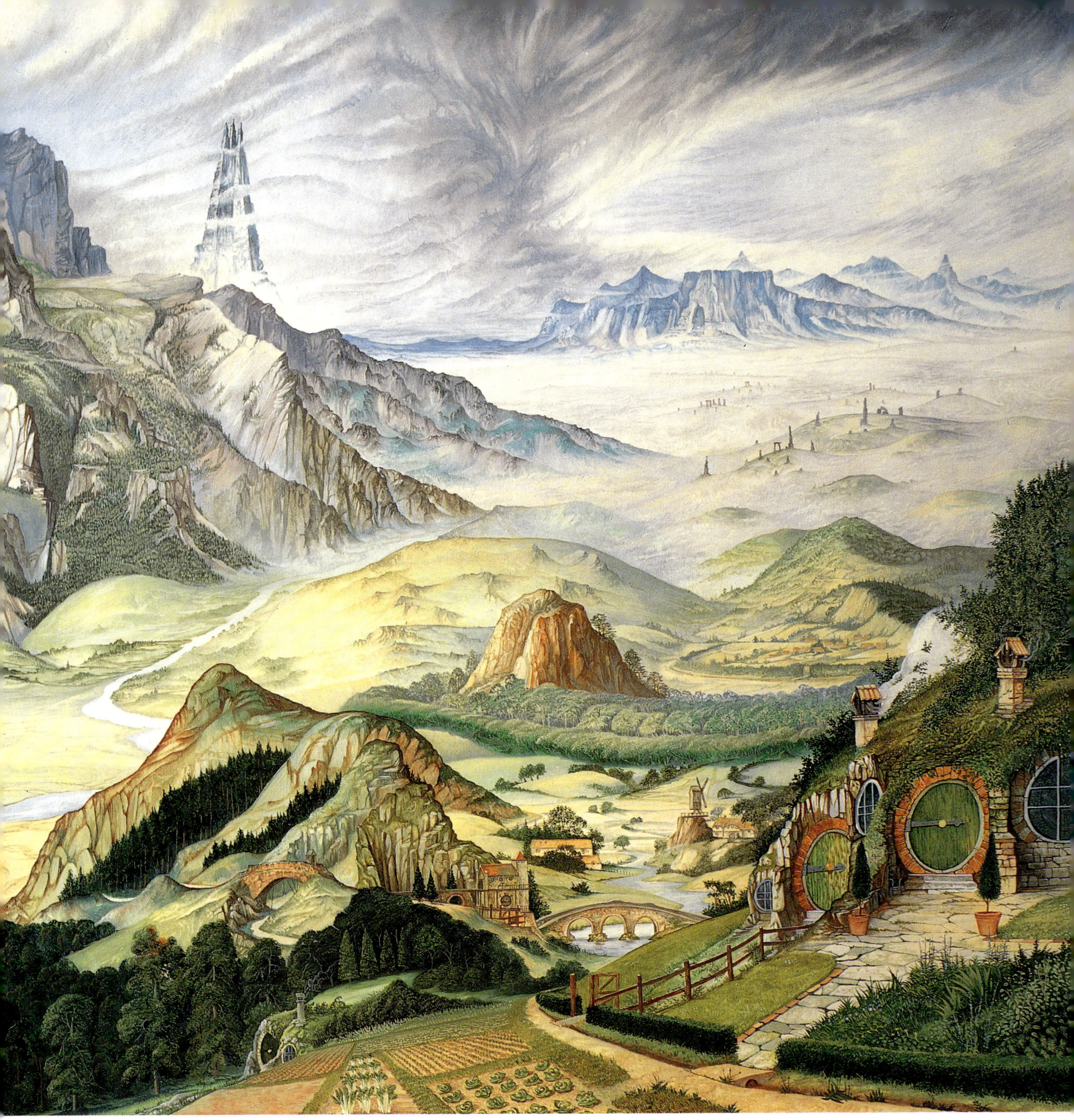

△ **Tolkien Landscape**
Roger 1987
Oils and Acrylic. 14 x 27in (36 x 69cm)
Trilogy box cover, Unwin Hyman.

This is an impossible picture, combining views of three totally separate places, but in a strange way it works. On the right is Bag End and a view over Hobbiton and the Shire. To reach the centre of the picture, one's eye should travel into the far distance, beyond the Shire, then back to the foreground in a circular sort of way, thus arriving at the falls of Rauros in far-off Rohan. To get to the left, another detour of some 300 miles, out through the back of your own eye, is needed, then forward to the haven of Pelargir, downstream from the falls. The image was broken down into its three elements for the 1989 calendar.

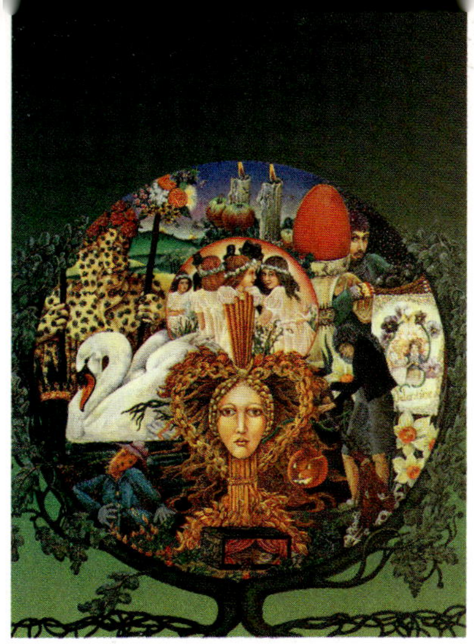

# FOLKLORE & LEGEND

*"The human psyche has to have something to believe in, and if established religion cannot satisfy the need, people will look elsewhere."*

The Garlands see Linda's path to fantasy being literary, while Roger's was instinctive, or visionary, but they led to much the same place. Roger's pictures tend toward heroic legend, Linda's to folklore, but they cross quite freely into each other's territory and undoubtedly complement each other's strengths.

They share many techniques, and often their styles are indistinguishable, but they do, in fact, go about their paintings quite differently. Roger has a fairly set formula of sky, landscape, and then working towards the foreground. Linda appears to start anywhere and jump around the picture at random, the whole thing coming together in the end like a jigsaw puzzle. It is not, of course, as random as it seems, but follows from what she sees as the principal problem, which is the interaction of the main figure with the background.

Mentally their approaches are different. Roger needs time to centre his thoughts before getting down to work, whereas Linda tends to jump straight in. She also likes working on three or four pictures at a time, finding that problems tend to resolve themselves by the time she comes back to them.

The greatest difference, though, is that Roger is basically a draughtsman, while Linda is a natural painter. Very often Roger prefers his rough drawings to the final painting, and tends to finish them to a higher standard than Linda. Her roughs are fairly functional, and only as finished as they need be for the next stage, when outlines are transferred to board with carbon paper ready for painting.

Roger has learned much from Linda about the use of colour and figure drawing, both of which came hard to him. He is happiest with pure fantasy landscapes, for which he rarely uses any reference material, just his imagination and memory – particularly of the coastline near St Austell, seen in all conditions during a decade of walking the dog along the cliffs. One problem with Cornwall, though, is that it has no real mountains, and for years Roger had to fight a tendency for his painted ones to resemble china clay tips.

△ **Folk Customs**
Linda 1977
Oils. 11 x 17in (28 x 43cm)
Cover for a book by Christina Hole, Granada.

This was Linda's second jacket commission. Among the many customs illustrated is that of hunting wrens on Boxing Day (the only day of the year on which it was not unlucky to do so). Once caught, children placed them in boxes and went round charging people for the privilege of 'seeing the king'. The custom arose from the ancient belief that the wren was the king of birds, being associated with Bran, or Saturn, who presided over Yule-tide.

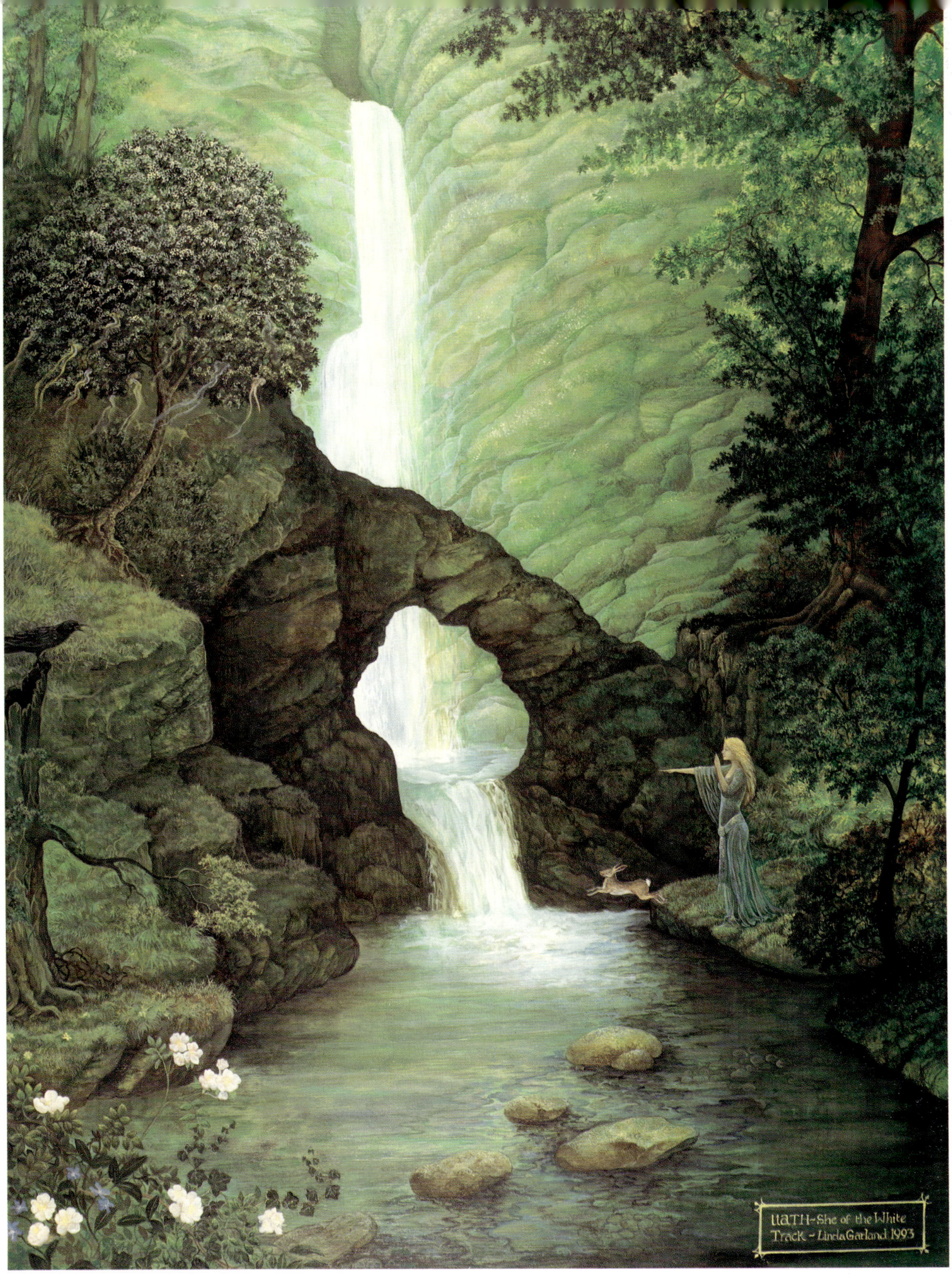


△ **Uath: She of the White Track**
Linda 1993
Oils. 18 x 24in (46 x 61cm)
Calendar illustration, Visionary Publishing.

The setting for this work is St Nectan's Glen, near Tintagel, in Cornwall, where the water falls into a wonderful chalice-like natural basin. Uath represents May, who is always preceded by a hare. The May tree on the left has scraps of material tied to it, which have been rubbed into wounds – a traditional Cornish way of banishing them.

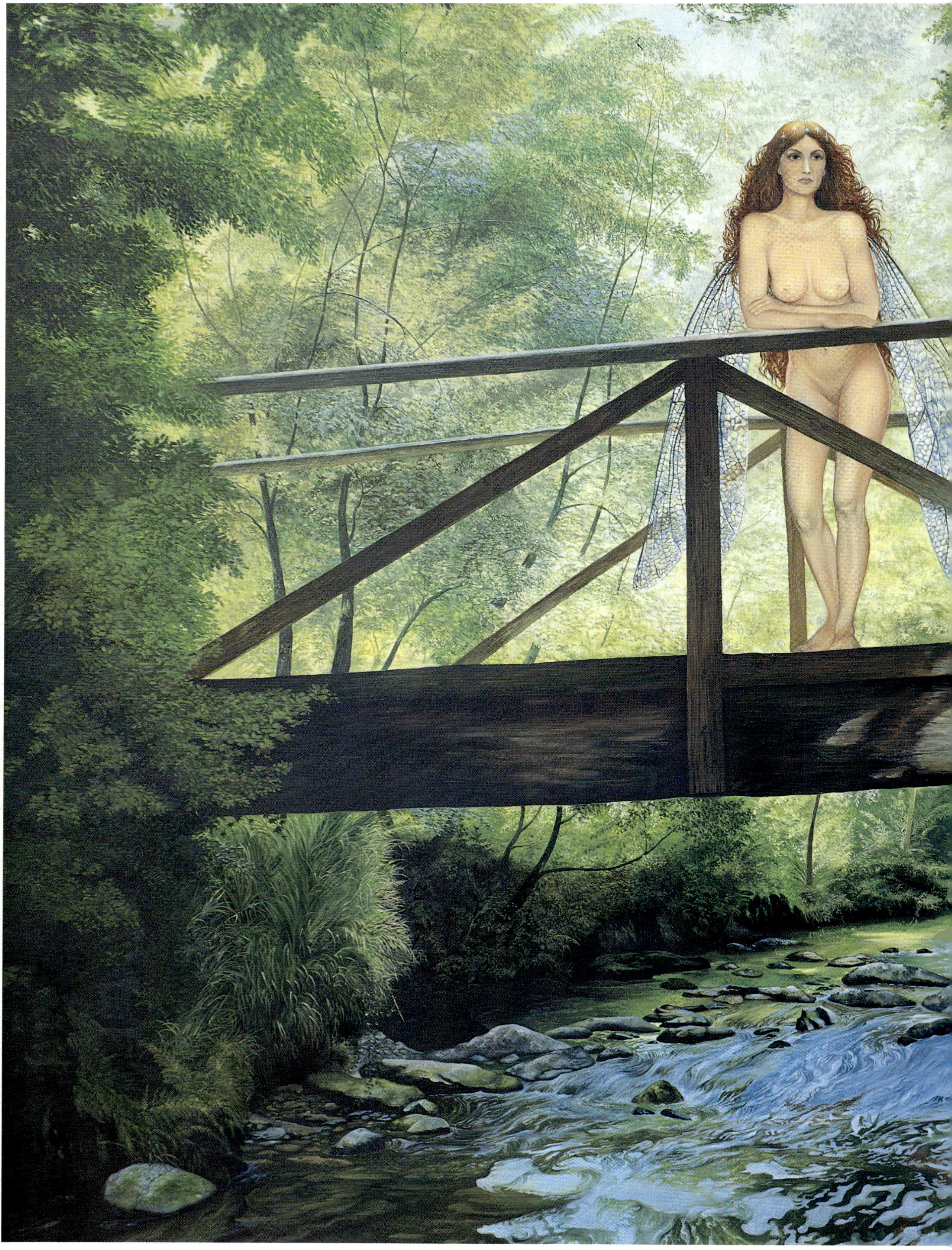

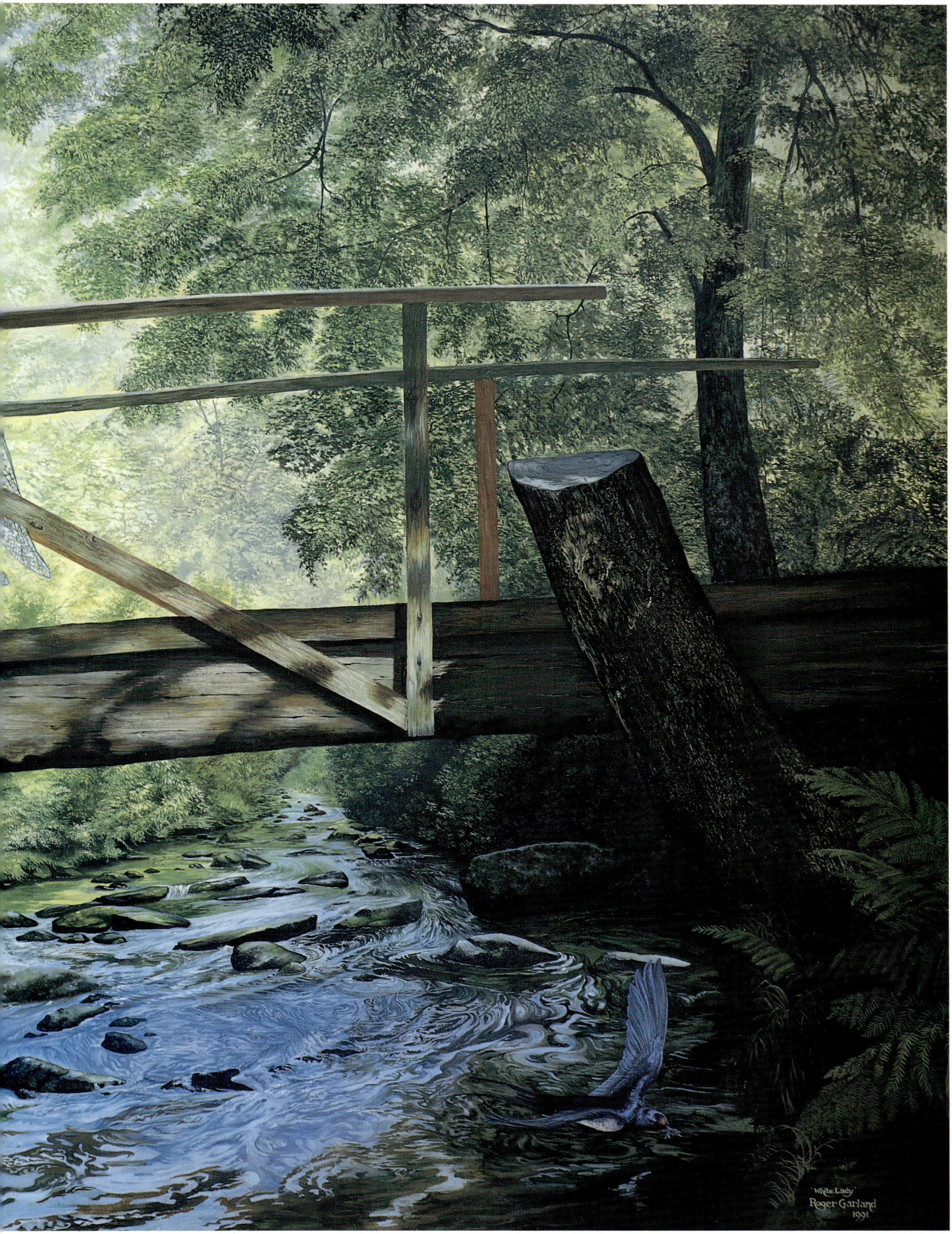
'White Lady'
Roger Garland
1991

**(Previous page)**
**White Lady**
Roger 1991
Oils. 24 x 36in (61 x 91cm)
Private work.

This work was inspired by Lifton Gorge, in Devon, whose high waterfall is known as the 'White Lady'. The scale is larger than usual, to test out a theory that this would speed up the work. It didn't.

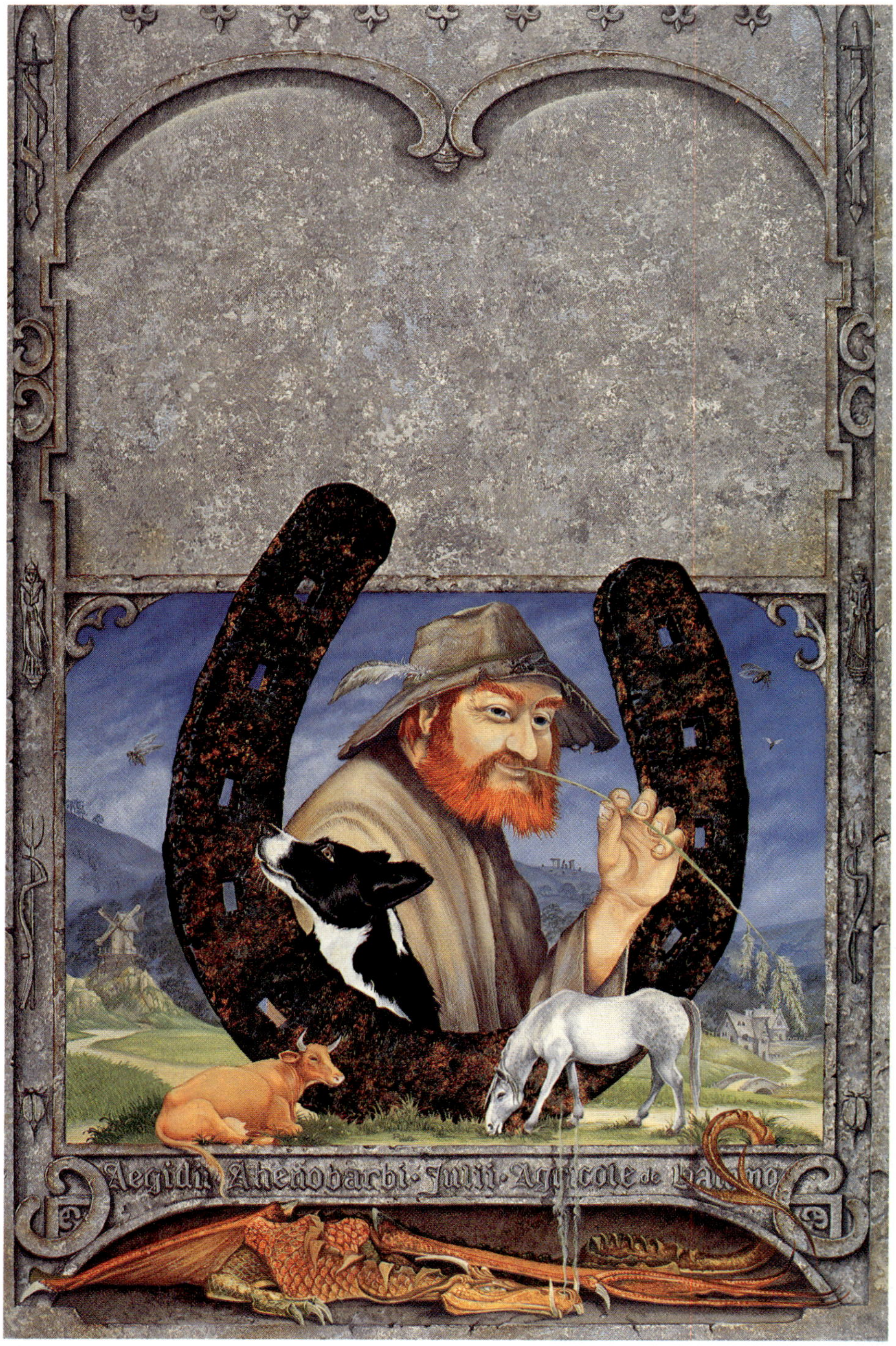

▷ **Farmer Giles of Ham**
Roger 1989
Oils and Acrylic. 9 x 13in (23 x 33cm)
Book cover, Unwin Hyman.

Roger: 'People don't usually think of Tolkien as having much sense of humour, but I find this book hilarious and a very true picture of village life.' The model for Giles was a farming neighbour, whose character had something in common with the hero of Ham.

The only previous illustrator of the story was Pauline Baynes, whose work Roger much admires. However, Roger did not feel that he was competing with her, since their styles and approach are very different.

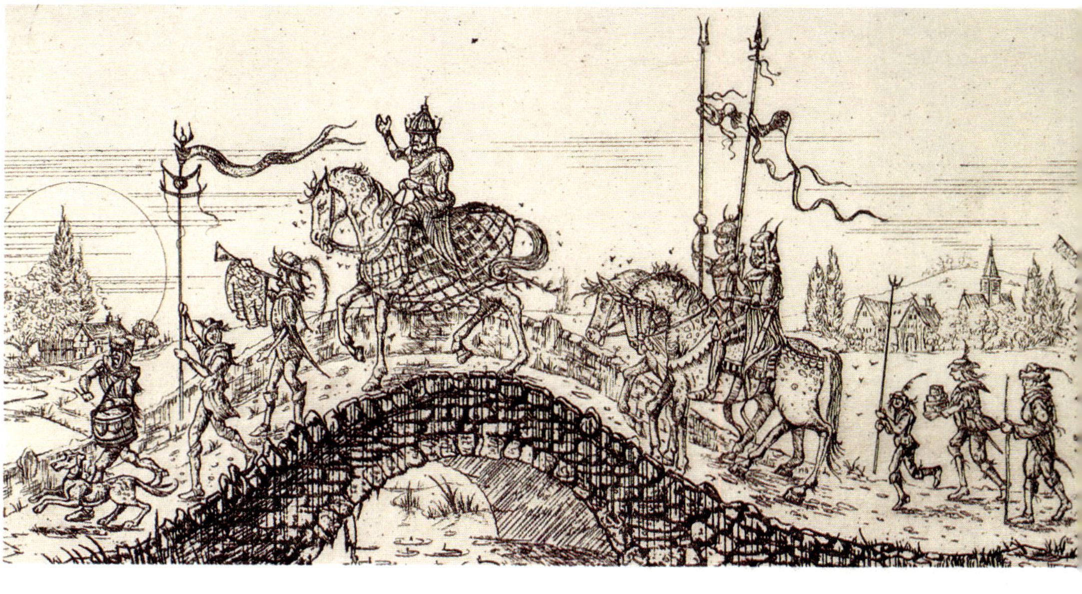

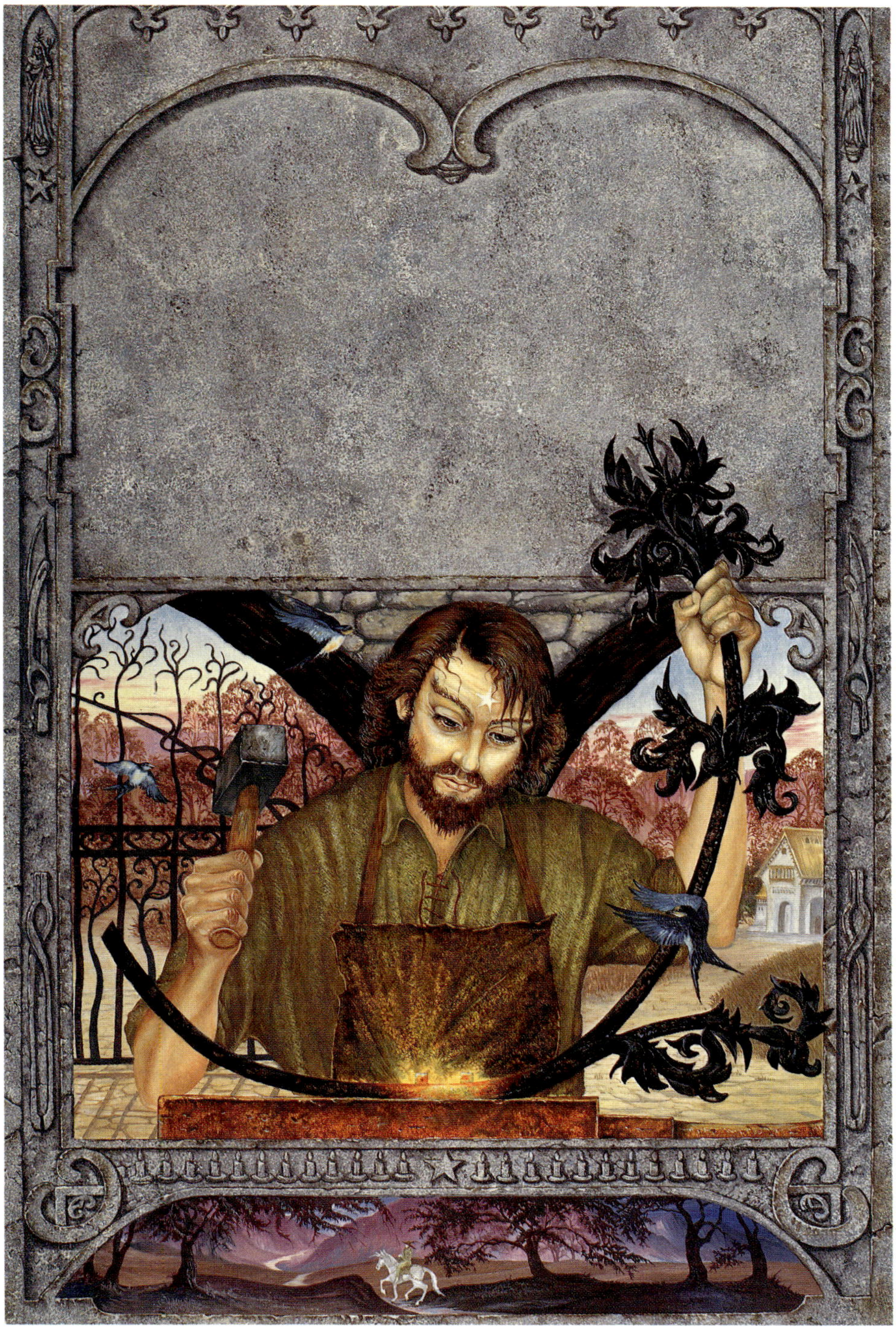

◁ **Smith of Wootton Major**
Roger 1989
Oils and Acrylic. 9 x 13in
(23 x 33cm)
Book cover, Unwin Hyman.

Roger was the model for this work, hirsutely modified to fit the part. The story is more ethereal than *Farmer Giles of Ham*, in that much of it is set in the land of Faery.

▽ **The King's Arrival**
Roger 1989
Copper etching. 3 x 10in
(7 x 26cm)
Illustration for *Farmer Giles of Ham*, Unwin Hyman.

Originally, Roger had wanted to etch many more of the internal illustrations for this, and the accompanying books – *Smith* and *Tom Bombadil* –, but there was too little time, and so he had to resort to pen and ink. Either way he was in his element, being able to indulge his passion for pure drawing. The composition was loosely inspired by Blake's *Canterbury Tales* engraving, and the etching style of Jacques Callot (1592-1635).

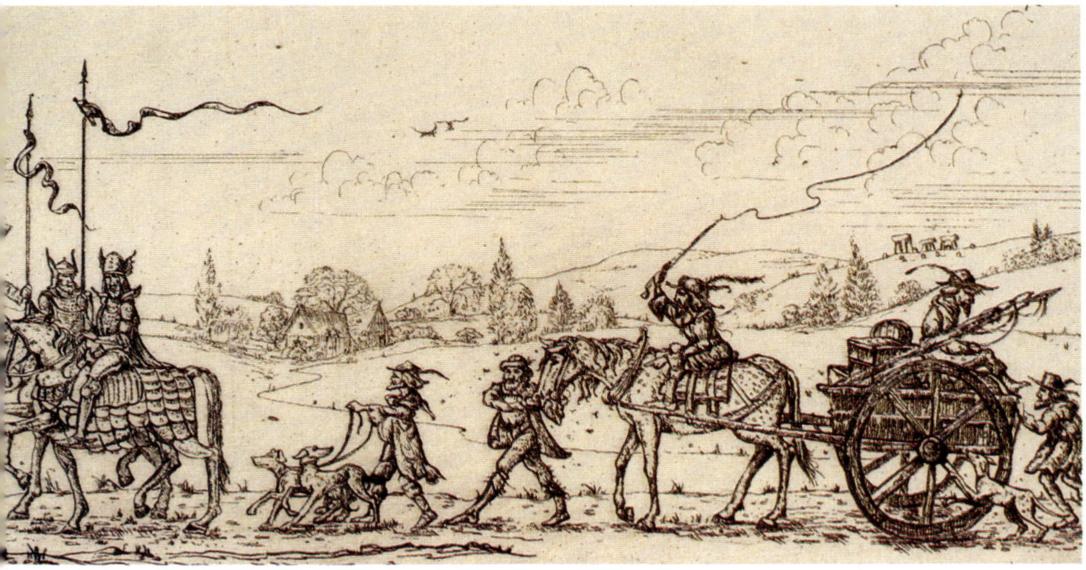

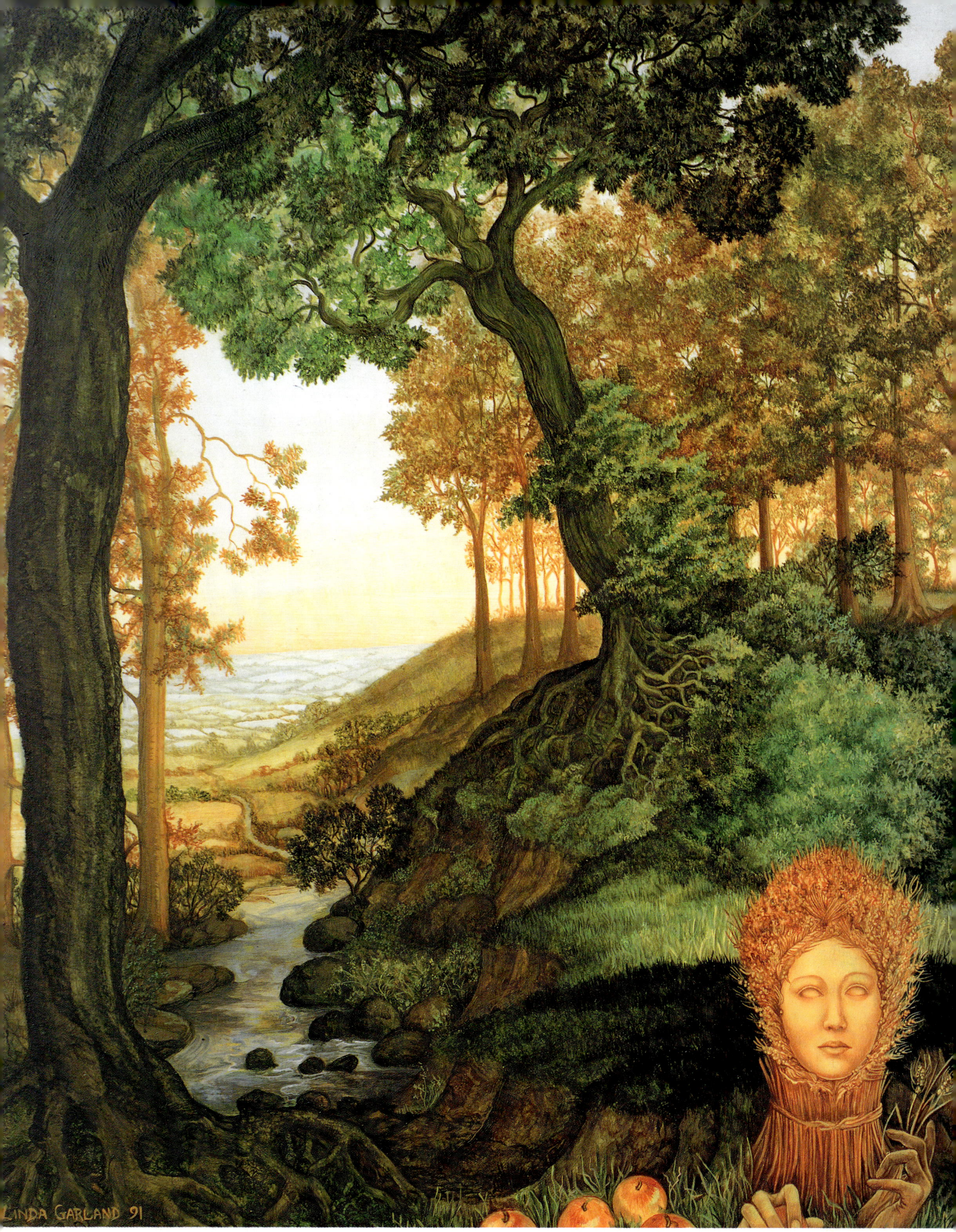
LINDA GARLAND 91

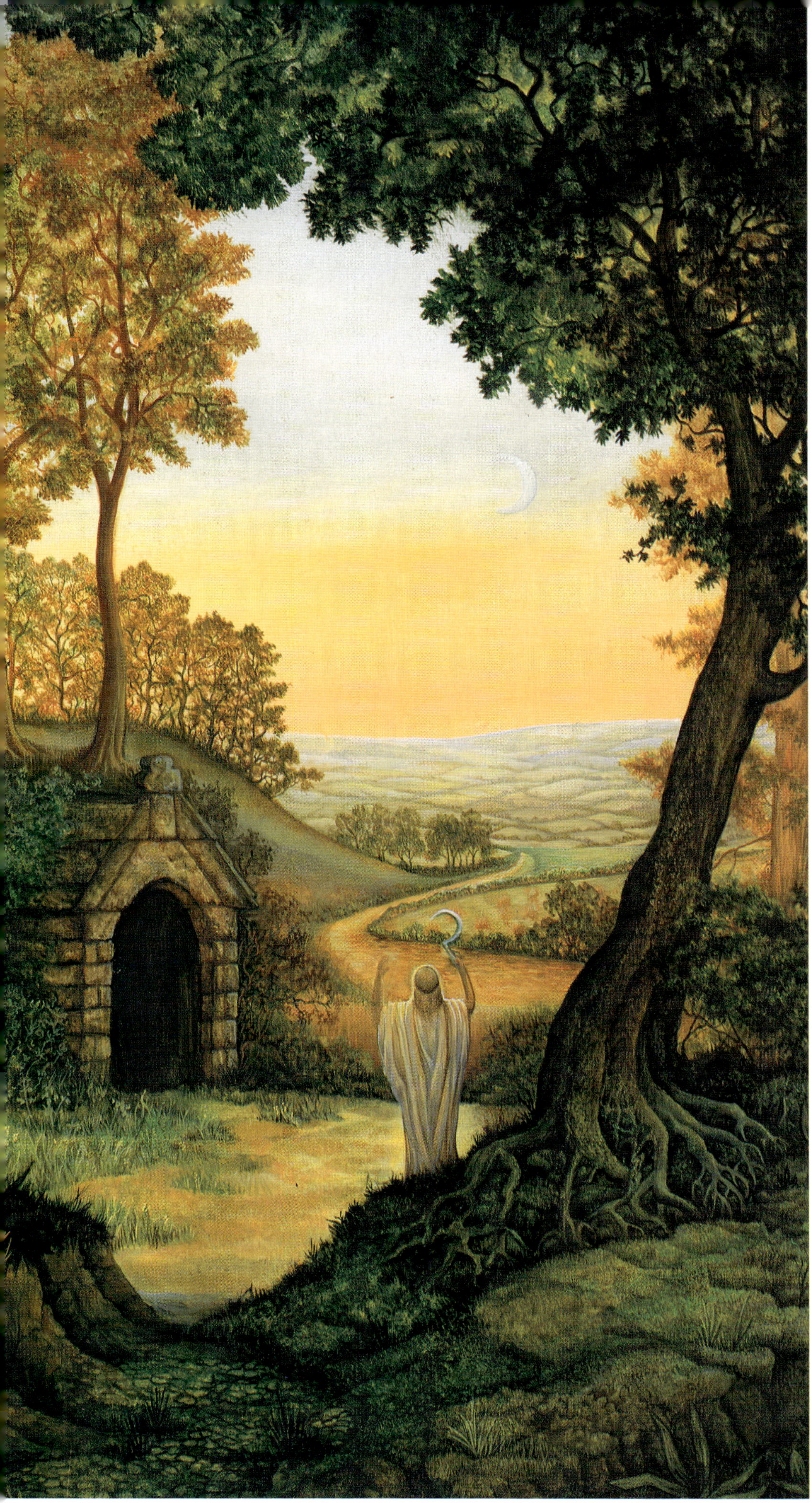

◁ **Cornish Well**
Linda 1991
Oils. 12 x 16in (30 x 41cm)
Cover for *Customs and Superstitions*, Tor Mark Press.

During the nineteenth century, Robert Hunt, a Cornish physician convalescing from the pace of life in London, spent a year roaming his home county recording all the folk-tales he could lay his ears on before they died out. In 1865, he published a range of these under the title, *Popular Romances of the West of England* which, in one form or another, stayed long in print. When Linda was first called in, extracts were being published as booklets, which it was felt needed new covers, the old ones being desperately dull. It says something for the power of illustration, that with her jackets sales soared.

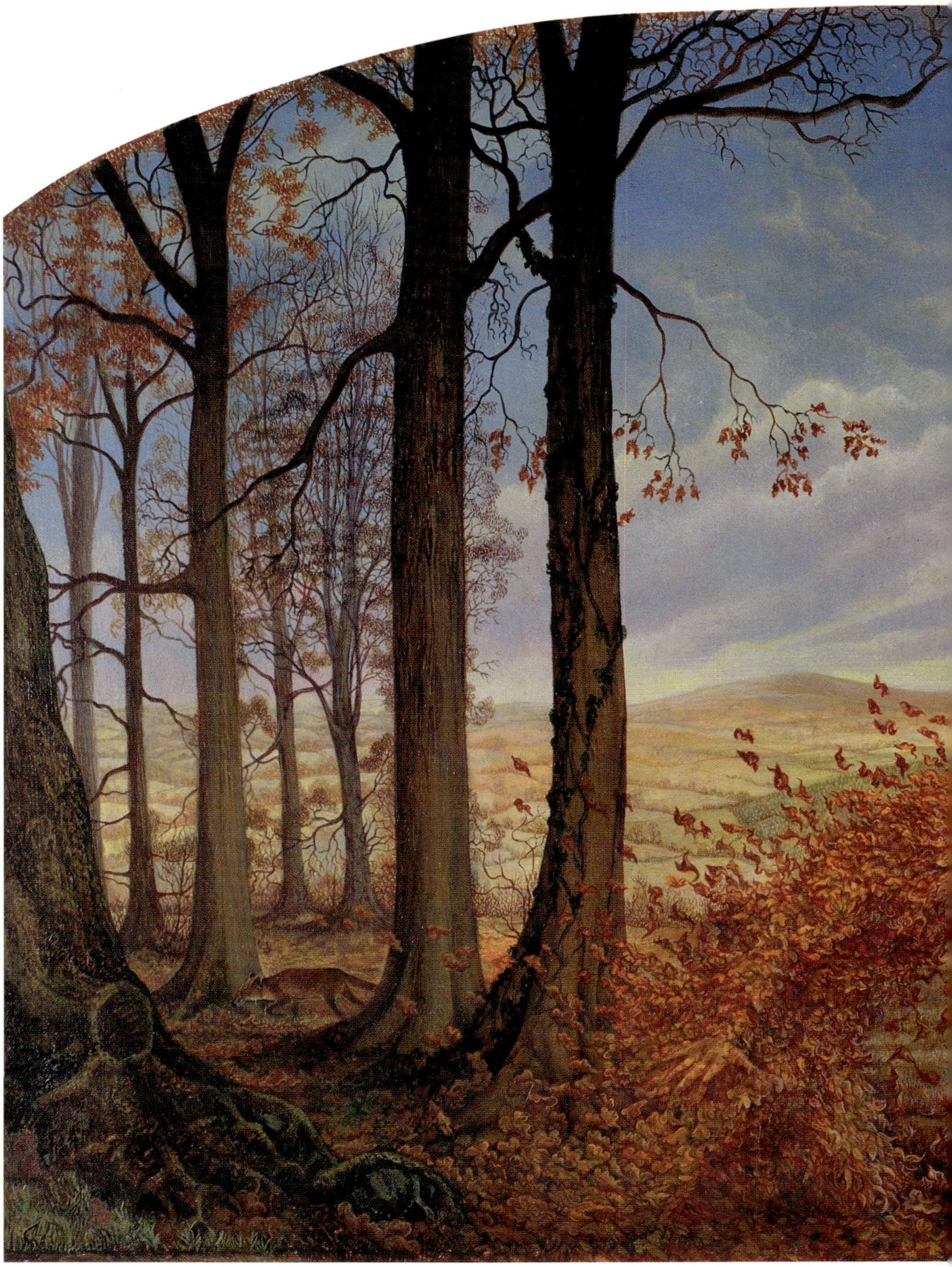

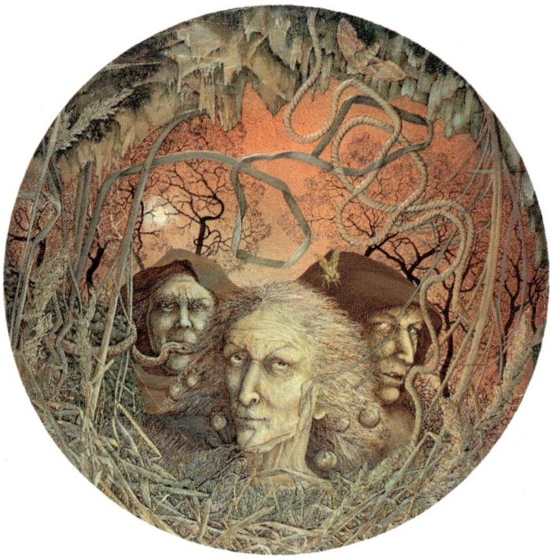

◁ Three Witches
Linda 1986
Mixed media. 15in diam. (38cm)
Private work.

The ground for this picture is a piece of Bockingford paper, which had been embossed by having pieces of string, knicker elastic etc., strewn over it, and being squeezed in an etching press. It was then turned over and given a collage of vegetation, before being painted. The effect is altogether very three-dimensional, and is powerful enough to give the Garland children the creeps when they have to pass it on the stairs.

△ Winter the Huntsman
Linda 1994
Oils. 10 x 16in (25 x 40cm)
Private work.

This work is an illustration for a poem by Osbert Sitwell, the final verse of which goes: 'Is it Winter the Huntsman/ Who gallops through his iron glades,/ Cracking his cruel whip/ To the gathering shades?' The red leaves and slinking fox feature in the poem, but artistic licence was used to animate the leaves and make the Huntsman a knight.

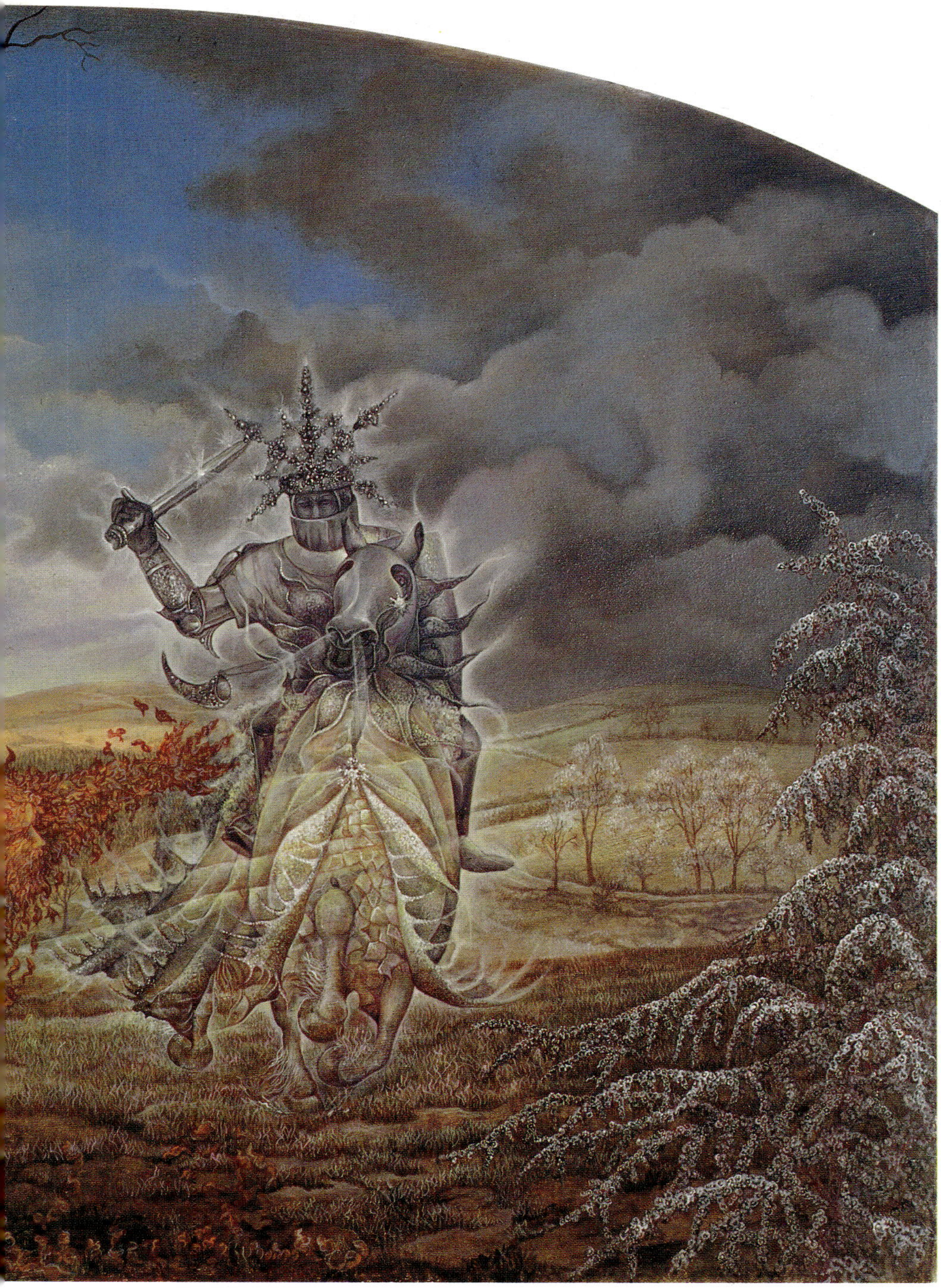

Correspondingly, Linda has learned much about line work from Roger, while also adopting some of the sponging and stippling techniques which have become his speciality. Cornwall is a lucky place to live if you are English and love folklore and legend, and it has probably had as much influence as anything on the Garlands' work. Linda: 'The curious thing about Cornwall is that it was the first part of the country to be Christianized, but is now the last bastion of paganism.'

The surviving relics of paganism in our culture have fascinated her ever since she first learned the origins of holly, mistletoe, and ivy at Christmas. Although many people frown on excessive interest in such matters, her parents were very tolerant and, in fact, have never had any problem with her work.

Roger was surrounded far more by such relics. His family was nominally Church of England, but during his childhood in rural Somerset the veneer was pretty thin.

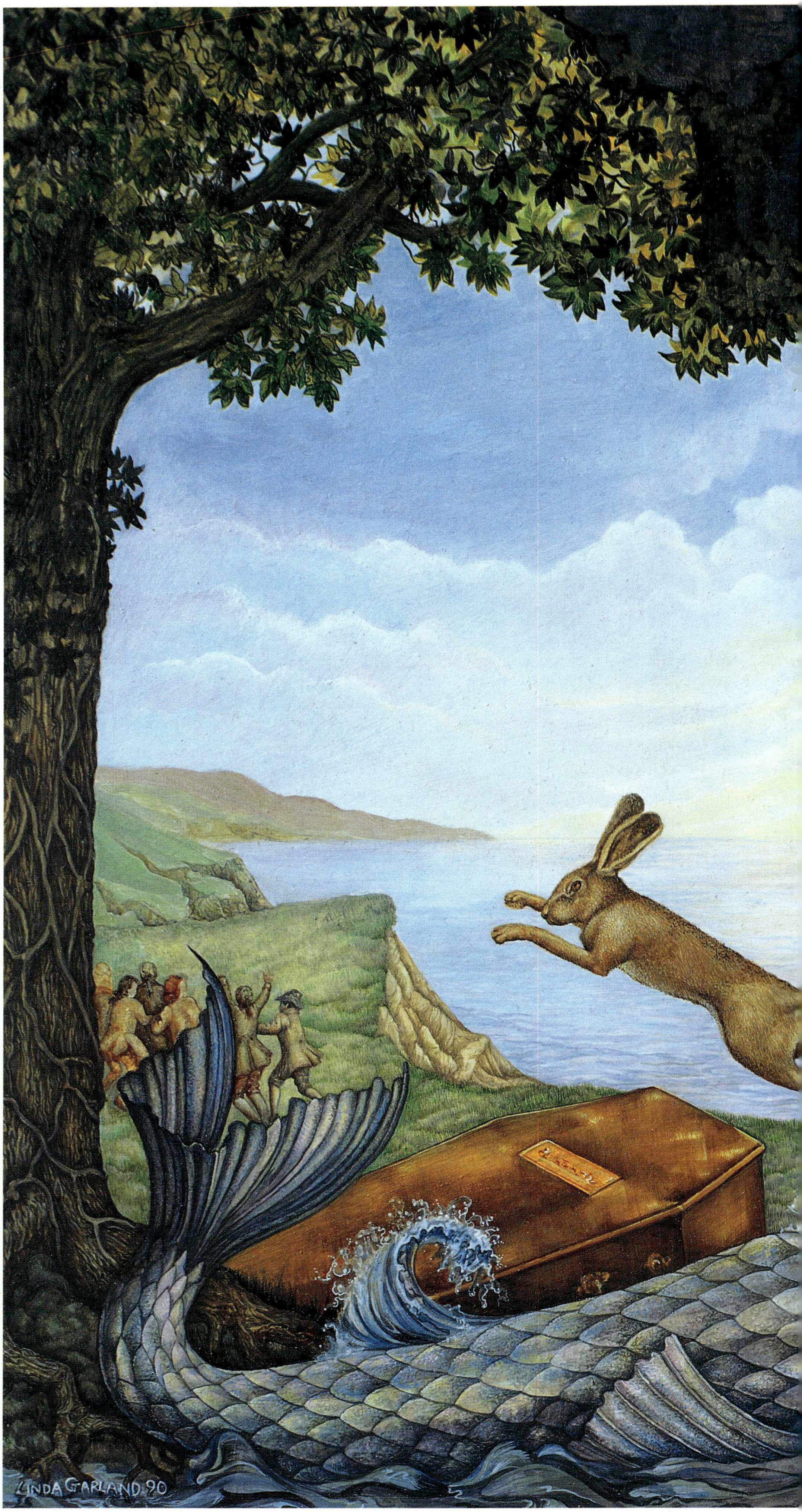


▷ **Cornish Legends**
Linda 1990
Oils. 12 x 16in (30 x 41cm)
Book cover, Tor Mark Press.

Cornwall has long been famous for its mermaids. In this picture, St Michael's Mount is in the distance, on the right. On the left is shown the tale of a witch who could not be buried, because every time the pallbearers came along, an ominous hare leaped across their path and frightened them away.

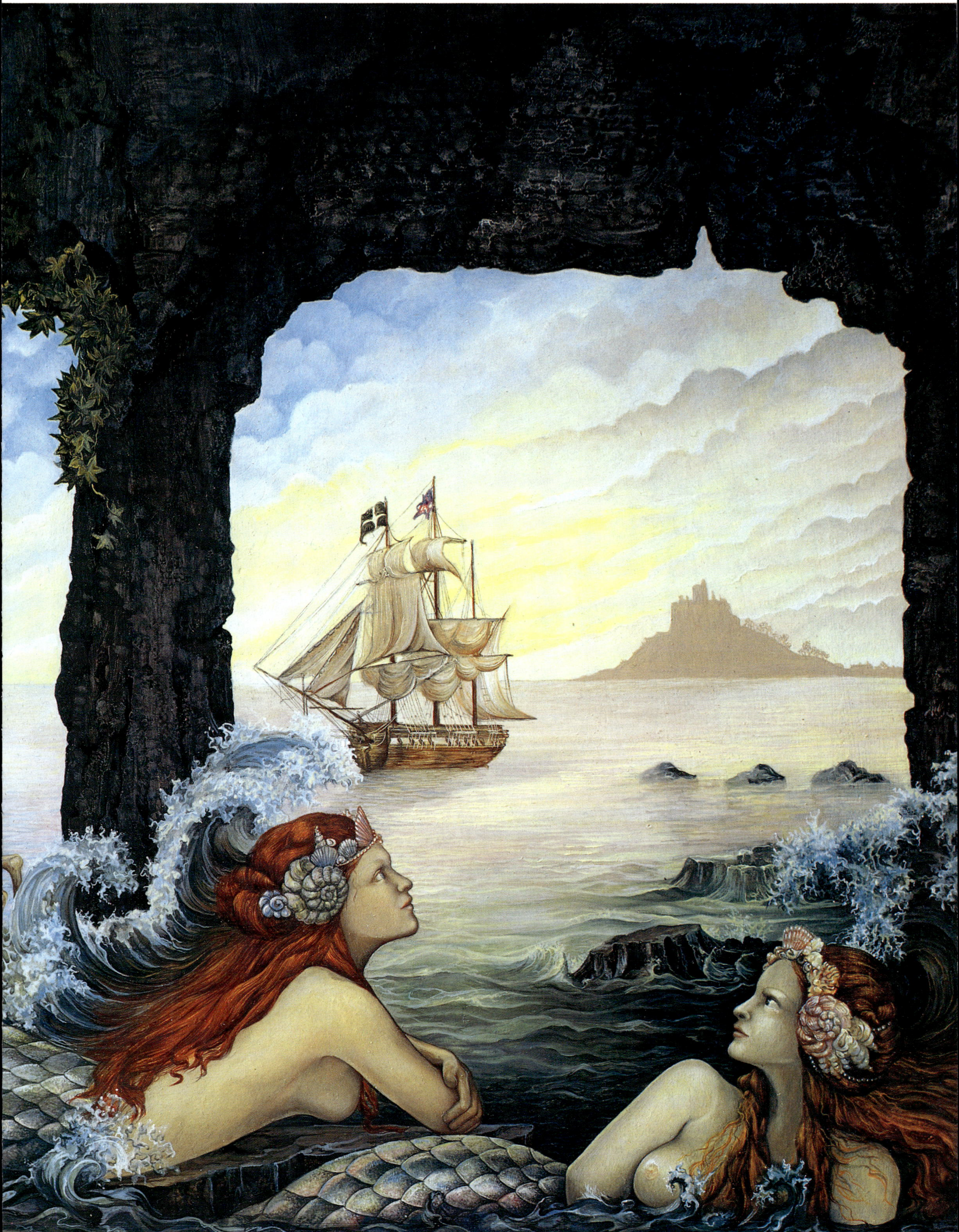

Superstition abounded, and he was quite old before he discovered that slugs did not fall out of the sky with rain, as his grandfather had said.

Living on a farm is in itself a tonic for their imaginations, being so close to the changing seasons and part of a tightknit community. To a town dweller they may seem isolated, but that is not how it feels, and it means that their daughter, Amy, can take off when she likes on a four-wheeled motorbike to play with the sheep, many of whom have become special friends.

For Roger, it is the best of both worlds. As a child he loved living on a farm, he just hated the work involved. Now he can get on with what he likes most, while enjoying all the benefits of rural life. But that is not to say that everything is perfectly idyllic for the Garlands; country life never has been. A beautiful location is all very well, but when life's complications strike, you are no more likely to notice your surroundings than in the inner city.

People find this hard to believe, though. One visitor to the gallery told Roger how envious he was, bemoaning his own lot in London's Metropolitan Police. It wasn't vandalism, joyriding or riots that got him down – he had an office job. It was the bureaucracy, having to live in an urban sprawl, and not being able to see any way out short of retirement. Roger tried reassuring him that life at the Lakeside Gallery was not quite the bed of roses it might seem, pointing out that the visitor could at least afford a shiny new car, and proper holidays. And this was not just said to make him feel better. But was the policeman even faintly convinced? No chance.

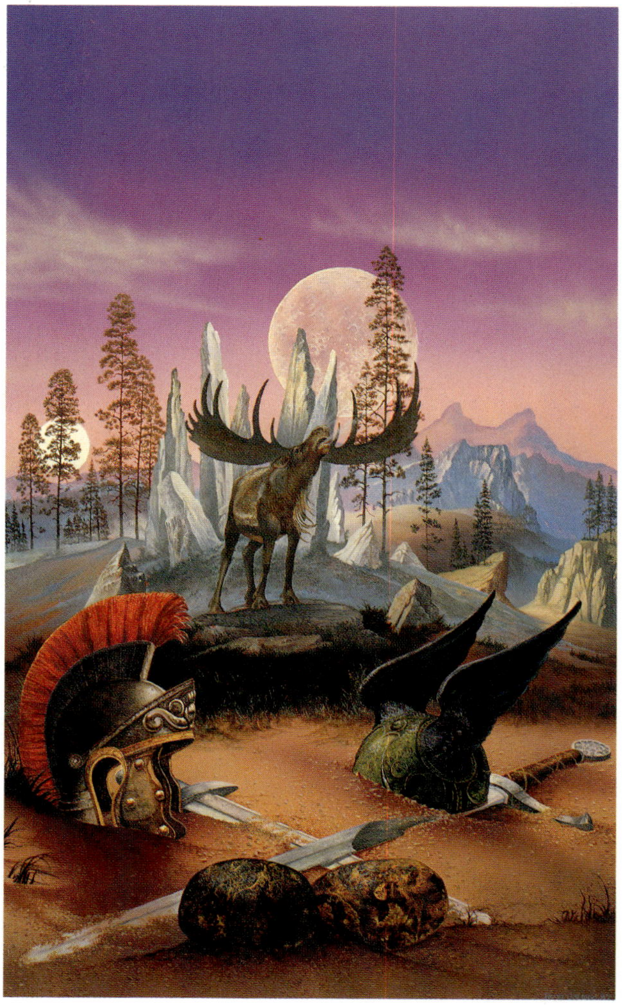

△ **Grail Quest**
Roger 1987
Oils and Acrylic. 11 x 17in (28 x 43cm)
Cover for *Rolynd* by David Gemmel, Century Hutchinson.

▷ **The Road to Underfall**
Roger 1988
Oils and Acrylic. 13 x 17in (33 x 43cm)
Cover for a book by Mike Jeffries, Fontana.

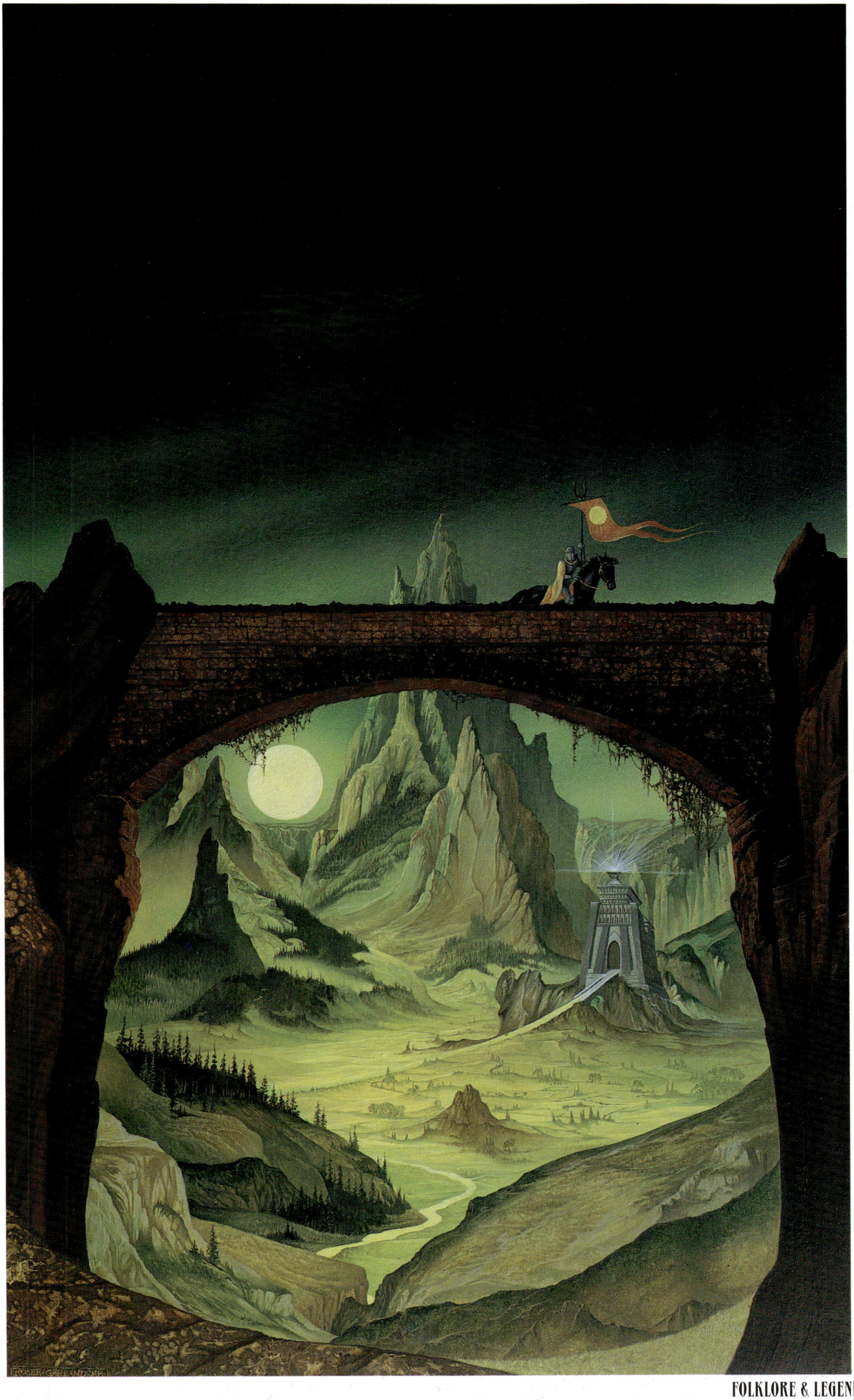

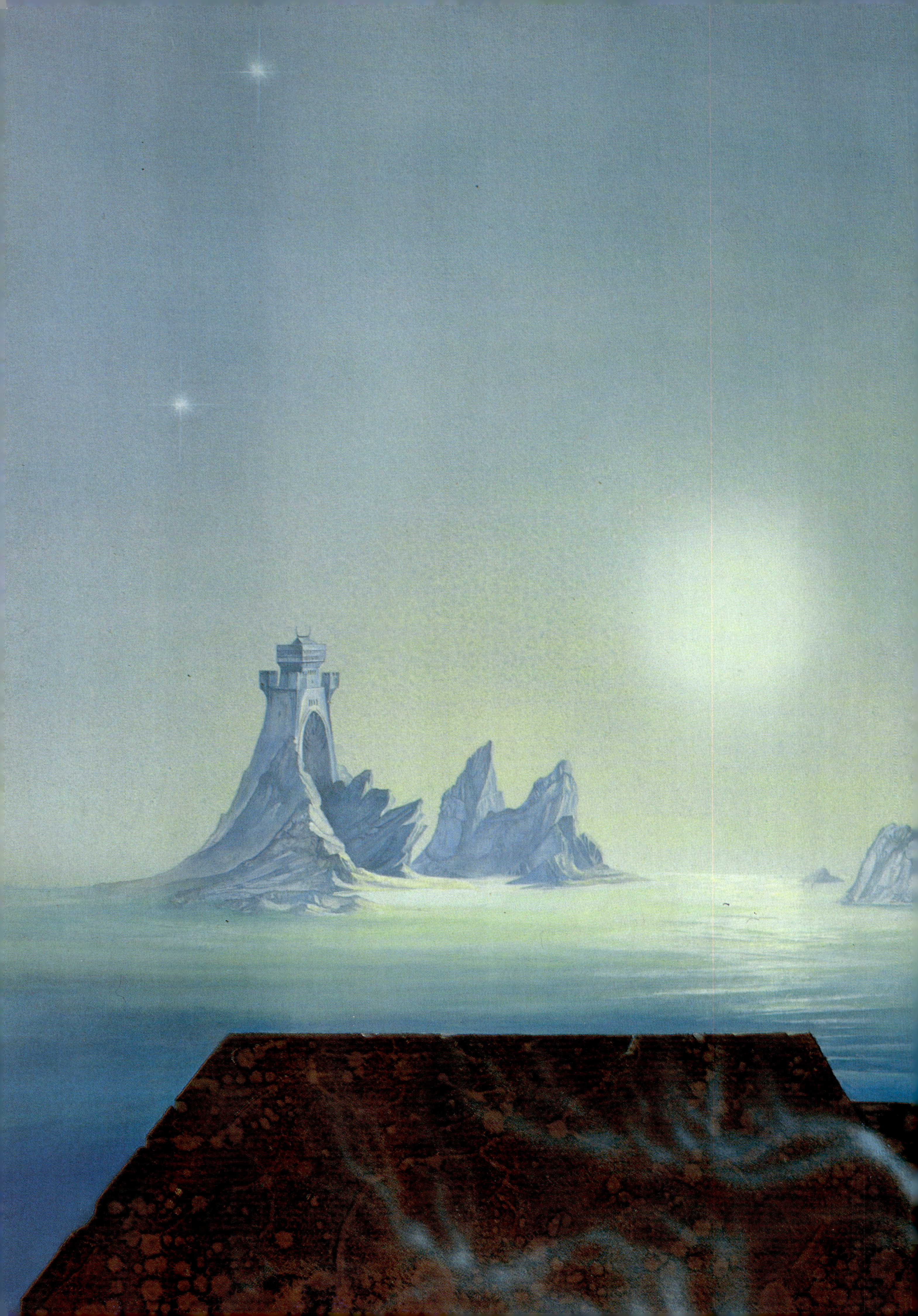

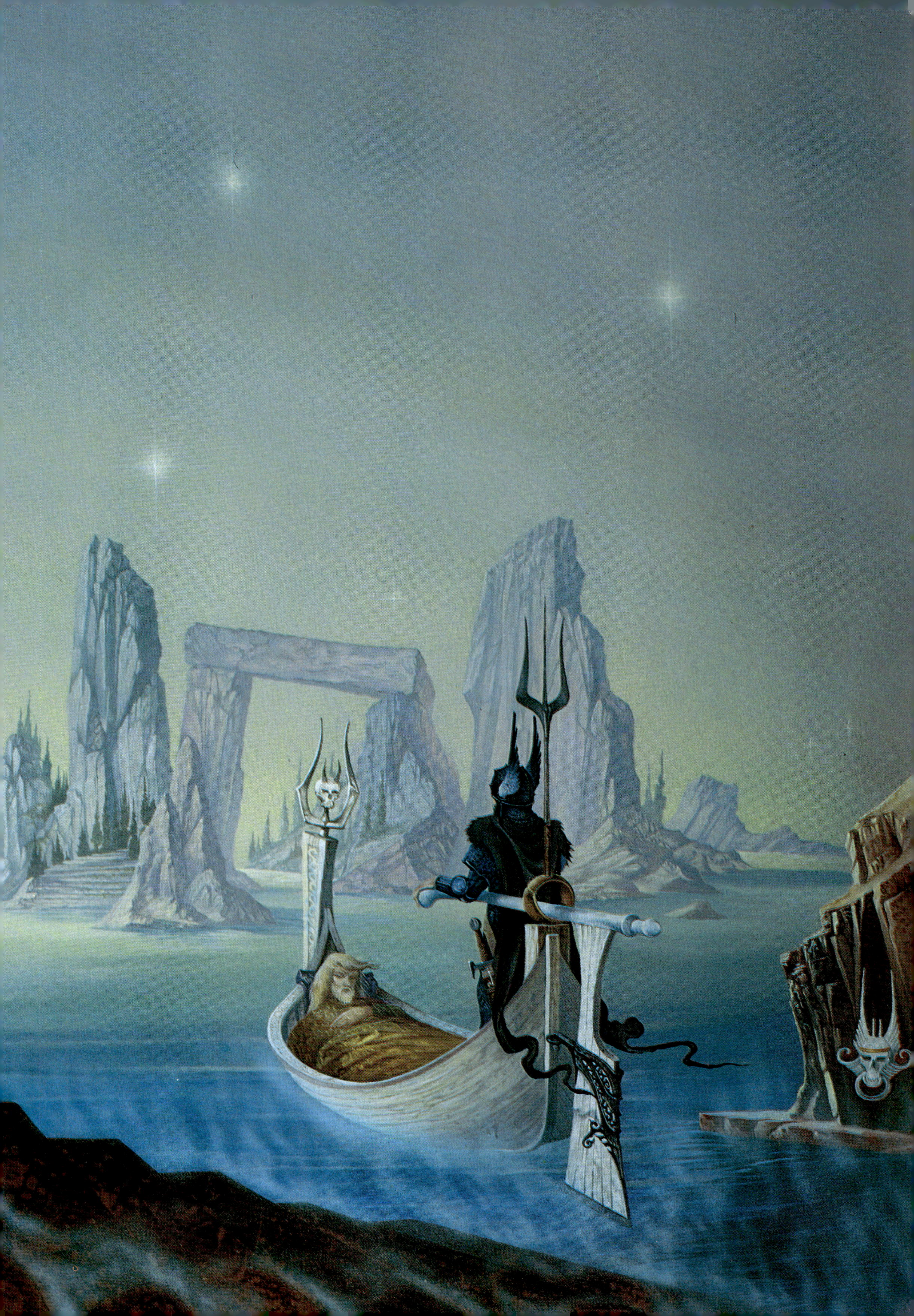

(Previous page)
Gates of Avalon
Roger 1988
Oils and Acrylic. 14 x 20in (36 x 51cm)
Cover for Last Sword of Power by David Gemmel, Century Hutchinson.

In this fantasy story, the dying Arthur is taken to Avalon for reincarnation, his boat being described as hovering, rather than floating, in the water.

▷ Merlyn
Linda 1990
Oils. 5 x 5in (13 x 13cm)
Book cover, Prism Press.

Among the details around Merlyn's face is a fossilized sea urchin, believed in ancient times to be a dragon's egg. It was a deliberate decision not to depict Merlyn as an old man, on the grounds that he must have been young once.

Cornwall is also a hotbed of New Age activity, the upsurge of which provided a welcome audience after a period in which the Garlands had felt out on a limb. For a while in publishing, it had seemed as if fantasy was being pushed aside by science fiction; but then everything goes in cycles. Their own theory is that science fiction went up a blind alley by tending too much towards 'faction', eventually forcing people with a more mystical turn of mind to look elsewhere for sustenance, and so back to fantasy.

There are, of course, wider issues involved in the rise, and semi-respectability, of New Age thinking, though they undoubtedly add up to some similar cyclical pattern. Linda: 'The human psyche has to have something to believe in, and if established religion cannot satisfy the need, people will look elsewhere.'

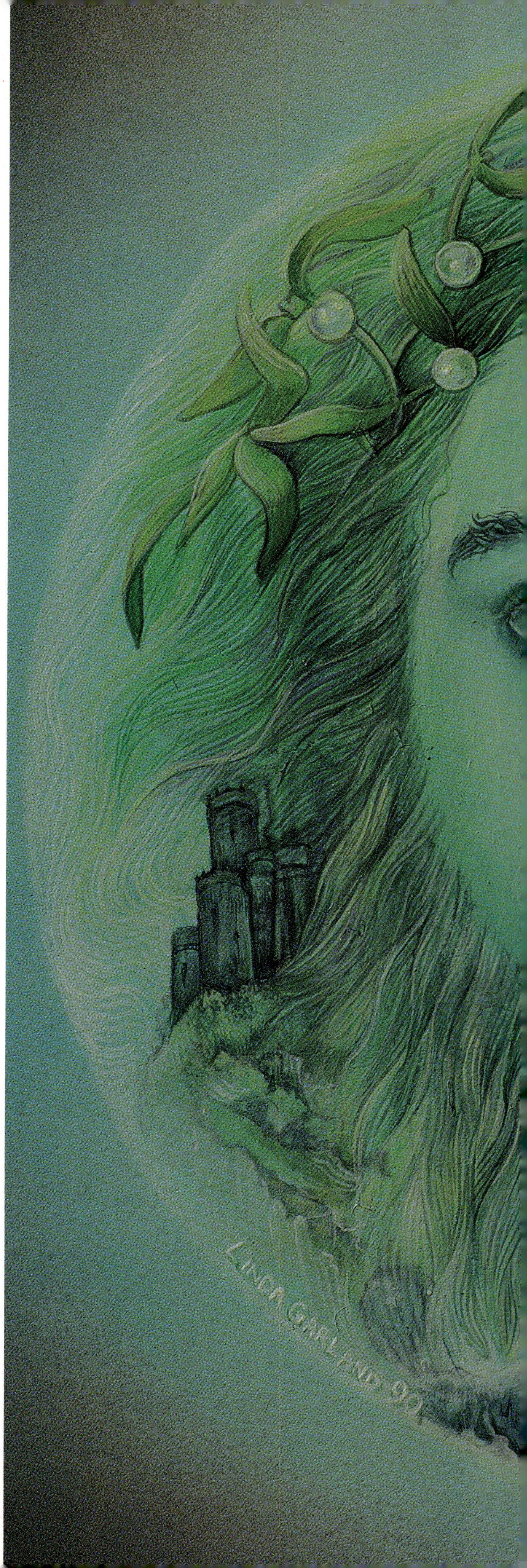

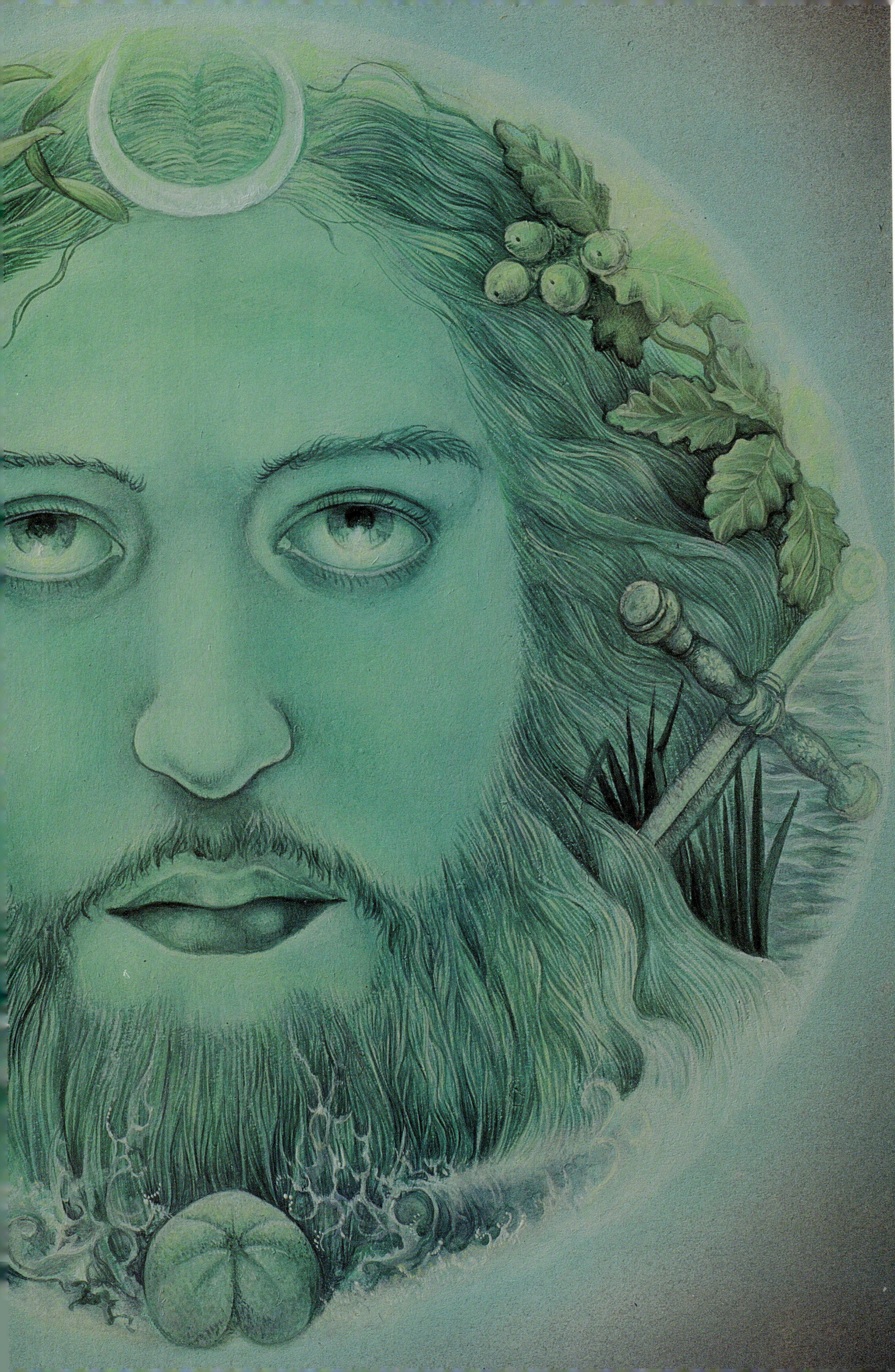

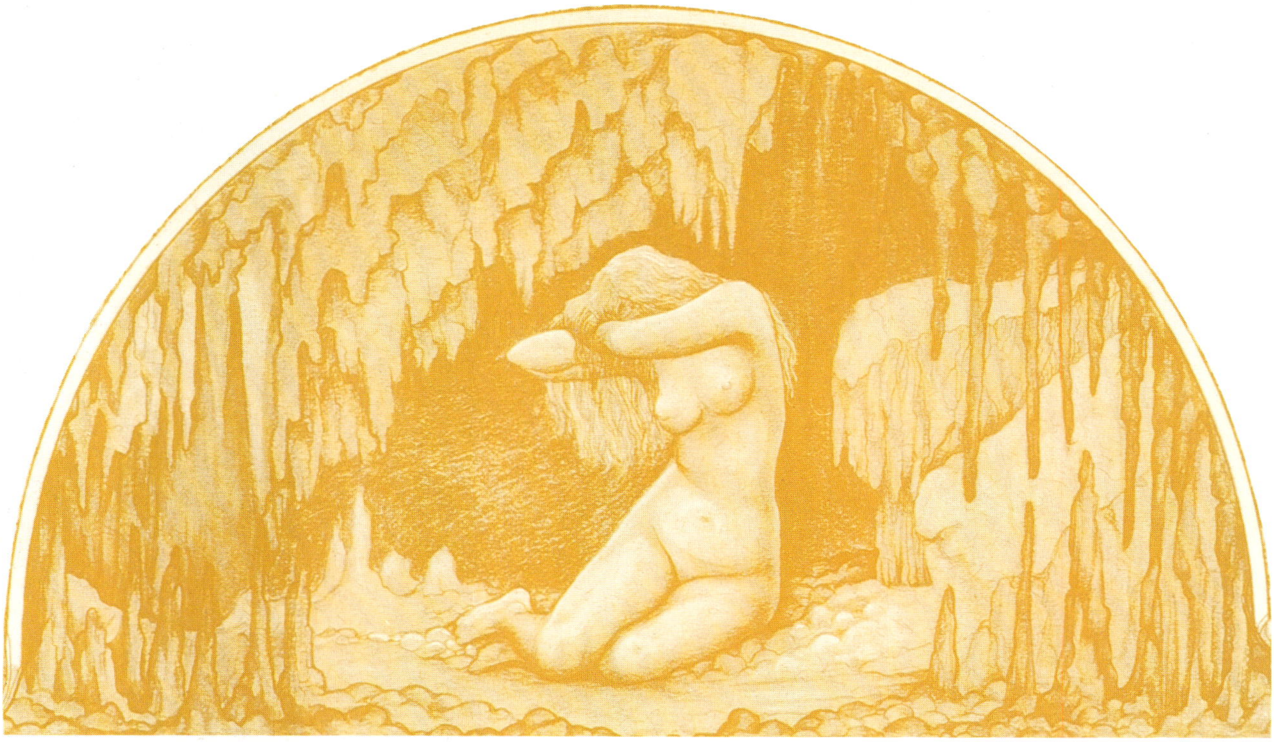

Being associated with the New Age means hearing some interesting ideas in the gallery. Like the US experiment in which rats across the country were made to solve the same maze problem at the same time. They were then given different problems at different times, which they solved a lot more slowly, suggesting that some kind of telepathy was at work in the first case. This led to a plausible theory that perhaps something similar happens with people, explaining the spread of ideas like writing and the wheel across the world even before the advent of global communications.

All of which, come to think of it, is possibly more entertaining than the office gossip on an average day in the London Met.

▷ **The Lady of Shalott**
Linda 1992
Oils and collage on embossed paper. 11 x 11in (28 x 28cm)
Private work.

Tennyson: 'She left the web, she left the loom,/ She made three paces through the room,/ She saw the water-lily bloom,/ She saw the helmet and the plume,/ She looked down to Camelot./ Out flew the web and floated wide;/ The mirror cracked from side to side;/ "The curse is come upon me", cried/ The Lady of Shalott.'

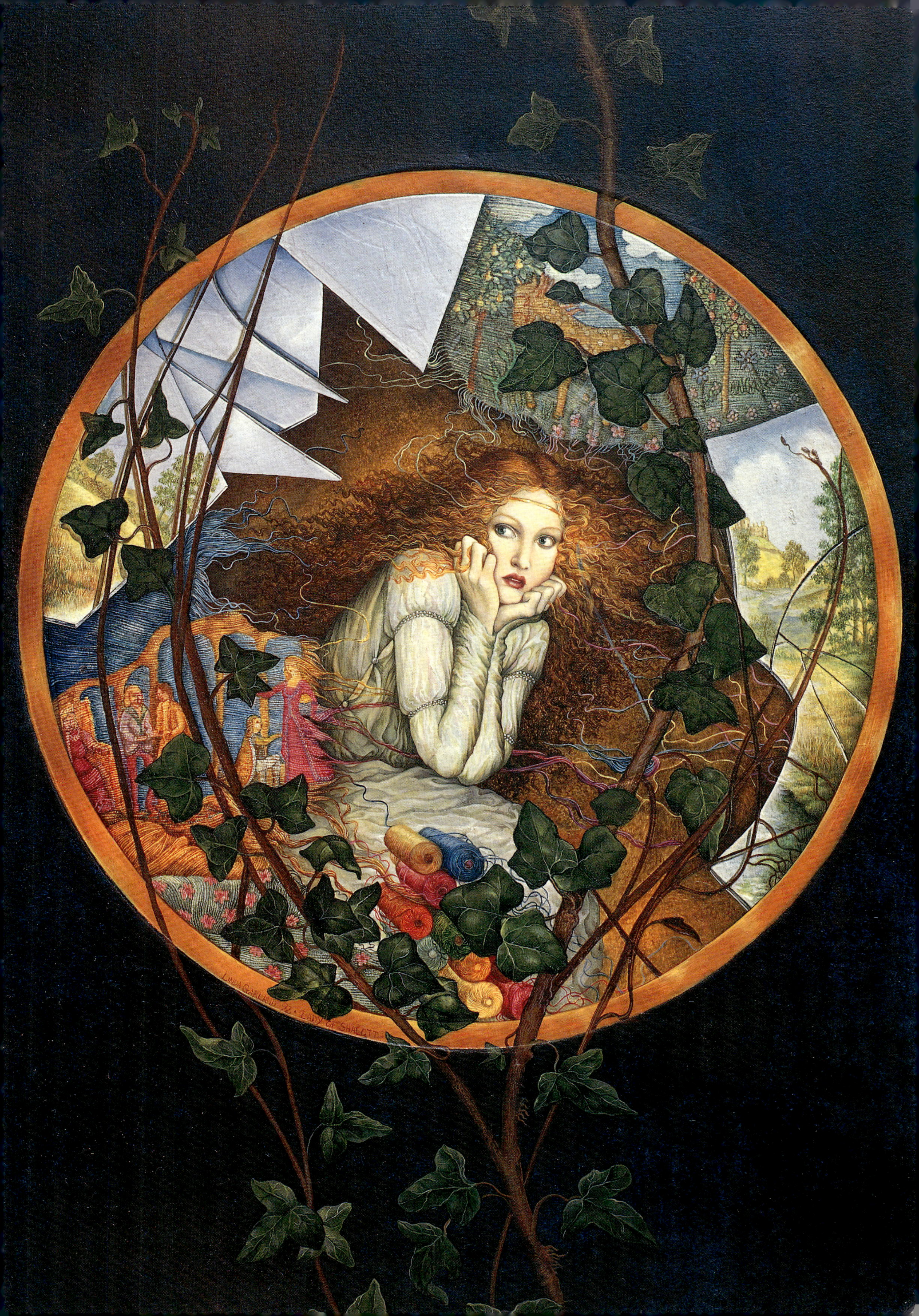
LINDA GARLAND '92 · LADY OF SHALOTT

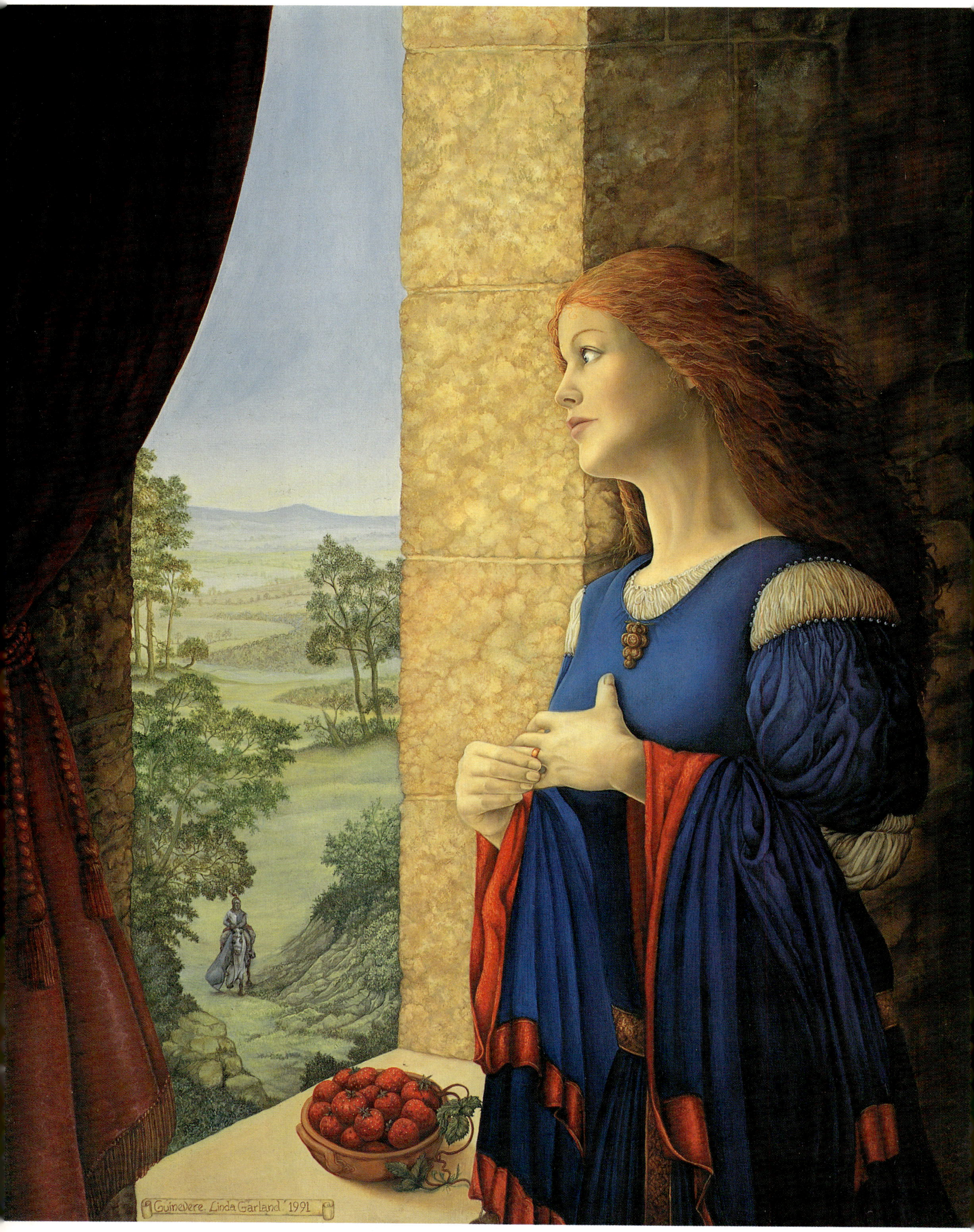
Guinevere. Linda Garland 1991

The Pre-Raphaelites were Linda Garland's first inspiration, and as she introduced Roger to them, it is fitting to close this book with a couple of paintings which show how close she has come to realizing her original ambition of joining their company. Although she would love to tackle all their favourite themes, the competition is daunting, and it generally takes a commission to provide the courage. This is how the painting *Queen Guinevere* came about, for which Linda posed by the living room window. Luckily, the same buyer would like a whole series of Arthurian characters, beginning with Morgan le Faye, so perhaps we will see a Pre-Raphaelite collection from her yet.

Overall, though, Linda and Roger Garland have collectively evolved a style and range of work that owes no great debt to anyone but themselves. And they have achieved this through an integrity which, while being flexible enough to bend to the commercial realities of the world, has also defied them at times in pursuit of a vision planted firmly in some other, more ethereal, sphere. Or perhaps, as Roger says, it is all around us, needing only the artist's eye and brush to render it visible.

◁ **Queen Guinevere**
Linda 1991
Oils. 14 x 18in (36 x 46cm)
Private commission, Geoffrey Vaulkhard.

Here we see Lancelot approaching Camelot, and the Queen, not without certain pangs of conscience, slipping the ring from her wedding finger. During the Middle Ages, strawberries were a symbol of wantonness, since they shamelessly carry their seeds on the outside.

**(Overleaf)**
**Door to Infinity**
Linda 1989
Oils. 7 x 7in (18 x 18cm)
Book cover, Prism Press.

This work was commissioned for a study of reported out-of-the-body experiences.

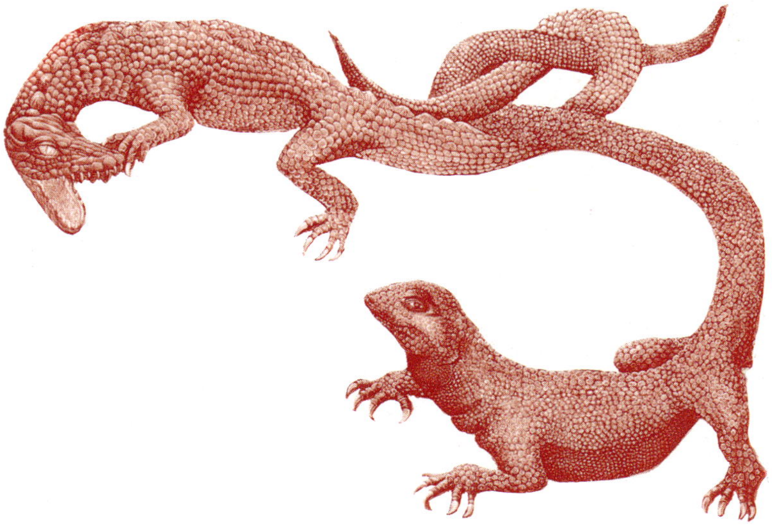

# ACKNOWLEDGEMENTS

## *Linda and Roger Garland wish to thank:*

The Tolkien Estate and HarperCollins for kind permission to reproduce the Tolkien illustrations, Colin Spooner and Julian King at Prism Press, Nigel Suckling, Jane Johnson, Valerie Pidgeon, Young Artists (Arena), John Munday, Richard Burgess, Lawrence Back, Alan Spain, Bob Hollingsworth, Rosemary Cheetham, Nick Eddison, Ian Jackson, Mike Bates, Janet Dymond, Andy Wadsworth, Michael Brown, the late Stephen Abis, the late Mike Jarvis, Spectrum Photo labs, Plymouth, Susan & Ian Anderson, Mary Butler, Francesca Marzotto Caotorta, Dougie the dog, Plymouth Sci-fi club, Paul White, Ivan Corbett, Strephon Kaplan-Williams, Brian Curry, John Knights and our parents, Doreen and Maurice Garland and Lilly and Stephen Eves.

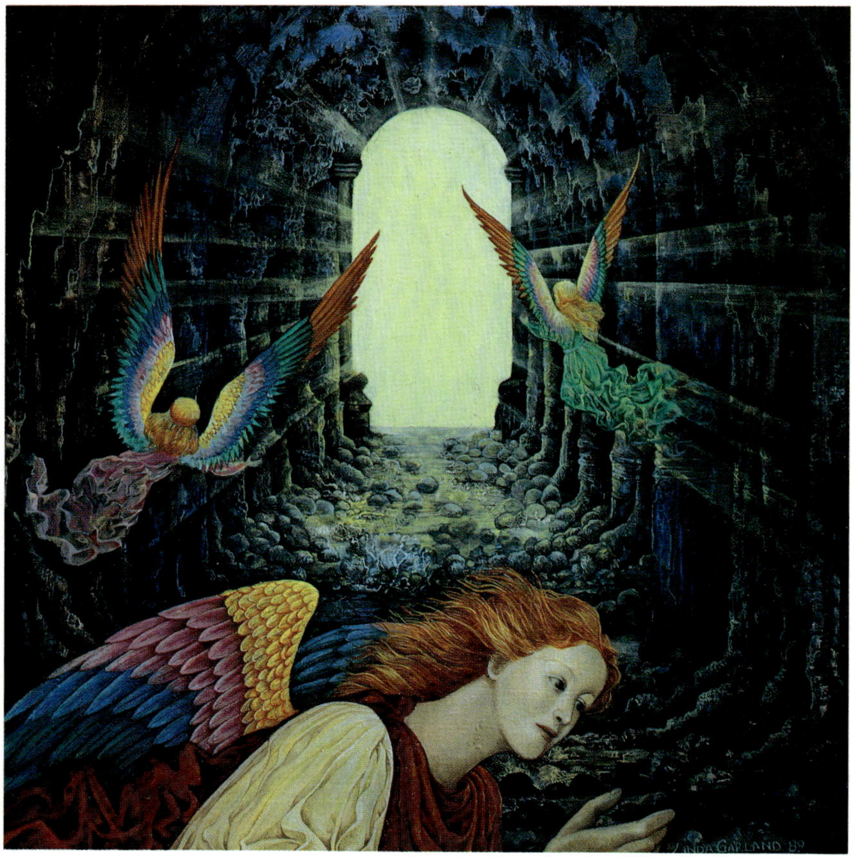